To

W. F. W.

With gratitude, appreciation
& affection.

B. W. B.

After a portrait by Nathaniel Hone, 1777

William Legge, Second Earl of Dartmouth
(1731-1801)

Lord Dartmouth

and the

AMERICAN REVOLUTION

by

B. D. Bargar

THE UNIVERSITY OF SOUTH CAROLINA PRESS
COLUMBIA   1965

Printed in the United States of America
by The State Printing Company, Columbia, South Carolina
Library of Congress Catalog Card Number 65-28498

PREFACE

IRONY is a quality which often appears in the course of human history. The life and political career of William Legge, the second Earl of Dartmouth (1731-1801), was filled with ironic incidents. Known to his contemporaries as "the good Lord Dartmouth," his principal interests were his family, his private estate, and his religious exercises. Left to his own devices, he probably would never have held an important political office. Yet, because he was related by marriage to Frederick, Lord North, he was compelled by his sense of family loyalty to accept the seals of office of the Secretary of State for the Colonies in 1772. His appointment pleased nearly everybody at the time: King George III, Lord North, various English officials on both sides of the Atlantic, colonial agents in England and numerous clergymen in the colonies. All agreed that the new Secretary of State was an excellent choice. During his brief tenure at the American Department (1772-1775), Lord Dartmouth participated, sometimes secretly, in several projects for reconciling the differences between Great Britain and her colonies. His chief wish was to establish harmonious and prosperous relations, on what he regarded as sound constitutional principles. But ironically, the policy of Lord North's administration provoked a major constitutional crisis which resulted in the War for American Independence.

What would have been the results, had Dartmouth's policy succeeded and a peaceful reconciliation occurred in 1775? The temptation to speculate is irresistible. Geographically, British North America would have remained united from the Gulf of Mexico to the Arctic. The subsequent process of westward expansion would have created a continental dominion from sea to sea, including as much, if not more, of Mexican territory as the United States now holds. Without an international boundary at the 45th and 49th parallels, the past history of American-Canadian relations would have been very different. There would have been no invasion of Canada in the non-existent War of 1812; no Fenian Raids, no Aroostook War, no Alaska boundary dispute, no nonsense about "54° 40′ or fight!" Recent arguments about atomic warheads for Canadian missiles and American investment in Canadian industry would have been groundless in a united British North America. The economic potential of such a united state, scarcely imagined in the brief period of its existence, 1763-1776, would develop without the complications of international dividing lines.

The passage of Time would have solved even the constitutional problems which Dartmouth found insuperable. Canada and the other dominions evolved an independent status within the Commonwealth, as fully sovereign as that of the United States. The larger dominions, like Canada and Australia, also succeeded in reconciling cabinet responsibility with a federal structure which permits varying degrees of states' rights. Whatever the virtues of the American constitution, few modern states have chosen to adopt its cumbersome system of checks and balances. The parliamentary system may not be perfect, but it obviates our periodic filibusters, stalemates, and mutual recriminations when different parties control executive and legislative.

The British Empire emancipated all slaves in 1833, with the British taxpayer providing compensation to the owners. The emancipation act would have been impossible without the establishment of the doctrine of parliamentary supremacy. Would the Southern States have attempted to secede thirty years earlier than they did, or would they have accepted the millions of pounds sterling offered by Britain? Lincoln's government not only refused to compensate slave owners, but crushed secession by armed force. The British Government recently opposed neither independence nor secession in the remainder of the empire. It sanctioned the secession of Nyasaland from a larger federation; it even granted full independence to Kenya. Apparently, if colonial radicals had been less impatient in the 1770's, Americans could have acquired all the "Liberty" they could agree upon in the next century or so. But there are enough "lost causes" in history. George III said that he would rather lose his possessions than admit their equality of status, and in spite of the "good Lord Dartmouth's" hopes for a peaceful reconciliation, that is what actually happened.

B. D. BARGAR

University of South Carolina
Columbia, South Carolina
25 July 1965

ACKNOWLEDGMENTS

TO EXPRESS adequately my appreciation to all those persons who have assisted me in the preparation of this volume would require more pages than the book itself. Some scholars will recognize their respective contributions to the whole project in various footnote references, which constitute very small Thank-you's for the information and stimulation they have provided. I must acknowledge several larger debts of gratitude more specifically. W. F. Woodring, Professor Emeritus of Ohio State University, first awakened my interest in the "good Lord Dartmouth" and he has consistently supplied much-needed advice and encouragement in subsequent years. Professor Emeritus D. J. McDougall, of the University of Toronto, listened to my early research problems and helped me solve most of them. The late V. T. Harlow, Beit Professor of Imperial History, Oxford University, supervised one phase of my post-doctoral research with unfailing and good-humored sympathy.

I am also indebted to the seventh Earl of Dartmouth and his gracious Countess. They made it possible for me to inspect the portraits at Patshull House, and they also accorded me unlimited access to the family manuscripts, without which my research would have been incomplete. Their warm hospitality and encouragement was deeply appreciated, so it is doubly regretful that death has prevented them from receiving the copy of this book which I promised them several years ago.

It seems churlish not to mention specifically the names of all the various librarians and archivists who have supplied so much grist for my mill, but it would require too many pages. Perhaps the underpaid, overworked staffs of the following institutions will accept an anonymous tribute with their customary patience and cheerfulness: the Public Record Office, the British Museum, the Bodleian Library, the Sheffield City Library, the William Salt Library of Stafford; the Public Archives of Canada, the Library of Congress, the William L. Clements Library, the South Carolina Archives, the South Caroliniana Library and the McKissick Library at the University of South Carolina. Without the manuscripts and books in their custody, my work would have been impossible.

I should like to thank the Librarian and the Archivist of Dartmouth College for the information which they have provided about portraits of the second Earl; the two which appear in this book are reproduced with the kind permission of the Trustees of Dartmouth College.

During the period of my research, I have enjoyed a number of scholarships, fellowships and grants. I must gratefully acknowledge the Mackenzie Fellowship of the University of Toronto, the Fulbright grant for research in England, the Duke University grant-in-aid, and the several grants of both time and money received from the University of South Carolina.

Finally, a word about style may be in order. The Eighteenth-Century rules of composition were rather more flexible than our own. Nouns were frequently capitalized, as in German, and numerous abbreviations. When Lord Dartmouth wrote "Y^r. Lord^p." he obviously meant "your lordship" and his reader understood it so. With modern methods of printing, it is unnecessary to follow the convolutions of a goose-quill pen, followed by [sic] in every case. Only in the case of printed sources have I retained Eighteenth-Century style. This may be inconsistency, but I submit that the meaning of a document is more important than the penmanship.

B. D. B.

CONTENTS

ILLUSTRATIONS

Portraits used by permission of Librarian and Trustees of Dartmouth College, Hanover, New Hampshire

Lord Dartmouth

and the

AMERICAN REVOLUTION

Chapter I

YOUNG MAN OF QUALITY

MANY elements were required to produce a man of quality in the well-ordered society of Eighteenth-Century England. A respectable family background, landed wealth, an educated taste for the arts, and good manners all contributed to one's position in the social hierarchy. William Legge, the second Earl of Dartmouth, possessed all of these qualifications, but the key to his social and political position will be found in his family connections. Persons to whom he was closely related and his reactions to those persons account for many of his most important decisions during the first three decades of his life. Even his entrance into politics, first with the Rockingham Whigs and later with Lord North's government, can best be explained by personal influences and family connections.

In the days of the Stuarts, Dartmouth's ancestors were Tories and royalists. One of them, Colonel William Legge, fought under Prince Rupert and Charles I, and lived long enough to enjoy the favor of Charles II after the Restoration.[1] Another, Captain George Legge, commanded a ship in the Dutch Wars and, with the assistance of the more famous Samuel Pepys, supervised the evacuation of Tangier in 1683. As a reward for his loyalty the Stuarts made him a Baron, but William III imprisoned him in the Tower of London.[2] Baron Dartmouth's son served Queen Anne in several offices, including President of the Board of Trade, Secretary of State, and Lord Privy Seal. In 1711, the Queen raised him in the peerage and he became the first Earl of Dartmouth. As a moderate Tory, he accepted the necessity for a Hanoverian Succession, but retired from active politics after 1714.[3] His caustic comments upon Bishop Burnet's *History*[4]

---

[1] *Dict. Nat. Biog.*, XXXII, 414-416. There are brief accounts of various members of the Legge family in: Burke's *Peerage;* Cokayne's *Complete Peerage*; and in the introductions to the three volumes of Dartmouth Manuscripts published by the Historical Manuscripts Commission, *Eleventh Report, Appendix, Part V* (1887), *Fourteenth Report, Appendix, Part X* (1895), and *Fifteenth Report, Appendix, Part I* (1896).

[2] *Dict. Nat. Biog.*, XXXII, 408-410. R. G. Howarth, ed., *The Letters and Second Diary of Samuel Pepys* (London, 1932), contains several references to Baron Dartmouth (see index) and a portrait facing p. 128.

[3] A. S. Turberville, *The House of Lords in the XVIIIth Century* (Oxford, 1927), 480.

[4] The first Earl's notes to Burnet's *History* appear in the edition by M. J. Routh (Oxford, 1823), 6 vols.

provide an interesting impression of his personality and political opinions.

From his grandfather, the first Earl, young William Legge inherited both his name and his title, for his own father, Lord Lewisham, died shortly after the birth of his son in 1731. Thus, when the old Earl died in 1750, his title passed directly to his namesake grandson. The family property was not extensive, but included houses in St. James's Square, in Blackheath, and Sandwell Park, near Birmingham, which proved in later years to be the favorite residence of the new Lord Dartmouth. The most valuable portion was probably the manor of Woodsome in Yorkshire, which Dartmouth would inherit from his mother.[5]

Lord Dartmouth's mother, Lady Lewisham, was the daughter of Sir Arthur Kaye. Judging from her portrait she was an extremely attractive woman but, judging from her letters, her intellect was at best shallow.[6] Her greatest bequest to her son was not the purely material consideration of the Yorkshire property; she introduced him into the North family circle by her second marriage in 1736 to Lord North and Grey. Young William was only five years old when he began a life-long association with Lord North's son Frederick. Although the two boys were properly stepbrothers, having no parental blood in common, their relationship was fully as intimate as many actual brothers. Here was a family connection that was to prove decisive in his political career thirty-six years later.

Having lost his own father soon after birth, Lord Dartmouth was especially fortunate in having Lord North as a stepfather. His mother's second husband looked upon this young stepson as his own, never making any distinction between Lord Lewisham's children and his own by a previous marriage.[7] The affection which the young boy enjoyed from his three closest relatives is well illustrated by their reactions to an accident which occurred when he was about ten years old. The grandfather, in referring to an operation which the lad was to undergo, called him "my dearest child" and thanked Lord North for "the tender concern, good nature and compassion" which he had shown.[8] Lady North happily reported a few days later that "the dear

---

[5] Estate accounts, Ms. North, c.74, c.75, c.76 (Bodleian Library).

[6] Letters from Lady North and Grey to the first Earl of Dartmouth, Dartmouth Manuscripts, William Salt Library, Stafford, England.

[7] Lord North and Grey (later, Earl of Guilford) left a copy of the inscriptions to be placed on the monument over his wives' graves. Lucy, the daughter of the Earl of Halifax, died in 1734, leaving the son who was known as Lord North during the American Revolution. Elizabeth, widow of Lord Lewisham, died in 1745, leaving three of her own and two of her second husband's children. The third wife, Katherine died in 1766 without issue. Ms. North, c.24, f.21.

[8] Earl of Dartmouth to Lord North and Grey, 15 January 1741/2, Dartmouth Manuscripts (William Salt Library, Stafford), 736.

boy" was recovering rapidly—"his arms are quite healed"—and that he would soon be home again.[9] A few years later the invasion by Bonnie Prince Charlie threatened the safety of the North household,[10] but a greater personal tragedy had already happened to young William. His mother had died unexpectedly in April of 1745.[11]

The loss of one's mother at the impressionable age of fourteen years can have serious consequences for a developing personality. Fortunately, young William Legge was not alone in his grief. Several brothers and sisters helped him sustain his loss. Besides his two older sisters and his stepbrother, Frederick North, there was also a half sister, Louisa, and a half brother, Brownlow, the surviving children of Lord North's second marriage. Since Lord North made no distinction between the Legge children and his own by two different wives, the children themselves ignored the nice distinction between stepbrother and half brother relationships.[12] Of all his relatives, however, Dartmouth was most intimately attached to Frederick North. They grew up in the same household together, attended Trinity College, Oxford, and between 1751 and 1754 toured Europe together.

The grand tour of the continent was an essential part of every gentleman's education in the Eighteenth-Century. Considering the low standards of university requirements, the tour might well exercise a more important influence in education and maturation. Dartmouth's later comment on his schooling was that mathematics had been his favorite subject,[13] but his letters from the continent reveal a developing awareness of the world around him. Although he complained, as tourists are wont to do, about the quality of the food, the lack of accommodations, and delays caused by necessary repairs to the coach, he had an enviable experience in seeing all the worthwhile sights.[14] The list of people he met in Europe reads like an abbreviated *Almanach de Gotha* and includes, the Princess Royal, the Landgrave of Hesse-Cassel, a princess at Wolfenbüttel, the Emperor of Austria and his ten children (many of whom, Dartmouth thought, had "beautiful countenances"), and the French royal family (Louis XV merely stared at his visitor, but the Queen spoke to him.)[15] Of far greater

---

[9] Lady North and Grey to Earl of Dartmouth, 19 January 1741/2, *ibid.*, 737.

[10] Lord North and Grey to Earl of Dartmouth, [December] 1745, *ibid.*, 769 and 770.

[11] Heneage Legge to Earl of Dartmouth, 23 April 1745, *ibid.*, 753. Lord North and Grey to Earl of Dartmouth, 30 April 1745, *ibid.*, 761.

[12] Brownlow North to Earl of Guilford, 20 March 1768, Ms. North, d.24, f.39, typically refers to his half brother as "Brother Dartmouth."

[13] To Lord Lewisham, 12 November 1771, British Museum, Additional Manuscripts, 39,311, f.277. In referring to correspondence written to or by William, second Earl of Dartmouth, his name will be assumed.

[14] To Dr. Huddesford, 28 July 1751, Dartmouth Manuscripts, 793 *et seq.*

[15] To the Duke of Newcastle, 16 February 1754, Add. Mss. 32,734, f.144.

significance than these brief encounters with continental royalty was
Dartmouth's continued association with North, for on the tour the
childhood companions developed into mature friends. At the end of
their travels Dartmouth reported that they were "as much one as we
were before we went abroad. . . ." In the same letter he also referred to North as "my other self."[16]

The immediate object of the tour was a course of study at the
University of Leipzig, but Dartmouth found Leipzig to be "as dull
as possible." He compared it unfavorably with his *alma mater,* saying
that it lacked "as much to put it upon a level with Oxford in point
of pleasure and amusement [as in] the number and variety of its
learned members."[17] By contrast with dull Leipzig, Dartmouth found
Italy to be full of both entertainment and instruction. There the
young man of quality acquired a new facet: patron of the arts. He
spent three weeks in Venice, looking at the "pictures and other remarkable sights,"[18] but the entire year 1753 was scarcely long enough
to see the rest of Italy. He bought a number of *objets d'art* and sat
for his portrait by Thomas Jenkins. At the same time, he engaged
Jenkins as his agent to purchase items from various Italian villas and
to ship them to England after his return.[19] Dartmouth's reputation
as a collector and a patron of the arts was soon well established.
During his life he sat for more than twenty portraits by painters who
ranged from the obscure Pompeo to the great Reynolds.[20] One interesting representation is John Zoffany's *Tribuna* in which Dartmouth
appears with a group of noblemen admiring a Madonna in the Uffizi
Gallery of Florence.[21]

Another important association dating from the tour was his acquaintance with the Duke of Newcastle. The old Duke was North's
cousin and his wife was similarly related to Dartmouth, so it was not
unnatural that the two young men of quality should visit the veteran
politician while he was attending the King in Hanover in 1752.[22] Two
years later, Newcastle arranged for the British Ambassador in Paris,

[16] To Dr. Huddesford, 10 April 1754, Dartmouth Manuscripts, 799.

[17] To Dr. Huddesford, 3 March 1752, *ibid.,* 794.

[18] To Newcastle, 10 December 1752, Add. Mss., 32,730, f.373.

[19] Thomas Jenkins' letters are printed in *Hist. Mss. Comm., 15th Report, App., Pt. I,* pp. 167 *et seq.*

[20] These portraits were hanging in Patshull House, the home of the seventh Earl of Dartmouth, as recently as 1959. C. R. Leslie and Tom Taylor, *Life of Sir Joshua Reynolds* (1865), I, 492 *et seq.* provides information about the dates on which Lord and Lady Dartmouth and their relatives sat for the great painter.

[21] The publishers of LIFE magazine have reproduced Zoffany's *Tribuna* in their issue of 13 September 1948 and again in *Life's Picture History of Western Man* (New York, 1951), 228-9.

[22] To Newcastle, 26 June 1752, Add. Mss., 32,727, f.435. From Newcastle, 3 February 1754, Add. Mss., 32,734, f.106.

Lord Albemarle, to meet the young travellers and introduce them to
the court at Versailles. While in Paris Dartmouth received a very
flattering message: Newcastle reported that King George II "has
often talked of you . . . with the greatest marks of distinction and
regard. . . ."[23]

To judge solely from his fulsome reply, Dartmouth was deeply
moved by Newcastle's flattery. He replied that, while the King's regard pleased him, it could not increase his "reverence and dutiful
affection" for George II. Upon returning to England, Dartmouth
continued, he hoped to be permitted to "throw myself at His Majesty's feet."[24] And yet, only six months earlier, Dartmouth had been
warned about just this type of flattery and its possible effects on impressionable young minds. His uncle, Heneage Legge, a lawyer who
had learned a great deal about the political facts of life in his career
as baron of the court of exchequer, recognized insincerity when he
saw it. Perhaps Dartmouth remembered his uncle's warning when
reading Newcastle's blandishments: "Nobody wishes your success
and good figure in the world more warmly than I do, . . . [but] I
can't help crying 'Fire!' when I see any danger coming towards you.
There is a huge dose of flattery preparing for you in high places,
against your return to England. . . . We have an excellent hand
at it in this country and if a young man of quality and fortune can
count twenty when he returns from abroad and does not absolutely
pick pockets, we all cry, 'Tertius caelo cecidit Cato!' But I thank God
you have sense and spirit enough to take the substantial benefits of
a good character and not let the flattery which will attend it turn you
[and North] into asses. You see . . . I can't help preaching a little
in the style of an uncle but I wanted to give you this hint and now
will have done."[25] Possibly this avuncular hint was well placed, for
more than a decade elapsed before Lord Dartmouth entered politics.
Yet, when he accepted Lord Rockingham's invitation to join the new
ministry in 1765, it was his "cousin" the Duke of Newcastle whose
urgings ended his hesitation. The grand tour of continent, then, created a friendly relationship which later contributed to his appointment to the Board of Trade.

After a month's stay in Paris, Dartmouth was eager to return to
England. During the three years he had spent on the continent a
number of changes had taken place in his family circle. For one
thing, his stepfather had been elevated in the peerage in 1752 and was
now the first Earl of Guilford.[26] As a result, his son and heir became

---

[23] *Ibid.* and letter to Newcastle, 16 February 1754, Add. Mss., 32,734, f.144.
[24] *Ibid.*
[25] From Heneage Legge, 2 August 1713, Dartmouth Manuscripts, 797. The
sarcastic epigram may be translated, "A *third* Cato has fallen from Heaven."
[26] Cokayne's *Complete Peerage,* VI, 213, explains Lord Guilford's various
titles.

"Lord North" by courtesy and would one day inherit the earldom. Lord Guilford had also taken a wife, his third and last, as time was to decree. She was Katherine Furnese, the daughter of Sir Robert Furnese of Waldershare, Kent. As Dartmouth's stepmother, the Countess of Guilford made at least two important contributions to the development of the young man of quality. She introduced him to his future wife and also to a new religious experience.

Soon after his return in the spring of 1754, Dartmouth became engaged to the daughter of Sir Charles Gunter Nicholl, Frances, a kinswoman of Lady Guilford. Their marriage, which took place in January, 1755, was blessed with nine children and remained unblemished by scandal. It is true that Dartmouth had developed an adolescent infatuation for a Miss Huddesford during his years at Oxford. When he wrote to her father, the president of Trinity College, he always included a message for her, calling her rather sentimentally, "my little wife."[27] But this innocent affair created no impediment to a long and happy marriage with Frances Nicholl.

Dartmouth's bride won the full approval of his family and his friends. Lord Guilford welcomed her as a daughter, remarking that she had "the fairest prospect imaginable"[28] in marrying one whom he had always considered a son. Louisa North wept at the wedding, but reported both what the bride wore and how merry the party was at Dartmouth's house in Blackheath.[29] Mrs. Delany, an old friend of the family, described Lady Dartmouth as "rather pretty . . . cheerful, civil, and easy in manner. . . . *She is as good as he is.* . . ."[30] The last remark was high praise indeed, for Mrs. Delany regarded Lord Dartmouth as the living embodiment of Richardson's hero *Sir Charles Grandison.* Although not as well known as the same author's portrait of the good woman in *Clarissa,* the novel is characteristically moralistic. Richardson had originally planned to call his work "The Good Man" and, after its appearance in 1753, volunteered the information that Dartmouth might have been the model for his hero.[31] As early as 1755, then, Dartmouth's friends had recognized his upright, moral character. The "good Lord Dartmouth" was very fortunate in finding a wife who could match his own qualities. Besides her goodness, the new countess brought a dowry of more than one hundred thousand pounds.[32] This additional income must have been welcome,

[27] To Dr. Huddesford, 28 July 1751, Dartmouth Manuscripts, 793 *et seq.*

[28] Guilford to Lady Dartmouth, 12 January 1755, *ibid.,* 803.

[29] Louisa North to Guilford, 13 January 1755, Ms. North, d.23, ff.44-5.

[30] Mrs. Delany to Mrs. Dewes, 31 January 1756, *The Autobiography and Correspondence of Mary Granville, Mrs. Delany* (Lady Llanover, ed., 1861-2), III, 405-6. Mrs. Delany's italics.

[31] *Dict. Nat. Biog.,* XVI, 1131. A. S. Turberville, *House of Lords,* 453-4.

[32] Mrs. Delany to Mrs. Dewes, 6 July 1754, *Correspondence* (Llanover, ed.), III, 283.

especially to one with a taste for imported Italian art objects and a growing family to support.

During the ensuing years, Dartmouth was deeply involved with personal and family affairs. Even in the periods when he held political offices, he had to deal with problems as diverse as his sons' education and his sister's marriage settlement.[33] There were compensations, of course, in the constant round of visits with friends and relatives. The ever-widening circle of the North clan[34] itself provided convivial entertainment for several weeks of each year. When at home in one of his residences, there were various improvements or refinements to be made, as for example the new walk leading to Lady Dartmouth's menagerie at Sandwell.[35] The menagerie itself included a number of specimens of North American fauna, sent by Dartmouth's well-wishers after the repeal of the Stamp Act. Sandwell was his favorite residence and Dartmouth often said that he disliked living in London.[36] He also felt a strong attraction for his Yorkshire property, the Manor of Woodsome, which he had inherited from his mother. Although he had no intention of living there, it contributed materially to his comfortable income, and he tried to visit his tenants at least once each year. This must have been a pleasant journey, for Dartmouth often mentioned it in his correspondence, always with regret in the years when other business forced him to forego his annual visitation.

Part of his pleasure no doubt stemmed from the fact that so many of his friends and relatives lived in the district through which his route led. Leaving Sandwell, which was then well outside rapidly expanding Birmingham, he rode north to Blithefield, the home of his aunt, Lady Bagot. Then, skirting the Derbyshire Peaks and passing through some delightful countryside, he continued through Sheffield, often turning from his route to visit the Marquess of Rockingham at Wentworth House. If he spent the night there, his own property was only a day's ride farther. In 1766, he told Rockingham that he had "so much business" at Sandwell and in London that he was forced to give up the Yorkshire expedition. Consequently, he would be unable to visit the Marquess that year. Although he assured Rockingham that he thought no less of him than before, he confessed that he had little appetite for political discussions.[37] Dartmouth pre-

---

[33] See various letters to Guilford in the North Manuscripts, especially d.14.
[34] For example, Dartmouth's letter to Guilford, 22 November 1771, *ibid.*
[35] To Guilford, 29 November 1769, *ibid.*, d.12, ff.154-5.
[36] To Guilford, 12 December 1769, *ibid.*, f.163, is one example.
[37] To Rockingham, 29 August 1766, Rockingham Manuscripts, R. 1, f.426. Woodsome is described in several places: D. F. E. Sykes, *Huddersfield and its Vicinity* (1898), 192 *et seq.*; T. Dyson, *History of Huddersfield and District* (1932), Chap. 17; *Country Life,* 22 December 1906.

ferred a quiet, family life and reluctantly entered politics out of a sense of duty.

By his twenty-fifth year, then, Dartmouth had already acquired most of the elements needed to produce a young man of quality. He possessed the title and estates of an earl. He enjoyed the affectionate and influential relationships of a wide family circle. He had married a wealthy woman whom he genuinely admired. Finally, he had acquired a taste for *objets d'art,* which established his reputation as a patron of the arts. The score of portraits of himself, which he was to commission during his lifetime, might suggest a note of vanity; but it might also indicate a desire to encourage many different artists by contributing to their incomes. If Dartmouth had any foppish inclinations at this point, they were sufficiently counterbalanced by his religious interests. Instead of living for pleasure and self-indulgence, like some young aristocrats of his day, he developed a pious nature which characterized the remainder of his life.

Chapter II

PIETY AND PHILANTHROPY

DARTMOUTH'S stepmother, the Countess of Guilford, introduced him to the religious circle formed by Selina, Countess of
Huntingdon. Lady Huntingdon regarded herself as a member of
the Church of England until 1779, and Dartmouth continued to communicate with the established church until his death. Both were interested in reforming the Anglican Church from within, stressing the
need for personal and "methodical" piety. As a peeress Lady Huntingdon contended that she had the right to maintain as many chap-
lains as her financial means could support. She appointed clergymen
whose ideas conformed to hers to as many as sixty chapels in various
parts of England and Wales. In 1779, however, an ecclesiastical
court ruled that Lady Huntingdon's "diocese" was too unorthodox
to be included in the national church. As a result, she had to declare
herself a dissenter and to seek shelter under the provisions of the
Toleration Act.[1]

Fortunately for Dartmouth's peace of mind, he was never placed
in the same position. He continued to practice his own personal piety
within the organization of the Church of England, following an attitude which today would be considered "Low Church" Anglicanism.
To refer to him as a "Methodist" without qualification would be less
accurate than to call him a sincerely pious Anglican. Before the
separation took place in 1779, however, Dartmouth formed many
lasting friendships among the Methodist leaders. Well known preach-
ers, like John Wesley, Augustus Toplady, Hervey, Romaine and
Venn, were all acquainted with him and occasionally enjoyed his
hospitality. Whitefield once administered the sacrament in Dartmouth's house and afterwards stood on a table near the door, in order
to preach to a large crowd of people who filled the room and over-
flowed onto the grounds outside.[2] When Lady Huntingdon was seri-

---

[1] Sarah Tytler, *The Countess of Huntingdon and Her Circle* (London, 1907).

[2] W. A. Withrow, *Makers of Methodism* (Toronto, 1898), 143. Toplady,
best remembered for his "Rock of Ages," was converted by a follower of
Wesley in 1755 or 1756, but by 1758 he had adopted Whitefield's Calvinistic
views and thereafter engaged in bitter controversy with the Wesleyans (*Dict.
Nat. Biog.,* XIX, 984). James Hervey was a tutorial student of Wesley's at
Lincoln College in the 1730's. After ordination in 1736 or 1737, he held
various curacies until he succeeded his father as rector of Weston Favell.
Although he also quarrelled with Wesley during the Calvinistic Controversy,
he remained unembittered, gentle and pious. His "Meditations among the

ously ill in 1767, Dartmouth was considered the logical one to take over her extensive obligations in the event of her death. Fortunately, she recovered her health and Dartmouth was spared the necessary of assuming such a great burden.[3]

Although the extent of his involvement was on a smaller scale than Lady Huntingdon's, Dartmouth engaged in numerous good works. His sincere piety naturally led him to follow the path of philanthropy. Cynics might sneer at the "good Lord Dartmouth" and call him unflattering names, like "Psalm-Singer,"[4] but those who recognized his sincerity praised his works. Among those who benefitted from Dartmouth's goodness were John Newton, the former slaver who wanted to become a parson, the poet William Cowper, and Dr. James Beattie, poet and essayist. When Newton encountered difficulty in obtaining holy orders, Dartmouth prevailed upon the Bishop of Lincoln to ordain him. He then secured a curacy at Olney for the former slave-trader and made generous contributions to his financial needs.[5] He also contributed to the support of William Cowper, when he lived in Olney. In one of his evangelical poems, Cowper referred to Dartmouth as "one that wears a coronet and prays. . . ."[6] This compliment was intended to mark the distinction between one member of the aristocracy who sympathized with the reform movement and other noblemen who preferred horse racing, gambling, and wenching. Dr. Beattie, professor of moral philosophy in Aberdeen, wrote an *Essay on Truth,* in which he attacked David Hume's theories, and a long, unfinished poem "The Minstrel," for which he is best

---

Tombs" is perhaps his best known work (*Dict. Nat. Biog.,* IX, 733). William Romaine, ordained in 1738, was also strongly influenced by Wesley and Whitefield. His enthusiastic sermons embarrassed the regular parishioners of the fashionable St. George's, Hanover Square, and he either resigned or was dismissed. Lady Huntingdon employed him as a chaplain in the 1750's and he preached in her kitchen and drawing room. Lord Dartmouth offered him a living in the country, but he preferred to work in London. He also declined Whitefield's suggestion that he go to Philadelphia and eventually obtained a City church in 1766, where he remained for twenty-nine years (*Dict. Nat. Biog.,* XVII, 175). Henry Venn abandoned High Church principles in favor of evangelicalism in the 1750's. As curate of Clapham after 1754, he began a lifelong friendship with John Thornton. In 1759 he became the vicar of Huddersfield for a period of twelve years, during which time he established a reputation for piety and earnestness (*Dict. Nat. Biog.,* LVIII, 207).

[3] *Dict. Nat. Biog.,* IX, 133-4.

[4] H. B. Wheatley, ed., *The Historical and Posthumous Memoirs of Sir Nathaniel William Wraxall* (London, 1884), III, 268.

[5] Richard Cecil, *The Life of the Rev. John Newton* (New York, American Tract Society, n.d.), 143.

[6] "Truth," *The Poems of William Cowper* (J. C. Bailey, ed., London, 1884), 128.

remembered. Dartmouth sponsored his petition to the King in 1773 and obtained a pension of £200 for him.[7]

In some times and places the cultivation of a religious and philanthropic attitude might serve an ulterior motive. It should be emphasized that Dartmouth was not attempting to court public favor by his good works. On the contrary, some members of the aristocracy regarded Methodist doctrines as unseemly and even subversive. The Duchess of Buckingham, for example, believed "these doctrines are most repulsive and strongly tinctured with impertinence and disrespect towards their superiors in perpetually endeavouring to level all ranks and do away with all distinctions, as it is monstrous to be told that you have a heart as sinful as the common wretches that crawl on the earth."[8] Dartmouth's religious views might even have hindered a political career. Early in the reign of George III, the Earl of Bute refused to appoint him to a place of honor in the royal household on the grounds that "so sanctimonious a man should gain too far on his Majesty's piety."[9] Actually, the King's attitude in religion was not too different from Dartmouth's, but even he had heard the rumor that Dartmouth was "enthusiastic"[10]—a highly opprobrious epithet in the Eighteenth-Century. Several years later, however, George III acknowledged Dartmouth to be "a true believer, one who shews by his actions that he is not governed by the greatest of tyrants, Fashion."[11]

It was not fashion which led Dartmouth to support Dr. Samuel Parr in the contest over the headmastership at Harrow. In seeking a suitable education for his sons, Dartmouth selected Harrow for his first-born, George, Viscount Lewisham. As the younger boys reached the appropriate age, they also attended Harrow before going on to Oxford. All his sons might have followed this procedure, had it not been for a riot which occurred in 1771 and which resulted in their

[7] When asked for his opinion of Dartmouth, Beattie told the King that he thought him "to be one of the best of men." George III and Queen Charlotte both heartily agreed. *Diary*, 24 August 1773, quoted in Sir W. Forbes, *Life of Dr. Beattie* (Edinburgh, 1806), I, 271, 347-354.

[8] Duchess of Buckingham to the Countess of Huntingdon, n.d., cited in Tytler, *Huntingdon*, 47. The writer of this letter was an illegitimate daughter of James II. Born Catharine Darnley, she married in 1705/6 John Sheffield, whom Queen Anne created Duke of the County of Buckingham and Normandy. Since the dowager duchess died in 1743, Dartmouth probably never knew her, but her famous letter constitutes an example of aristocratic opinion toward the new evangelicalism. *Dict. Nat. Biog.*, XVII, 1124. Turberville, *House of Lords*, 445. S. Watson, *Reign of George III*, 3, note 1.

[9] *Dict. Nat. Biog.*, XXXII, 417. Horace Walpole, *Memoirs of the Reign of George III* (G. F. Barker, ed., London, 1894), I, 331.

[10] Dr. Beattie's *Diary*, above 7. Turberville, *House of Lords*, 453.

[11] From the King, 17 July 1773, Hist. Mss. Comm., *Eleventh Report, App., Part V*, 438.

following Dr. Parr to less "fashionable" schools. The Harrow riot resulted from the selection of an unpopular headmaster to replace Doctor Robert Sumner. Dartmouth had placed his sons in Sumner's immediate care, because he approved of his policies and those of his assistant, Samuel Parr. Upon learning of Sumner's death, Dartmouth asked Parr to look after his sons and expressed the hope that the school's governors would promote Parr to the headship. He felt strongly enough about Parr's qualifications to recommend him to two of the governors, Sir John and Mr. Rushout.[12] The governors, however, regarded Parr as too young (he was not yet twenty-five) and may have suspected that he was too radical (he had voted for John Wilkes). They chose Mr. Heath as Sumner's successor.[13]

Parr's disappointment was surpassed by that of his pupils. To register their disapproval of the newly chosen headmaster, they stoned and destroyed a carriage belonging to Mr. Bucknell, one of the governors.[14] Although not directly involved in this incident, Dr. Parr decided to withdraw from Harrow and to establish his own school at Stanmore. Approximately forty pupils accompanied him, including the Messrs. Legge. Dartmouth not only agreed to his sons' transfer from Harrow but continued to support Dr. Parr in all his subsequent migrations and difficulties.[15] When Parr moved his school to Colchester in 1777, the Legges went with him.[16] Eventually, even the youngest son, born in 1773, attended Dr. Parr's school, by then located in Hatton.[17] Dartmouth's confidence in Parr was unwavering, for as late as 1783 he secured a prebendary of St. Paul's for him. Apparently, this support was based upon Parr's educational ability, for his religious views were quite different from Dartmouth's. Parr was a High Churchman who denounced the errors of evangelicalism and attracted more than a little suspicion of being a Roman Catholic.[18] Nevertheless, Lord Lewisham had a highly favorable opinion of his former teacher[19] and probably encouraged his younger brothers to follow the peripatetic Parr.

---

12 Samuel Parr, *Works* (J. Johnstone, ed., London, 1828, 8 vols.), I, 63-64. To Parr, 15 September 1771, *ibid.*, 56.

13 From Parr, 4 October 1771, Hist. Mss. Comm., *15th Report, App. Pt. I*, 195.

14 P. H. M. Bryant, *Harrow* (London, 1936), 29. Percy M. Thornton, *Harrow School and Its Surroundings* (London, 1885), 166-7.

15 To Parr, 10 October 1771, *Works*, I, 67-8.

16 From Parr, 4 February 1777, Hist. Mss. Comm., *15th Report*, 230-2.

17 *Parr's Works*, I, 57. The birth of Dartmouth's youngest son was reported in the *Massachusetts Gazette*, 5 August 1773, and the clipping has been preserved in the Dartmouth Manuscripts, 675.

18 *Dict. Nat. Biog.*, XV, 362. Rev. Wm. Field, *Memoirs of the Life . . . of the Rev. Samuel Parr . . .* (London, 1828), I, chap. 6.

19 Lewisham to Parr, 26 December 1771, *Parr's Works*, I, 68.

The Harrow Riot produced a number of perplexing problems for
Dartmouth as a father. The principal problem, his sons' education,
was eventually solved satisfactorily, but during the weeks immediately
following the riot he was extremely worried. His deep concern is
reflected in a letter to his stepfather in which he assured Lord Guilford that Parr's role had been quite correct. He could not, however,
excuse the boys who destroyed private property, even though Mr.
Bucknell had provoked them.[20] Dartmouth's fear that his sons might
have been involved in the fracas gave way to relief which other members of the family shared when this "sad affair" finally ended.[21]

Dartmouth's philanthropy involved him with an American educational institution, very different from Dr. Parr's various schools. The
New Hampshire school which has been known as Dartmouth College
since 1769 began as an Indian Charity School fourteen years earlier.
The founder, Eleazar Wheelock, was a graduate of Yale and a friend
of George Whitefield. He was determined to train Indian boys to
preach the gospel to their own people. His work attracted the interest
and support of many evangelicals in England, including Dartmouth's
good friend, the Countess of Huntingdon. When Whitefield suggested
that an Indian be sent to England to campaign for further funds,
Wheelock selected his first native pupil, Samson Occum. Many persons were undoubtedly attracted by sheer curiosity to hear a noble
savage preach, but Occum preached well enough to attract a large
sum of money for his cause. King George III contributed £200,
Dartmouth contributed £50 and more than two thousand other con-
tributors raised the total to £11,000 during Occum's mission.[22]

Occum dined with Dartmouth in February, 1766, reporting that
he "appeared like a worthy lord indeed." George Whitefield recorded
that on this occasion Occum had dined "with the Daniel of the age,
the truly noble Lord Dartmouth."[23] Dartmouth's reputation marked
him for the added responsibility of acting as trustee for the funds
collected in England. With him on this board of trustees were several
other prominent evangelicals, including John Thornton. Thornton, a
father of the Clapham Sect, had contributed to the support of John
Newton and the poet Cowper at Olney, besides giving generously

[20] To Guilford, 24 October 1771, Ms. North, d.14, ff. 80-2.
[21] Lord Willoughby to Guilford, 20 October 1771, *ibid.,* f. 75.
[22] James Dow McCallum, *Eleazar Wheelock: Founder of Dartmouth College*
(Hanover, N. H., Dartmouth College Publications, Manuscript Series #4,
1939), 166, citing L. B. Richardson, *History of Dartmouth College* (1932),
I, 66-67. Compare M. D. Bisbee, "A Historical Sketch of the College," *General
Catalogue of Dartmouth College . . .* (Hanover, 1900), 27-8. The charter
bears the date 18 December 1769, *ibid.,* 11-21.
[23] McCallum, *Wheelock,* 156. George Whitefield to Eleazar Wheelock, 27
February 1766, Frederick Chase, *A History of Dartmouth College and the
Town of Hanover, N. H.* (J. K. Lord, ed., Cambridge, 1891), I, 51.

to Occum's mission fund. During the years between 1766 and 1775, the English trustees dispensed the monies to the Indian Charity School. Their most serious disagreement with Wheelock arose over the issue of whether to incorporate the institution. Wheelock believed that there were many advantages to incorporation, after he moved the school to its present site in New Hampshire. The trustees, however, feared that the clergy of the established church and Anglican officials in New Hampshire would gain too much control over the religious policies of an incorporated institution. Wheelock pursued his own plan, eventually persuading Governor Wentworth to issue a charter in 1769. The Governor rejected Wheelock's first suggestion to name the college Wentworth and insisted that the name of the new institution be Dartmouth College.

The English trustees were deeply offended when they heard of the incorporating charter. Not even the compliment of an eponym would persuade Dartmouth to forgive Wheelock at first. Just as they feared, the Anglican Governor of New Hampshire had insisted that the Bishop of London be included in the new board of trustees named in the Charter. When Dartmouth wrote to the Bishop, he made it clear that the latter's acceptance would cause considerable embarrassment, explaining that "the case and situation appear to [the trustees] to be misunderstood on the other side of the water." Instead of troubling him with an invitation, they had already returned a negative answer to Governor Wentworth.[24] Far from being offended, the Bishop replied that since there was no provision for an Anglican headmaster, nor the use of the liturgy in the college chapel, and since all the other trustees were dissenters, he could not see "what use a Bishop of London would be under the circumstances."[25] Although Wheelock had agreed to Wentworth's conditions in order to obtain his charter, he was much relieved by the episcopal refusal.[26] The offended trustees soon conquered their sense of grievance and resumed their correspondence with Wheelock in July, 1770.[27] The fund which they administered continued to support the Indian Charity School of Dartmouth College until the American Revolution. There is more than a touch of irony in the fact that the only remaining monument to the "good Lord Dartmouth's" concern for the American colonies should have been named without his permission and incorporated against his known wishes.

24 To the Bishop of London, 5 July 1771, Dartmouth Manuscripts, 347.
25 From the Bishop of London, 9 July 1771, *ibid.*
26 McCallum, *Wheelock*, 172-3.
27 Robert Keen, secretary to the English Trustees, wrote to Wheelock, 30 July 1770. This letter is printed in Chase, *Dartmouth College,* I, 241.

Chapter III

POLITICAL APPRENTICESHIP

LORD DARTMOUTH took his seat in the House of Lords on the last day of May, 1754. He was not very much interested in political matters, but preferred to devote his time to his family and his philanthropy. In the years preceding his entrance into the Rockingham administration, only two political issues excited his interest enough to draw him into debate. One concerned the cider tax of 1763 and the other involved Brecknock's pamphlet, *Droit le Roi,* the following year. In both instances, he opposed the government's policy and gained modest praise from competent observers. It was his manner of speaking, rather than any originality of his comments, which these observers noted. Nevertheless, these rare occasions reveal Dartmouth's intention to follow an Old Whig line. The group led by the Marquess of Rockingham and the Duke of Newcastle would look to him for support, when they formed a new ministry.

The cider tax, proposed by Francis Dashwood, the Chancellor of the Exchequer in Bute's administration, aroused a storm of opposition. In the first place it was an excise and according to John Wilkes: "The very word is hateful to an English ear. . . ."[1] Its proposed enforcement would deny defendants a trial by jury, while the right of search would infringe the Englishman's right to regard his house as his castle.[2] Furthermore, the measures especially discriminated against the apple-growers of six western counties.[3] One of these so-called "cider lords," Lord Lyttelton, was a friend of Dartmouth, which may help to account for his participation in the debate. He did not attend the dinner at Devonshire House on March 8th, where the principal leaders of the opposition discussed their strategy. On March 30th, however, when the bill was read in the House of Lords, Dartmouth let his voice be heard for the first time in a major debate. The Duke of Bedford's agent, Rigby, reported that "Many young lords spoke yesterday for the first or second time, but I think nothing

---

[1] *North Briton,* XLI (12 March 1763) and XLIII (26 March 1763). Compare the Petition of the Lord Mayor, Aldermen and Commons of the City of London against the Cider Bill, 28 March 1763, *Journals of the House of Lords,* XXX, 380.

[2] Basil Williams, *Life of William Pitt, Earl of Chatham* (London, 1914), II, 153-4.

[3] Turberville, *House of Lords,* 313. *Parl. Hist.,* XV, 1307-16. *Lords' Journals,* XXX, 378-387.

extraordinary except Lord Dartmouth, who did remarkably well."[4]
According to Horace Walpole, Dartmouth attacked the bill "with
decency and propriety."[5] We must be grateful to Rigby and Walpole
for recording their considered judgment of Dartmouth's speaking
ability, but it is unfortunate that no one bothered to write down
what he said. Nevertheless, it is possible to conjecture what his arguments might have been. In the first place it should be noted that this
debate on the cider tax marked the first occasion when the House of
Lords divided on a money bill.[6] Many members, opposed to the bill
in principle, doubted whether the house was competent to attack a
tax which had already passed the lower house. An undated paper in
Lord Dartmouth's hand may well explain the grounds for his opposition to the cider bill. The second point in this paper says, in part,
"We think it an high indignity and affront to his House to insist upon
words which bind down our future proceedings and preclude the
freedom of debate and the power of rejection, in case we should hereafter see reason not to agree with the Commons. . . ."[7] Whether
or not Dartmouth used these words, they apparently represent his
feelings in the matter of the lords' position in the legislative process.

In spite of combined efforts of William Pitt, John Wilkes, the Duke
of Newcastle and other opposition leaders, the cider bill became law.
Lord North was among those who voted for the measure, with the
curious consequence that his kinsman, Sir William Pynsent, burnt
him in effigy and changed his will, leaving his estate to William Pitt
instead of North![8] Many of Bute's contemporaries—including Horace
Walpole—attributed his resignation shortly afterwards to the inten-
sity of the opposition on this occasion. This interpretation of Bute's
resignation is no longer accepted by modern historians,[9] but it is significant that Walpole believed it to be so. Considering the strong
antipathy which George III's favorite aroused among the Whigs, his
resignation could only be regarded as a great victory. Anyone who
played even a small part in the assumed cause of that resignation
would certainly share the Whig leaders' elation and possibly their
gratitude. Lord Dartmouth's decent and proper attack on the cider
bill did not prevent its passage, but the Whig politicians would con-

[4] Rigby to Duke of Bedford, 31 March 1763, *Correspondence of John, Fourth Duke of Bedford* (Lord John Russell, ed., London, 1842-6), III, 222.

[5] Walpole, *Memoirs*, I, 200.

[6] *Parl. Hist.*, XV, 1316.

[7] Paper in Lord Dartmouth's handwriting, headed, "Dissentient," n.d., Dart-mouth Manuscripts, 1933.

[8] North to Guilford, 15 January 1765, Ms. North, d.23, f.178. Keith Feiling, *Second Tory Party, 1714-1832* (London, 1938), 78.

[9] Walpole, *Memoirs*, I, 197-204. Compare, Romney Sedgwick, ed., *Letters from George III to Lord Bute, 1756-1766* (London, 1939), nos. 285, 288, 289, & 290; also Richard Pares, "George III and the Politicians," *Transactions of the Royal Historical Society*, Fifth Series, Vol. I (1951), 141-2.

sider this failure less serious, if they believed that the opposition had forced Bute to leave office. One final comment with respect to the cider tax may be allowed; it was repealed by the Rockingham ministry while Dartmouth was serving at the Board of Trade in 1766.[10]

In February, 1764, a year later, Dartmouth had addressed the House of Lords. The occasion was the condemnation of a pamphlet entitled *Droit le Roi,* by a hack writer, Timothy Brecknock.[11] Briefly, the author argued that the royal prerogative remained the most potent force in the British constitution. Brecknock stated that the king had never acknowledged any superior authority on earth;[12] also that royal power was not limited by Parliament.[13] This thesis was anathema to all Whigs, who regarded parliamentary partnership in a "balanced constitution" as the only possible alternative to despotism. Horace Walpole, for example, denounced Brecknock's effort as "a collection from old statutes and obsolete customs of the darkest and most arbitrary ages [which failed to take into account] all the immunities obtained since by the Civil War, by the Revolution, and by various other struggles of Parliaments and the Crown."[14] Dartmouth was especially moved by this attack upon the Whig interpretation of the constitution. It was even rumored that the young Earl was going to lead the condemnation movement. When Newcastle heard such a rumor, he wrote to inquire if it were true. Dartmouth replied: "Your Grace mistakes in supposing that the motion is to come from me; it is in much abler hands and I think myself much honored that I am allowed to second Lord Lyttelton upon such an occasion."[15]

We have already noticed that Lyttelton and Dartmouth joined in opposition to the cider tax. Dartmouth's support of his resolution to censure *Droit le Roi* emphasizes again the importance of personal relationships in Eighteenth-Century political practice. Before leaving for the continental tour in 1751, Dartmouth had visited Lyttelton and later corresponded with him from Europe. Lyttelton had sent him a list of places he recommended visiting in the vicinity of Rome and requested some Italian perfumes and pieces of music for his wife.[16] In 1765 the government had already succeeded in expelling the con-

---

[10] *Parl. Hist.,* XVI, 206-7. Feiling, *Second Tory Party,* 88. A. D. Winstanley, *Personal and Party Government* (Cambridge, 1910), 269.

[11] *Droit de Roi: or, The rights and prerogatives of the imperial crown of Great Britain.* By a member of the Society of Lincoln's-Inn. London, Printed and sold by W. Griffin, 1764. Compare *Notes and Queries,* First Series, and Library of Congress *Catalog of Printed Cards,* Vol. XVIII.

[12] *Droit le Roi,* p. 2.

[13] *Ibid.,* 31 & 63.

[14] Walpole, *Memoirs,* I, 304-5.

[15] To Newcastle, 16 February, 1764, Add. Mss. 32,956, f.8.

[16] From Lyttelton, 6 February 1753, Dartmouth Manuscripts, 796.

troversial John Wilkes from his seat in the House of Commons. The argument still raged, however, about the methods they had used to procure evidence. In the midst of this ferment about the use of general warrants, lean, lank Lyttelton made his motion on February 21st. Reproving the ministry for seizing allegedly seditious literature on the questionable authority of a general warrant, Lyttelton accused them of overlooking a pamphlet which was subversive of all liberty.[17] *Droit le Roi* was not only "Jacobitical," he insisted, but also in violation of the Bill of Rights and the Glorious Revolution. Lord Dartmouth seconded the motion and "treated the book with still more severity," according to Walpole.[18] The motion was carried, a committee was appointed, including Dartmouth among its members, and a resolution was prepared condemning the pamphlet as a "false, malicious and traitorous libel . . ." to be burnt by the hangman.[19] Brecknock himself escaped any punishment, possibly because he had influential friends, although twenty years later he was hanged as an accessory to an atrocious murder in Ireland.

Dartmouth's friendship for Lyttelton and his sincere sympathy with Old Whig views might have required him to speak occasionally in the House of Lords. The key to his more active participation in politics is provided by another and more powerful friendship. The Duke of Newcastle was strong and decisive in influencing Dartmouth's early career. When the young Earl hesitated to accept Rockingham's invitation to join the new administration, it was Newcastle whose letter ended Dartmouth's hesitation. Later, in the midst of the Stamp Act crisis, Newcastle urged the Marquess to consult more with Dartmouth. Even as the Rockingham Ministry was crumbling, the Old Duke could still spare a thought for Dartmouth's career, vainly urging the powerless Rockingham to promote him.

Their acquaintance began with the grand tour, as we have seen. There were several occasions between 1752 and 1765 when Dartmouth and Newcastle corresponded with each other. The record of this exchange will help to reveal the nature of their friendship and set the stage for Dartmouth's entrance upon the political scene. While visiting Vienna, Dartmouth wrote to Newcastle on behalf of a certain Mr. Dillon, soliciting the Duke's recommendation for a post in Ireland.[20] Whether this particular request was successful, we do not

---

[17] Earl of Albemarle, *Memoirs of the Marquis of Rockingham* (London, 1852), I, 205-6. Lord Lyttelton was the victim of this bit of doggerel:
> "But who be dat bestride a pony,
> So long, so lean, so lank, so bony?
> Dat be de great orator Littletony."

[18] George, Lord Lyttelton, *Memoirs and Correspondence* (Robert Phillimore, ed., London, 1845), II, 650. Walpole, *Memoirs*, I, 304-6.

[19] *Lords' Journals*, XXX, 476-485. *Parl. Hist.*, XV, 1418.

[20] To Newcastle, 10 September 1752, Add. Mss. 32,729, f.252.

know, but Dartmouth's friendship with Newcastle became closer. By the time of his marriage he could say, "I have always been honored with particular marks of esteem from your Grace. . . ."[21] Perhaps encouraged by the old man, Dartmouth occasionally asked for small favors for others, never for himself. He secured a military promotion for Colonel Oughton by writing to Newcastle in 1759.[22] He forwarded with his warmest recommendations a petition from Rowland Friend, an eighty-eight-year-old man, nearly blind, who wished to be admitted to Charterhouse.[23] Whether these requests be considered political or philanthropic in nature, Dartmouth was beginning to learn the importance of maintaining a friendly understanding with a great and influential man. More important, he was also accumulating a small obligation to Newcastle with every request or petition which was granted. (Granting favors without obligation may be a work of charity, but it is not practical politics.)

In addition to their brief visit in Hanover, the flattering attention in Paris, and these few requests for favor, there was another tie between Dartmouth and Newcastle. Dartmouth's uncle, Henry Bilson Legge, and Newcastle had both served George II. In 1764 the Duke expressed great concern for Mr. Legge's declining health. Dartmouth wrote frequently to report the latest developments in his uncle's last illness until his death in August.[24] The Duke's letter of condolence praised Mr. Legge's virtues, integrity and resolution, and expressed a desire to be of service to those left behind.[25] In the meantime, the practical politician had already secured Dartmouth's promise of support for his candidate in the Cambridge election.[26] Thus, Dartmouth was learning some of the rules of the political game, whether they be designated favors, services, or *quid pro quo*.

There is no reason to suppose that Dartmouth was entering blindly into the political arena, nor that he unwillingly repaid Newcastle with his support. His uncle's political ideas were similar to Newcastle's and Dartmouth greatly admired his uncle's principles.[27] With so much in common, it is not surprising that Dartmouth gravitated into Newcastle's circle. By 1765 they were exchanging invitations to

---

[21] To same, 14 January 1755, Add. Mss. 32,852, f.168.

[22] To same, 17 September 1759, Add. Mss. 32,895, f.443. Also 26 March 1760, Add. Mss. 32,904, f.38.

[23] Petition of Rowland Friend to Newcastle, Received 9 June 1761, Add. Mss. 32,923, f.429. Endorsed by Dartmouth.

[24] To Newcastle [27 January 1764], Add. Mss. 32,955, f.285. See also folio 358 in this volume and 32,957, f.414.

[25] From Newcastle, 28 August 1764, Add. Mss. 32,961, f.388. Henry Bilson Legge's widow, the Baroness Stawell, later married the Earl of Hillsborough, Dartmouth's predecessor in the American Department.

[26] To Newcastle [11 March 1764], Add. Mss. 32,956, f.398.

[27] To same, 28 August 1764, Add. Mss. 32,961, f.261.

dinner, and no doubt discussing the political situation over bottles of port.[28]

As Dartmouth's apprenticeship progressed, he became more familiar with practical politics. Although he spoke seldom in the House of Lords, he gained a reputation as a staunch Whig which more than compensated for his Tory family background. He co-operated with Old Whigs like Newcastle and, in joining Lyttelton's attack, discomfited the Grenville Whigs who were in power. He was less interested in gaining an office for himself, however, than in seeing the government stabilized. During the last days of the Grenville ministry, Dartmouth wrote to his stepfather: "I am afraid your observation that the old ministry is settled again is rather premature. I hear of no further alterations than those which were talked of when your lordship was here. . . ."[29] The need for a stable ministry was great, for "several events that have happened lately discover [i.e., reveal] some sparks of a discontented and turbulent spirit which, if not timely suppressed, may break out into a flame which will not easily be quenched. May God avert the dismal effects of lawless rage and fury!"[30]

In spite of his fears for the future, Dartmouth was not immediately concerned with the downfall of George Grenville. He was taken completely by surprise in July, 1765, when Lord Rockingham invited him to become a member of the newly formed government. He had not been a party to the devious negotiations between the Whig leaders and the King's brother, the Duke of Cumberland, concerning the formation of a new ministry, but his name occurs in most of the lists of proposed ministers. The principal question was whether to offer Dartmouth the presidency of the Board of Trade or a position at the Treasury under Rockingham himself. A "Plan of a New Administration," dated June 30th mentions Dartmouth as one of the junior lords of the Treasury.[31] Various lists of proposed ministerial arrangements, drawn up during the first week of July, show either the Board of Trade or a junior lordship of the Treasury reserved for Dartmouth.[32] It was intended to offer the Board of Trade to the Earl of Shelburne, but it was already assumed that he would decline; thus, the choice of the two positions was almost entirely in Dartmouth's hands. The great Whig leaders agreed to include Dartmouth in the

[28] To same, 21 February 1765, Add. Mss. 33,068, f.382.

[29] To Guilford, 28 May 1765, Ms. North, d.10, ff.16-17.

[30] Ibid.

[31] "A plan of a new administration . . .," 30 June 1765, Sir John Fortescue, ed., Correspondence of King George the Third, 1760-1783 (London, 1928), I, 126.

[32] Fortescue prints several "Lists of Removals" in the King's Correspondence, I, 130-153.

ministry during a conference at Cumberland House on July 5th.[33] Three days later, Rockingham cordially invited Dartmouth to join the new government. If he chose the Treasury lordship, said the Marquess flatteringly, his presence there would compensate for Rockingham's own deficiencies. But Newcastle had informed him of Dartmouth's preference for the Board of Trade. Giving the young Earl his choice of the two positions, Rockingham acknowledged that the Board of Trade would be equally "proper for your Lordship's dignity and equally if not superiorly advantageous to the public."[34]

Once he had recovered from his surprise, Dartmouth began to draft, with many corrections and alterations, his reply. He stated that he had "never entertained a serious thought of taking part in [any] administration," but that he had once remarked in "accidental conversation" with his uncle that he would rather be a Lord of Trade than preside at a board of commissioners. The honor of Rockingham's invitation was great and Dartmouth deeply appreciated it, but his answer was couched in typically hesitant terms. He asked Rockingham to allow him more time to consider his proposal, "but if the urgency of the case should require an immediate determination, I beg your Lordship will consider me as having declined employment. . . ."[35] Since Dartmouth indicated that he preferred to continue his private life, without the obligations of office, this letter, or his subsequent interview with Rockingham, was interpreted as a refusal. Lord Shelburne also refused to preside over the Board of Trade, although for different reasons. A follower of William Pitt whose motto was "measures not men," Shelburne based his refusal on "the total ignorance I am under in regard to the measures you propose to pursue. . . ."[36]

By the 12th of July the old Duke of Newcastle was beginning to worry seriously about the construction of the ministry. He pointed out to the young and inexperienced Rockingham that all the junior lords of the Treasury had been chosen, but many other posts remained unfilled. "As I have had a long intimacy with my Lord Dartmouth," Newcastle continued, "I shall take the liberty . . . to write a very pressing letter . . ., to engage him to accept the First Lord of Trade. For, indeed, if he does not, I don't know where another

---

[33] Newcastle to John White, 29 June 1765 [?], Mary Bateson, ed. *A Narrative of the Changes in the Ministry, 1765-1767* . . ., Camden Society, New Series (London, 1898), LIX, 30. Newcastle apparently misdated his letter, for in it he mentions the meeting of July 5th.

[34] From Rockingham, 8 July 1765, Dartmouth Manuscripts, 818.

[35] Dartmouth's draft reply, *ibid.*

[36] Shelburne to Rockingham [11 July 1765], Rockingham Manuscripts, R. 1, f.244. "The Letters and Papers of the 2nd Marquis of Rockingham," Wentworth Woodhouse Muniments in the Sheffield City Library, are designated "Rockingham Manuscripts" for the sake of brevity.

proper man can be found."[37] In carrying out his intentions, Newcastle began his letter by apologizing for failing to keep Dartmouth
informed of the details of the negotiations over the new cabinet.
Now, however, he insisted that it was "essential in forming an administration" to have the young Earl's presence in some position of rank.
Adding to this piece of flattery by pointing out that Rockingham
would have preferred to have Dartmouth "with himself, in the
Treasury," Newcastle urged him to reconsider his refusal. "The Duke
of Grafton and my Lord Rockingham are both about your Lordship's
age, and if they had not got the better of their own inclination for
the sake of the King, and the public, I don't know where the King
would have got a Secretary of State, or a Treasury." Newcastle of
course exaggerated the difficulties, but he applied excellent psychology in urging Dartmouth to hear the call of duty before the siren
song of private inclinations. He also referred to "our intimacy at
Hanover."[38] The combination of all these appeals to duty, former
friendship and the implication of past favors, must have appeared
insufficient to Newcastle, for he felt impelled to add a postscript,
praising Dartmouth's reputation and forestalling any plea of inexperience by pointing out: "That in the present state of our plantations, and new acquisitions in America, a man of your Lordship's
most excellent character and known disinterestedness is more wanted
at the head of the Board of Trade than in any other station in his
Majesty's service; and this makes it in my opinion incumbent upon
you to accept it."[39] Unable to resist such a complimentary statement
of his own indispensability, Dartmouth reluctantly agreed to join the
Rockingham ministry. He accepted the position of First Lord of
Trade on July 19th.[40] Rockingham's difficulties in constructing a
ministry, however, were not yet at an end. As late as August 5 the
remaining lords commissioners still had not been appointed. Rigby,
who reported this deficiency to the Duke of Bedford, noted face-
tiously that Dartmouth had not yet used his position to recommend
the evangelical Whitefield for the Catholic bishopric of Quebec![41]

Entrance into the Rockingham ministry continued a political difference between Dartmouth and his stepbrother. Lord North had entered the political arena several years earlier, when he became a
junior Lord of the Treasury in 1759. He continued to serve there
until the formation of the Rockingham ministry. The two "brothers"
had voted on opposite sides in the cider tax debate, as we have seen.

---

37 Newcastle to Rockingham, 12 July 1765, Rockingham Manuscripts, R. 1,
f.246.
38 From Newcastle, 12 July 1765, Dartmouth Manuscripts, 819.
39 *Ibid.* Compare Add. Mss. 32,967, f.365 (Library of Congress Transcripts).
40 Entry for 19 July 1765 in George Grenville's Diary, W. J. Smith, ed.,
Grenville Papers (London, 1853), III, 220.
41 Rigby to Bedford, 5 August 1765, *Bedford Correspondence*, III, 313.

While North co-operated with the Grenville administration, Dartmouth supported the Rockingham group during their wilderness years. Rockingham would have welcomed North's adherence to his ministry. An early "list of removals" shows that Newcastle intended to offer him the paymaster-generalship.[42] Possibly it was in this connection that Dartmouth was entrusted with a secret mission in November, to persuade someone, probably Lord North, to join the recently formed and none too strong ministry. At any rate, Newcastle noted that the unnamed person had been unattached three weeks earlier and, if properly managed, could be brought into the administration.[43] Although Newcastle regarded Dartmouth as the best person to handle the negotiations, the latter confessed his failure to persuade "our friend" to join the government. Neither the friend's name nor his reasons for declining appear in the letter, because Dartmouth intended to explain the details of his interview in person. He did, however, admit that he sympathized with the principles on which the friend based his refusal.[44] Since Dartmouth himself lacked enthusiasm for his new position, it is not surprising that he failed to convert this anonymous friend into a supporter. He could have learned many lessons in the art of persuasion from that veteran politician, the Duke of Newcastle.

---

[42] "List of Removals," 9 July 1765, Rockingham Manuscripts, R. 1, f.241.
[43] Newcastle to Rockingham, 26 November 1765, Add. Mss. 32,972, f.60.
[44] To Newcastle, 28 November 1765, *ibid.*, f.70.

Chapter IV

REPEALING THE STAMP ACT

THE ROCKINGHAM ministry is best remembered for repealing the Stamp Act in 1766. At the time of its formation, however, there were many uncertainties. Not only did they lack a clearly defined policy but it was very difficult to say who would support and who would oppose their administration. Rockingham's followers were so anxious to taste again the joys of office-holding that they accepted the King's invitation on the last day of June, 1765, with only a vague hope for a parliamentary majority. They rationalized their love of office-holding and political patronage by referring to "sound Whig principles." Yet, about the only "principle" still operating in Whiggism was the rather irrational hatred for the Earl of Bute, George III's former tutor and first minister.[1] The great Whig Party had degenerated into a number of quarrelling factions, each following the leadership of a political personality, rather than a set of principles or party platform. Each faction hoped to place its leader in the King's Cabinet, in order to influence the distribution of patronage plums. While it would be foolish to deny that men of principle sometimes entered politics, it would be naive to assume that great policy decisions were always based upon principle and never upon expediency.

The Rockingham group of Old Whigs needed the support of some other faction in Parliament, in order to maintain a majority. They could count upon a large number of votes from the independent members who generally supported the "present system" so long as it enjoyed the King's approval. They might be able to purchase the support of the Duke of Bedford's following, "the Bloomsbury Gang," if they could satisfy their demands for jobs. They would almost certainly face the opposition of George Grenville and his followers, recently displaced from office, especially if they changed the policy which had produced the Stamp Act in 1765. Even a combination of Bedford-Grenville opposition would not injure the ministry, if that great enigma William Pitt decided to support the government. The number of his own followers was small, but the power of his voice would sway many votes among the uncommitted and inde-

---

[1] G. H. Guttridge, *English Whiggism and the American Revolution* (*University of California Publications in History Series,* vol. XXVIII, Berkeley, 1942), 138-142. Richard Pares, *King George III and the Politicians* (The Ford Lectures, Oxford, 1953), 56 n.1.

pendent gentlemen in the House of Commons. If he opposed Rock-ingham's administration, however, its life would be short indeed. Hoping to persuade Pitt to lend his support, Rockingham included two of his followers in the new administration. The Duke of Grafton became the Secretary of State for the Northern Department and General Conway accepted the seals of the Southern Department in July of 1765. Within six months, however, it was obvious that the Great Commoner would not join any ministry which he did not lead himself.[2]

When the list of ministers was complete, it was notable only for youth and inexperience. Dartmouth, as President of the Board of Trade, was only thirty-four and had held no other office except the largely honorary position of Recorder of Sheffield. Many of his fellow ministers, including the Marquess of Rockingham, were equally inex-perienced. None was a statesman of the first rank, and only Dowdes-well, the Chancellor of the Exchequer, possessed any remarkable ability. It is difficult to assess Dartmouth's relative position in this decidedly mediocre group of ministers. His office yielded precedence to several others: the Lord Chancellor (Northington), the two Secre-taries of State, the First Lords of the Treasury and the Admiralty, for example, were all greater offices than his. Yet, in character and intelligence he was equal to any of the present holders of those offices. Given a little experience, he would have made an able minister. The life of this administration was too short to provide this experience and, furthermore, the office which he held entailed some constitu-tional problems which Rockingham left unsolved.

Contemporary accounts did not estimate Dartmouth's abilities as more than modest. Even his old friend, the Duke of Newcastle, men-tioned him only twice in his account of the rise and fall of the gov-ernment.[3] Rockingham's biographer allots Dartmouth little space and even that brief paragraph follows the descriptions of all the other ministers.[4] Apparently, his fellow ministers ignored him early in the administration, for in December Newcastle wished "that my Lord Dartmouth was more consulted than he is. . . ."[5] From then on Dartmouth attended the meetings of the party leaders and took a more active part, especially as the American crisis became more serious. Rockingham was a most reluctant speaker in public,[6] and

[2] Grafton's *Autobiography*, 54-93. Pitt to Shelburne, December 1765, *Life of William, Earl of Shelburne* (Lord Fitzmaurice, ed., London, 1912), I, 256. Newcastle to Page, 7 January 1766, Add. Mss. 32,973, f.55 (L.C. Transcripts).

[3] Newcastle's *Narrative* (Bateson, ed., Camden Society), 47 & 78.

[4] Albemarle, *Memoirs of Rockingham*, I, 237.

[5] Newcastle to Rockingham, 10 December 1765, Add. Mss. 32,972, f.193 (L. C. Transcripts).

[6] King to Rockingham, January 1766, *Memoirs of Rockingham*, I, 271.

more of the burden of explaining the government's policy to the House of Lords fell to Dartmouth.

Soon after the new president took his seat at the Board of Trade, the most alarming reports began to arrive in his office.[7] The Virginia House of Burgesses passed four resolutions introduced by Patrick Henry, denying the right of Parliament to levy a tax on the people of Virginia.[8] Similar sentiments were expressed by other legislatures, including a strong statement from the General Court of Massachusetts protesting that the Stamp Act violated their Charter.[9] The Governors of the various colonies reported to the Board of Trade that not only their legislatures but the populace in general were determined to resist the new tax. Lieutenant-Governor Colden described the New York riots which forced the stamp officers to resign.[10] This disorderly state of affairs was confirmed by the newly arrived Governor, Sir Henry Moore, who told Dartmouth that the courts of the colony were closed to all business. The Stamp Act had been virtually "suspended" by the action of the mob.[11]

The greatest violence occurred in Massachusetts, however, where the mob attacked not only the stamp distributors but the private property of several leading officials, including Lieutenant-Governor Hutchinson.[12] They destroyed both private papers, including notes for Hutchinson's *History of Massachusetts,* and the public records of the court of Vice Admiralty.[13] Even more ominous than mob actions was the summons of the Massachusetts House of Representatives to hold an intercolonial congress in October. Governor Bernard did not anticipate any difficulty from this meeting. He thought it would be dominated by "friends of government," but the Board of Trade could only view with alarm a meeting unauthorized by the Crown.[14] Private letters from various parts of North America, relayed

---

[7] "Intelligence," Dartmouth Manuscripts, 100, is only one of many examples and contains copies or extracts of letters from the colonies dated variously 4 July to 5 November.

[8] "Resolutions" *ibid.,* 66, sent by the Lieutenant-Governor of Virginia on 5 June 1765.

[9] Rhode Island's resolutions, *ibid.,* 85. Resolves of the New Jersey Assembly, *ibid.,* 118. Petitions of the Massachusetts Council and Representatives, *ibid.,* 55, 95.

[10] Colden to Board of Trade, 6 December 1765, *Documents relative to the Colonial History of the State of New York* (O'Callaghan, ed., Albany, 1853-87), VII, 791-3.

[11] From Gov. Moore, 21 November 1765, *ibid.,* 789. From Moore, 16 January 1766, Dartmouth Manuscripts, 153.

[12] Thomas Hutchinson, *History of the Colony and Province of Massachusetts-Bay* (L. S. Mayo, ed., Cambridge, Mass., 1936), III, 90.

[13] Gov. Bernard to the Lords of Trade, 30 November 1765, Dartmouth Manuscripts, 116.

[14] Same to same, 8 July 1765, *ibid.,* 70. "Representation from the Board of Trade," 1 October 1765, *Parl. Hist.,* XVI, 121-2.

to the Board of Trade by interested persons in Britain, confirmed the seriousness of the situation.[15]

The Board of Trade was not an executive office and had no power to initiate policies or actions. Their greatest power was restricted to drawing up reports based upon the information gathered in their office, and presenting these representations to the Privy Council for implementation. Dartmouth proceeded to utilize this limited power, issuing on October 10th a representation relating to the "outrageous behaviour of the people of the town of Boston in opposition to the Stamp Act."[16] The principal ministers, however, were in a worrisome dilemma. The Stamp Act was George Grenville's measure and none of their own. General Conway, one of the Secretaries of State, had voted against it and, like some others in the Rockingham group, would have gladly seen it repealed. Any discredit that could be cast upon the Grenville Whigs would naturally reflect some glory upon the Old Whigs. On the other hand, repeal might be construed either as weakness, or worse, abandonment of the right to tax the colonies. Since this reflected upon the supremacy of Parliament, no true Whig could be expected to support unconditional repeal.

As the crisis deepened in America, so did the dilemma in the minds of the ministers. On Christmas Day, Newcastle was still proposing the query: "Stamp Duty—What is intended to be done with it. . . .[?]"[17] Some members were in favor of enforcing the measure, while others would modify it and a few would repeal it. According to one report, Dartmouth was among those who met a deputation of merchants on December 12th, telling them that a suspension of the act was the most that they could expect and insisting that the right to tax America would never be given up.[18] This may be true, but Dartmouth had much earlier expressed his view that the Stamp Act was inopportune,[19] although he would never agree with the American contention that it was unconstitutional. The lamentable fact is that the Rockingham government lacked a clear idea of what action to take until William Pitt declared his intentions in January, 1766.

Edmund Burke, serving as Rockingham's secretary, was hard at work forging a link between his master's political faction and powerful mercantile interests. The merchants trading to North America

---

[15] Copy of a letter from Trenton, New Jersey, 5 November 1765, Dartmouth Manuscripts, 100. William Smith to Rev. George Whitefield, 6 December 1765, *ibid.*, 820.

[16] *Parl. Hist.*, XVI, 123.

[17] Add. Mss. 32,972, f.333 (L. C. Transcripts).

[18] Basil Williams, *Life of William Pitt, Earl of Chatham* (London, 1914), II, 186, supplies this information, but without documentation.

[19] From Andrew Symmer, 21 September 1765, Dartmouth Manuscripts, 88, contains the statement, "I *agree* with your Lordship that there never could have been a more unlucky time in imposing a tax. . . ." Italics are mine.

and to the West Indies were for once united in their detestation of
the Stamp Act. The colonial non-importation agreement had aggra-
vated a depression, coupled with a scarcity of specie. English merchants found that they could neither sell goods to the colonies nor
receive payment for previous shipments. The repeal of the Stamp
Act seemed to them the only way to re-open channels of exchange.
The merchants, led by Barlow Trecothick, working behind the scenes
but with the full knowledge of the government leaders, planned a
petitioning campaign. Their heart-rending complaints about the decline in trade resulting from the Stamp Act would give Rockingham
the solution to his problem. Pressure upon Parliament would favor
repeal on the grounds that the act damaged British trade, not because
American colonists denounced it as unconstitutional.[20]

After Newcastle's letter of December 10th Rockingham consulted
Dartmouth more frequently on American affairs. He attended some
of the meetings between the Old Whig leaders and the City of London
merchants in December. Among his papers there are many memoranda based upon information received at the Board of Trade, carefully arranged according to the date received. These lists enable the
reader to gauge Dartmouth's reaction to the available information
and to conjecture the nature of any report he might have given to
meetings of politicians and merchants. The letters from America
received during the summer and autumn reflected the violence of
the reception of the Stamp Act. Later reports, however, indicated the
return of some calmness. General Gage, for example, insisted that
many persons would soon "repent of their opposition" and "wish to
take the stamps."[21] As long as the non-importation agreement was
in effect, however, the weight of the merchants' complaints must be
considered.

When Parliament met on December 17th the government was still
unprepared to present a statement of policy. The King's speech was
purposely vague, referring only to "matters of importance" which had
occurred in the colonies. During the Christmas recess the petitioning
movement gained momentum, as mercantile interests in the north
joined the London group. Samuel Garbett informed Dartmouth that
his fellow merchants in Birmingham were unanimous in their opposition to the Stamp Act. The stagnation in the iron trade had reduced
their exports by 75% to 90% and had resulted in unemployment for

[20] L. S. Sutherland, "Edmund Burke and the First Rockingham Ministry,"
English Historical Review, XLVII (January, 1932), 63. V. T. Harlow, *Founding of the Second British Empire* (London, 1952), I, 181. C. R. Ritcheson,
British Politics and the American Revolution (Oklahoma, 1954), 47-50. E. S.
& H. M. Morgan, *The Stamp Act Crisis* (Chapel Hill, 1953). E. S. Morgan,
ed., *Prologue to Revolution: Sources and Documents on the Stamp Act Crisis,
1764-1766* (Chapel Hill, 1959).
[21] From General Gage, 4 November 1765, Dartmouth Manuscripts, 139.

10,000 workers. The failure of American remittances and the count-ermanding of orders would result in an enormous dead stock of iron-ware unsalable elsewhere. Garbett expressed the opinion of the merchants that "no palliative measure or any but an instant repeal of the Stamp Act" would revive trade. Otherwise, the thousands of jobless persons would constitute a serious threat to peace and order, for Garbett included the ominous reminder: "Your Lordship knows their manners are daring and dissolute. . . ."[22]

From the point of view of the imperial government, the Stamp Act Congress was an extra-legal meeting. The colonial assembly was the only properly constituted body which could claim to represent and petition in behalf of its citizens. Claiming to represent all the colonies, however, the Congress addressed a petition to the King, a memorial to the House of Lords and a petition to the House of Commons.[23] The arrival of these several documents in Britain caused great interest among the political leaders who were searching for a policy before the re-opening of the parliamentary session. When Newcastle wrote to Dartmouth on the last day of the year, he said that he had heard ("though not from the Ministers") that the Board of Trade had received a "very decent, moderate and proper application from the representatives of the colonies . . . for redress."[24] He asked to see a copy. In returning the papers, Newcastle took exception to the de-nial of Parliament's right to tax the colonies, but otherwise agreed with the petitioners' complaint that the tax itself was improper.[25] Following Newcastle's advice to consult Mr. Speaker Onslow for his opinion, Dartmouth replied, "He thinks that such part of the petitions as tend to deny the right are unreasonable and unwarrantable, and that it would be extremely dangerous to give way in that point, be-cause the ground upon which they would build their claim of exemp-tion from taxation will equally support a denial of the authority of the British Legislature in any other instance. On the other hand, he thinks there is so much weight in the reasons they allege against the expediency of the late measures and so much propriety and decency in the manner of stating them as will be sufficient to induce Parlia-ment to give them relief, provided a mode of doing it can be formed which shall not be liable to be construed by them into an acknowl-edgment of the justice of their claim."[26] These are Onslow's words, but they represent Dartmouth's opinion too. The government's quan-dary still persisted into the new year: how to give relief to the

---

[22] From Samuel Garbett, 21 December 1765, *ibid.*, 130.

[23] Morgan, *Prologue to Revolution,* documents nos. 23-26.

[24] From Newcastle, 31 December 1765, Dartmouth Manuscripts, 134. Add. Mss. 32,972, f.386.

[25] From same, 2 January 1766, Add. Mss. 32,973, f.15.

[26] To Newcastle, 3 January 1766, *ibid.*, f.31.

merchants and satisfaction to the Americans without abandoning parliamentary supremacy.

When Parliament resumed its session on January 14th, the petitioning movement had produced some additional sentiment in favor of repeal. George Grenville and his supporters, however, were determined upon enforcement of the act. The majority of the members probably preferred some modification in its provisions, but the tide was turned by Pitt's famous speech.[27] Appearing in the House after a prolonged illness, Pitt demanded total repeal of the Stamp Act, "because it was founded on an erroneous principle." According to his interpretation of the constitution, Parliament had no right to tax the colonists, who were unrepresented in the House of Commons. Attempting to draw a line of distinction between the right to tax and the right to legislate, the Great Commoner pointed out that King, Lords and Commons all participated in the law-making process, whereas taxes were the "voluntary gift and grant of the Commons alone." The Commons in Britain could not give away portions of wealth belonging to Englishmen overseas, but the Parliament could exercise "supreme governing and legislative power" in regulating colonial trade and manufacturing—"in everything [said Pitt], except that of taking their money out of their pockets without their consent."

When George Grenville replied in defense of his policy, he said he could see no difference between internal and external taxes. He went so far as to blame the "factions in this House" for the "seditious spirit of the colonies."[28] Pitt's response insisted that "there is a plain distinction between taxes levied for the purpose of raising a revenue, and duties imposed for the regulation of trade. . . ."[29] Far from apologizing for any encouragement he may have given the colonists, Pitt declaimed, "I rejoice that America has resisted." He proposed, however, that the repeal of the tax measure go hand in hand with a statement of parliamentary authority over the colonies in "every point of legislation whatsoever." Pitt would never join a ministry in a secondary position but this speech gave the Rockinghams the necessary cue for their policy. Abandoning all suggestions for enforcement or modification, they proceeded to consider total repeal. They hoped that Pitt's eloquence would sway the majority and counterbalance the opposition of Grenville, Bedford and Bute.[30]

---

27 Mr. West's Paper, 14 January 1766, *ibid.,* f.133.

28 *Parl. Hist.,* XVI, 97-108.

29 *Ibid.,* p. 105. The role of William Pitt is documented in Morgan's *Prologue,* no. 56. E. S. & H. M. Morgan, *Stamp Act Crisis,* demonstrates that the colonists themselves did not draw this line between internal and external taxes in their denial of Parliament's right to tax them.

30 O. A. Sherrard, *Lord Chatham and America* (London, 1958), chaps. 13-14.

The Stamp Act crisis brought Dartmouth into a more prominent position in the political arena. From a minor post in which he was seldom consulted, he now progressed to the inner circle. A draft of the King's speech delivered on January 14th, containing several emendations in Dartmouth's handwriting, still remains among his papers. The Ministry obviously found it difficult to write this particular speech, for they had not yet agreed upon their policy. The phraseology had to be vague. Dartmouth contributed some phrases concerning the "alterations" which "might be found expedient in the regulations of the commerce" of the empire.[31] Whether those alterations would be modifications of the existing statute or its repeal was still left open to speculation until Pitt's speech. After Grafton presented the papers relating to the colonial disorders to the House of Lords, Dartmouth was appointed to the committee to draft the reply to the King's speech. Foreshadowing the Declaratory Act, the reply assured the King that the lords would exert their "utmost endeavours to assert and support . . . the legislative authority of this kingdom over its colonies. . . ."[32]

While the two houses of Parliament proceeded to the consideration of the papers presented to them by the Secretaries of State, the cabinet held several meetings to shape their policy. The veteran Duke of Newcastle was excluded from these conclaves, much to his chagrin, but Dartmouth attended.[33] His importance to the inner circle of political leaders was paralleled by the increasingly active role he was assuming in the House of Lords. Rockingham's own hesitation to speak in public drew Dartmouth more and more into the limelight.[34] The chief impediment to action was a division within the ranks of the ministerial leaders: Lord Barrington, the Secretary at War, Lord Chancellor Hardwicke and his brother Charles Yorke, were opposed to repealing the act, while Newcastle, Rockingham and Dartmouth were among the first to commit themselves in favor of repeal.[35] The solution of this problem lay in compromise: offer a bill to declare that Parliament had the right to tax the colonies, in spite of the withdrawal of Grenville's particular application of the right.

The Declaratory Act is significant not only for its effect in consolidating the divided Rockingham ministry but also for the important role it played in Dartmouth's own thinking. There never was a doubt

---

[31] King's Speech [14 January 1766], Dartmouth Manuscripts, 150.

[32] House of Lords to the King, draft reply with corrections in Lord Dartmouth's hand, *ibid.*, 151. Compare *Lords' Journals*, XXXI, 234-5.

[33] Winstanley omits Dartmouth from his list in *Personal and Party Government*, 262, but compare Newcastle to Portland, 20 January 1766, Add. Mss. 32,973, f.241-2.

[34] Draft of a speech in the House of Lords, Dartmouth Manuscripts, 247.

[35] Rockingham to Newcastle, 2 January 1766, Add. Mss. 32,973, f.11. Fitzmaurice, *Life of Shelburne*, I, 259-60.

in his mind about Parliament's right to legislate "in all cases whatsoever," but the act crystalized this basic tenet of Whiggism. As a
member of the ministry which was to repeal the Stamp Act, Dartmouth earned considerable reputation as a friend of the colonies,
but he remained consistent throughout his political career in his
loyalty to the Declaratory Act. The only question in his mind was
whether a particular measure was expedient, not whether it was
within the power of Parliament to pass it.

Ministerial problems were not completely solved by this compromise, and Rockingham seriously considered resigning in February.
The quarrels within the ministry, the gathering strength of the opposition, and the lukewarm support of the King all conspired to over-
whelm the young Marquess with defeatism. Dartmouth, who had
entered the government with the greatest reluctance, found himself
in a position of ever-increasing responsibility. Trying to instill into
his leader some of the enthusiasm which he was only beginning to
experience himself, he wrote, "you ought by all means to stand it
out to the last moment, and for the sake of your country to cling
with the same tenacity that others would use for the sake of themselves; the case is not yet desperate, and while there is the least
shadow of hope of doing good, I would on no account give up the
game to those who will undoubtedly do mischief. The act once repealed, I shall heartily congratulate your Lordship upon a release
from your fatigues."[36]

The Declaratory Act passed both houses easily and succeeded in
reassuring some opponents to the repeal of the Stamp Act.[37] The
debate on the latter measure raged long and heatedly, revealing weakness rather than strength in the ministry. Lord Chancellor Hardwicke,
who opposed the repeal, left an account of the debate which took
place on March 11th. Dartmouth was one of the speakers, urging
repeal as a measure to restore tranquillity between Great Britain and
her colonies.[38] Repeal would have been impossible without the declaration of parliamentary sovereignty, but only the Pittites seriously
questioned Britain's power to tax all parts of the empire.

Dartmouth's role in repealing the Stamp Act was well known to
his contemporaries, who showered him with gestures of appreciation.
British merchants framed petitions thanking him for his "assiduity,"
his "distinguished part" and his "important services" in promoting

---

[36] To Rockingham [12 February 1766], Rockingham Manuscripts, R. 1,
f.344.

[37] For example, Charles Yorke; see Newcastle to Archbishop of Canterbury,
1 March 1766, Add. Mss. 32,974, f.115.

[38] "Debate on the . . . Repeal of the Stamp Act," *A.H.R.*, XVII (April,
1912), 577.

the repeal, and some offered him the freedom of their city.[39] The
colonists were naturally elated at the success of their resistance and,
while some of them erected statues to Pitt, others acknowledged
Dartmouth's assistance to their cause by sending him letters and gifts.
Colonel John Randolph of Virginia sent him a young eagle in honor
of the occasion.[40] That Dartmouth was touched by these demonstra-
tions of gratitude is reflected in a letter which he wrote to a member
of the Virginia clergy after resigning from the Board of Trade:

> I suppose nothing can afford greater or more reasonable satis-
> faction to the mind of any man, who is engaged in the service
> of the public, than the approbation of the sound and sober part
> of that community whose welfare he is endeavoring to promote.
> Upon this principle I confess it gives me very great pleasure to
> hear that the most respectable people of the Province of Virginia
> have expressed their confidence in the integrity of an adminis-
> tration, whose upright intentions and real zeal for the public
> good, will I am persuaded be remembered with honor to the
> latest posterity, and of which I had the happiness to make a
> part. The measures they pursued had so evident a tendency to
> remove all cause of jealousy and misunderstanding between
> different parts of the British Empire, and to promote the true
> interests of the whole, that I am persuaded they must receive
> the hearty approbation of every dispassionate and candid mind
> in all parts of his Majesty's dominions. . . .[41]

The House of Representatives in Massachusetts voted unanimously
to thank Dartmouth for his "noble and generous patronage of the
British colonies."[42] He replied that "as I shall always hope to be able
to consider Great Britain and her colonies as one and the same
people, it will always be my endeavor in all public transactions in
which I may any way be concerned equally to consult the interests
and benefit of all parts of the British Dominions."[43] To Dartmouth's
mind it was perfectly logical that, if the people of Britain and the
colonies were one and the same people, they must naturally have but
a single head—the King-in-Parliament. To limit the supremacy of
the legislature by reserving certain essential functions, such as taxation, to the individual colonial assemblies would be tantamount to

---

[39] These congratulatory messages are in Dartmouth Manuscripts, ff.201
et seq. See especially, ibid., ff.212, 219, & 228.

[40] From Col. John Randolph, 15 June 1766, Dartmouth Manuscripts, 214.
A statue of William Pitt, erected in 1766, still stands in Charleston, South
Carolina.

[41] To Rev. Giberne, in answer to his letter of 30 May 1766, Dartmouth
Manuscripts, 201.

[42] From Thomas Cushing, 21 June 1766, ibid., 215.

[43] Dartmouth's draft reply, ibid.

dissolving the empire. If he thought that the colonists agreed with his interpretation of the constitution, he might have considered the warnings expressed by some of his correspondents that the Declaratory Act was considered only a matter of form.[44]

Dartmouth's year at the Board of Trade established his reputation as a friend of the colonists. Those who knew of his religious convictions were pleased that he shared some of the experience of the Great Awakening with them. The fact that he was a member of the ministry which repealed the Stamp Act further enhanced his reputation for goodness. Yet, as his replies to congratulations demonstrate, his view of the imperial constitution varied considerably from theirs. In their moment of triumph, the colonists chose to overlook his endorsement of the Declaratory Act. This failure to appreciate his position would lead to further misunderstanding in 1772, when he became Colonial Secretary. In the meantime, however, Dartmouth had other problems, stemming directly from the constitutional limitations of his office and his ill-fated desire to create an executive office out of the weak presidency of the Board of Trade.

---

[44] From Charles Williamos, 3 July 1766, *ibid.*, 218.

Chapter V

MOST AGREEABLE EMPLOYMENT

REPEALING the Stamp Act was certainly the most significant event in Dartmouth's year in office, but it would be a mistake to assume that this was the only political problem to concern him. The Board of Trade had a wide variety of business to transact, in addition to gathering information about the American crisis. During these months, Dartmouth began to feel the restrictions imposed upon his office and to believe that a greater degree of power and responsibility would be desirable.

The Board of Trade was in a period of declining influence when Dartmouth was called to preside in 1765.[1] One of his predecessors, the Earl of Halifax, had led the Board to its greatest heights in 1752 and had nearly succeeded in obtaining for himself the powers and dignity of a secretaryship of state. Pitt had thwarted Halifax's ambition, when he assumed the leadership of the government in 1756. Ten years later, history repeated itself when Dartmouth's hopes of achieving a similar status were frustrated by the same William Pitt, about to become the Earl of Chatham. The weaknesses of the Board's position and the complexity of the problems with which it was supposed to deal had by then conspired to convince Dartmouth that he must either acquire more power or resign.

Although the empire was more than 150 years old, no branch of the British government was primarily and exclusively responsible for colonial policy before 1768 when a third Secretary of State was appointed. Responsibility was divided among several offices, including the Admiralty, the Treasury and the War Office, in addition to the Board of Trade. Some co-ordination was provided by the Secretary of State for the Southern Department, but neither he nor the Board of Trade was exclusively concerned with colonial affairs. The Board's principal concern was the commercial policy of the realm; the plantations were no more important than general European trade.

---

[1] The following are the most valuable detailed accounts of the Board of Trade: C. M. Andrews, *Guide to the Materials for American History to 1783 in the Public Record Office of Great Britain* (Washington, 1912 & 1914), I, 82-103; A. H. Basye, *The Lords Commissioners of Trade and Plantations: Commonly Known as the Board of Trade, 1748-1782* (New Haven, 1925); M. P. Clark, "The Board of Trade at Work," *A.H.R.*, XVII (October, 1911), 17-43; and O. M. Dickerson, *American Colonial Government, 1696-1765* (Cleveland, 1912).

Under Lord Halifax, the Board had nearly succeeded in monopolizing colonial business. An order in council gave Halifax the complete control of colonial trade as well as the very important power of nominating colonial officials. By these means, especially the control of patronage, Halifax became a colonial secretary of state in all but name. Pitt, however, had other plans and, by revoking the order in council, in 1761, began the process of rapid decline which the Board suffered thereafter. By the time Dartmouth succeeded to the First Lord's chair, the Board once again shared its work in colonial matters with the Secretary of State for the Southern Department. Both the power of correspondence and the patronage were entirely in the Secretary's hands. The Board's power had been reduced to gathering information and drawing up representations for the Privy Council to implement or to reject.

In spite of these changes, Dartmouth was a very faithful and conscientious president. He attended one hundred twenty-five meetings during his term, missing only three.[2] The monetary reward for his services was a salary of £1,000, to which was added an annuity of another thousand pounds during His Majesty's pleasure.[3] Reduction in power was not accompanied by a simplification of business, for Dartmouth's Board was still responsible for a wide variety of matters. The Duke of Grafton had once refused to accept the presidency on the grounds that it was "as difficult a post as any whatever."[4] The Stamp Act crisis, as we have seen, created additional work for the Board, receiving reports and preparing papers for Parliament.[5] But several other major items of business required the Board's attention, especially the Sugar Act, the Free Port in Dominica and policies for the newly acquired portions of the empire.

In some respects Grenville's Sugar Act of 1764 was more important than the Stamp Act. The Molasses Act of 1733 had imposed a duty of sixpence, which had merely encouraged smuggling. Grenville reduced the duty on sugar to threepence, but he had every intention of enforcing its collection in the colonies. The Sugar Act not only attempted to raise a revenue for defense by means of import duties but it also sought to strengthen the mercantilist system.[6] Dartmouth had scarcely assumed the presidency when he received complaints against this measure. Dennys de Berdt, a London merchant with valuable trading connections with North America, hoped that Dartmouth would be the means of reviving American trade and specifi-

[2] Basye, *Board of Trade,* Appendix A, p. 225.

[3] Add. Mss. 33,056, ff.171 & 172.

[4] Grafton's *Autobiography,* 43 *et seq.* "Duke of Cumberland's Account," Rockingham Manuscripts, R. 13, f.15.

[5] From Grafton, 10 March 1766, Dartmouth Manuscripts, 177.

[6] Harlow, *Second British Empire,* I, 179-181.

cally deplored the revenue measures of the Grenville government.[7] Dartmouth also read the opinion of the Massachusetts Assembly to the effect that the Sugar Act imposed an unconstitutional tax.[8] The argument that the tax of threepence per gallon was too high probably sounded more convincing. Andrew Symmer gave Dartmouth a lesson in the facts of the triangular trade when he pointed out that one hogshead of rum equalled the cost of a slave in Africa. The slave would bring £27 profit when sold at Antigua, which not only represented a gain in bullion but also gave employment to many colonists. The threepenny duty destroyed this profitable enterprise.[9] Dartmouth and the Board of Trade were interested in trade problems, but the Treasury and the merchants of Britain were much more vitally concerned. The initiative in the new Molasses Act lay with them, but the Board was consulted about matters of detail.[10] The result was the passage of an act in 1766, reducing the duty to one penny, which pleased the American colonists in spite of the fact that it was a form of taxation without representation.

Dartmouth's Board of Trade was also concerned with the problem of trade with Spain's Caribbean colonies. In theory the empires of both Spain and Britain were governed by mercantilist principles which prohibited any exchange between their colonies. In fact, however, many exceptions were made to the general rule and Spanish ships often purchased British manufactured goods, paying in gold bullion. Grenville's legalistic mind had spawned an order to British customs and naval officers to intercept all foreign shipping in American ports, with the result that the Spaniards stopped trading there.[11]

When Dartmouth came to the Board of Trade, he received many complaints and suggested remedies for this situation. An unsigned letter from Philadelphia, for example, told him of the serious results of Grenville's regulations upon several merchants of that city. Upon the invitation of the Governor of West Florida, they had sent English goods worth £100,000 to Pensacola in anticipation of trade with the Spanish colonies. When a Spanish vessel from Vera Cruz arrived with half a million dollars in hard money, the captain of a British man-of-war threatened to seize the Spaniard if so much as one dollar landed. This narrow view of the mercantilistic regulations prevented

---

[7] From Dennys de Berdt [Received July 1765], Dartmouth Manuscripts, 73.

[8] Massachusetts Representatives to Mr. Mauduit, 13 June 1765, *ibid.*, 51.

[9] From Andrew Symmer, 21 September 1765, *ibid.*, 88.

[10] Roger Hale to William Dowdeswell, 8 November 1765, *ibid.*, 106. Merchants' Resolutions, 10 March 1766, *ibid.*

[11] A. M. Schlesinger, *The Colonial Merchant and the American Revolution, 1763-1776* (New York, 1939, Second Edition), 85. Frances Armytage, *The Free Port System in the British West Indies: A Study in Commercial Policy, 1766-1822* (*Imperial Studies Series*, V. T. Harlow, ed., London, 1953), 24-27.

American merchants from paying their English creditors.[12] The Governors of Georgia and West Florida confirmed the impressions of the Philadelphia merchants that the naval patrols had acted with undesirable severity.[13]

Dartmouth participated in various conferences of government leaders with British merchants who were seeking a solution to this problem as one aspect of the general depression. One such meeting, on the last day of December, 1765, was attended by Rockingham, Dowdeswell and Dartmouth together with two important City merchants.[14] Here as in the Sugar Act problem, the initiative lay with the merchants and the details of the solution were the work of the Treasury. Dartmouth's interest and participation in the discussions, however, are evidenced by the several papers which he preserved long after the event.[15] One of these manuscripts is Colonel Dalrymple's report on American trade which contains the recommendation that a free port be established in Dominica, one of the British West Indies.[16] The logic of this argument must have convinced Dartmouth, for he supported the Free Port Bill of 1766. This act opened the port of Dominica to the free exchange of British manufactures for Spanish and French produce.[17] It was hoped that this measure would relieve the depression but it had more than immediate significance. As the first legal breach in the mercantilists' dike, it foreshadowed the policy of free trade many decades later.[18]

Included in the variety of problems with which Dartmouth became acquainted at this time were several he had to consider again after 1772. The disposition of territory conquered from France in the Seven Years' War plagued every administration before the American Revolution.[19] The Province of Quebec lacked a settled

---

[12] Unsigned letter from Philadelphia, 11 October 1765, Dartmouth Manuscripts, 100. De Berdt identifies the writer as John Rhea, in his letter of 3 December 1765, *ibid.,* 119.

[13] Governor Wright to Board of Trade, 28 June 1765, *ibid.,* 69. Governor Johnstone to John Pownall, various dates, 1764 & 1765, *ibid.,* 53 *et seq.*

[14] L. B. Namier, *England in the Age of the American Revolution* (London, 1930), 281.

[15] For example, draft Treasury minute, 15 November 1765, Dartmouth Manuscripts, 111. Draft of a clause of an Act of Parliament [1766?], *ibid.,* 243.

[16] "Colonial Dalrymple's Report of the State of Trade, presented soon after his return to England to the first Lord of the Treasury and Board of Trade," *ibid.,* 1052. See also, Dorothy B. Goebel, "The 'New England Trade' and the French West Indies, 1763-1774: A Study in Trade Policies," *William and Mary Quarterly,* XX (July, 1963), 345.

[17] Armytage, *Free Port System,* 42-43.

[18] Harlow, *Second British Empire,* I, 182.

[19] C. W. Alvord, *The Mississippi Valley in British Politics* (Cleveland, 1917) explores this theme in two volumes. Jack M. Sosin, *Whitehall and the Wilderness: The Middle West in British Colonial Policy, 1760-1775* (Lincoln, Nebr., 1961), undertakes a revision of Alvord's thesis.

constitution until the Quebec Act of 1774, which Dartmouth was to introduce in the House of Lords. As early as 1765, however, he was dealing with certain aspects of the problem. The problem of the judicature was especially difficult, owing to the lack of experience with the jury system under French law. The Board of Trade prepared instructions to Governor Murray to declare all the King's subjects, both French and English, competent to act as jurors and to insure fair trials for the *habitants*.[20] This policy was endorsed by the law officers of the Crown, and approved by the Privy Council, but the ministry was too near its dissolution to implement it.[21]

Western lands were no longer disputed by France, but problems of settlement and government remained. Grenville and Shelburne had sponsored the Proclamation of 1763 as a temporary restriction of western migration, in order to prevent certain conflict with the Indians, until a permanent policy could be formulated. The actions of the Rockingham administration helped to make this policy of prohibiting white settlement endure until the Revolution. Dartmouth learned some of his first lessons in the complexities of imperial administration of western lands in his year at the Board of Trade. In accordance with Old Whig policy, he rejected applications, such as that of Major Mant, to establish white settlements in Indian country.[22] Other territory was open for settlement, however: The Earl of Moira requested 5,000 acres in West Florida,[23] while another of Dartmouth's correspondents expected to take up lands in East Florida.[24] These and similar petitions must have excited Dartmouth's interest, for eventually he secured substantial grants of Florida land for himself and members of his family. Thus, he gained a reputation for sympathy with the expansionists, whereas his successor in the Board of Trade and his predecessor in the colonial secretaryship (the Earl of Hillsborough), was noted for his opposition to such plans.

Numerous other problems appeared on the table of the First Lord of Trade: sericulture in Georgia, the improvement of the harbor in Barbados, clarification of the legislative power in Senegambia, recommendations for colonial councillors, the establishment of a new consulate at Naples, and the solution of problems arising from the trade with Portugal, to cite only a few examples.[25] In dealing with this wide variety of business, Dartmouth's board showed a great deal

20 Additional Instructions to Governor Murray, 15 November 1765, Dartmouth Papers, Public Archives of Canada (Ottawa), 2264. Report of the Attorney and Solicitor General, 14 April 1766, *ibid.*, 2269.

21 C. R. Ritcheson, *British Politics and the American Revolution*, 65.

22 From Major Mant, 30 April 1766, Dartmouth Manuscripts, 194.

23 From the Earl of Moira, 19 August 1765, *ibid.*, 79.

24 From R. Charles, 21 September 1765, *ibid.*, 86.

25 Public Record Office of Great Britain, C.O. 391/72 & 73. *Journal of the Commissioners for Trade and Plantations* (London, 1936), XII.

of efficiency, but little of the initiative and enthusiasm for its work demonstrated by earlier Boards.[26] Part of the explanation for this lack of enthusiasm may have been the reduction in authority imposed by Pitt long before Dartmouth became president. Then, too, Burke's policy of alliance between political and mercantile leaders allowed the merchants to exercise a great deal of initiative in commercial matters. Whatever the reasons, it was not long before Dartmouth began to feel cramped in his new office. Expected to deal with a large number of complex problems, he lacked the power to initiate or implement policies. The solution to this administrative claustrophobia lay in the direction of a true secretaryship.

He had known at the beginning of his term that great difficulties lay in his path. Lord Hillsborough, who both preceded and succeeded Dartmouth in the first lord's chair, had warned him that it was absolutely necessary for the president of the Board of Trade to have complete control of colonial business.[27] Dartmouth may have read the book written by Thomas Pownall, former Governor of Massachusetts, in which he recommended ending the division in authority over the colonies shared by the Board and the Secretary of State.[28] His own experience with government business, especially during the Stamp Act crisis, showed him that these recommendations and warnings were valid. Just when he was feeling most uncomfortable in his office, the Duke of Grafton's resignation in April, 1766, gave him an opportunity to press for an improvement. Grafton's desertion, however, seriously weakened the ministry. Rockingham would be interested in Dartmouth's elevation to a secretaryship only if it strengthened the administration in some way. In one proposal, Newcastle suggested creating a third secretaryship for Charles Townshend.[29] The constitutional difficulties connected with appointing a member of the House of Commons to a third secretaryship, however, were too great and Newcastle proceeded to draw up other suggestions.[30] One of these plans would have transferred Dartmouth to the Admiralty, but most of them placed him in charge of the colonies. The principal question was whether he should be First Lord of Trade with greatly expanded power or a Secretary of State in name as well as fact.

[26] Basye, *Board of Trade*, 153.

[27] From Hillsborough, September 1765, Hist. Mss. Comm., *15th Report, App., Pt. I*, p. 179.

[28] Thomas Pownall, *The Administration of the Colonies* (London, 1765, Second Edition), 23-24.

[29] Newcastle to Rockingham, 6 May 1766, Add. Mss. 32,975, f.89 (L. C. Trans.).

[30] Newcastle to Conway, 7 May 1766, *ibid.*, 104. It would be necessary to grant Townshend a peerage, for the third secretaryship might be considered a new office, as defined in the Act of 1707. Betty Kemp, *King and Commons, 1660-1832* (London, 1957), 59-61.

Everyone concerned approved of Dartmouth personally. Even the new Secretary of State, the Duke of Richmond, had no objection to transferring the colonial business from his department to Dartmouth.[31] The King, however, preferred giving Dartmouth fuller powers in his old position at the Board of Trade rather than creating a new secretaryship.[32] The ministry was rapidly reaching the end of its existence, so that major alterations were impossible. At the end of the parliamentary session, Secretary at War Barrington noted that "it was agreed that America should be given to the Board of Trade or a third Secretary of State [but] this is not done, or at present much talked of."[33] When no action was forthcoming in July, Newcastle became quite concerned and asked Rockingham, "For God's sake, why don't you settle my Lord Dartmouth's affair?"[34] The King had already decided to send for Pitt, however; the Rockingham ministry was moribund.

In modern practice the resignation of one Prime Minister and the appointment of another usually leads to the replacement of all members of the government by supporters of the victorious party. By Eighteenth-Century standards, however, there was nothing unusual in a member of an out-going administration retaining his position or obtaining a different one in the new ministry. Pitt expected to construct a "broad-bottomed" administration, including Whigs from every group, so that there was some reason to assume that Dartmouth might secure a secretaryship after all.

Pitt's principal goal at this time was to ensure his parliamentary support by breaking up the factions, like Rockingham's, and detaching individual members who clustered around the great Whig leaders. Whether Dartmouth went or stayed would matter little to him, if the Old Whig group ceased to act together as a political unit. Pitt invited Dartmouth to remain in office, but was cool, to say the least. According to a close friend of the family, "he never condescended to visit him or even in the most indirect way to convey a single message to him. . . ."[35] Although Dartmouth may have been hurt by this rude-

---

[31] Richmond to Rockingham, 19 May 1766, Rockingham Manuscripts, R. 1, f.369.

[32] Rockingham to Newcastle, 18 May 1766, Add. Mss. 32,975, f.207 (L. C. Trans.). King to Egmont, 18 May 1766, Fortescue, ed., *Correspondence of George III*, I, 309.

[33] Barrington to Gov. Bernard, 8 June 1766, *Barrington-Bernard Correspondence* (Edward Channing and A. C. Coolidge, eds., Cambridge, Mass., 1912), 108.

[34] Newcastle to Rockingham, 5 July 1766, Add. Mss. 32,976, f.13, cited in Basye, *Board of Trade*, 151, n.125.

[35] Fitzmaurice, *Life of Shelburne*, I, 279. W. Talbot to Guilford, 5 August 1766, Ms. North, d.10, f.143-4. Edmund Burke noted that "Dartmouth, who has firmness and feeling enough, will never endure the cutting off his American pretensions by the New People. . . ." Burke to Charles O'Hara, 29 July [1766], *Correspondence* (T. W. Copeland, ed.), I, 262.

ness, it was Pitt's attitude toward the third secretaryship which proved decisive. At the end of July, Rockingham informed him that there would be no promotion for the First Lord of Trade. Dartmouth replied that he would rather retire than continue in the same position.[36] The correctness of his decision was confirmed by his successor's actions. Lord Hillsborough requested a reduction in the Board's powers, since an increase in responsibility had been denied and a continuation of the *status quo,* he believed, was undesirable.

Dartmouth's resignation caused great disappointment among his friends. DeBerdt, for one, had found the amiable Earl sympathetic and easy to work with. Consequently, he urged him to remain in his present office. Dartmouth replied that he had found the "employment . . . most agreeable" and had left it reluctantly. He continued then, to give his views of both the American colonists in general and his own experience with the newly-formed ministry: "notwithstanding the late excesses, I believe there are many [Americans] possessed of sound and sober principles both of religion and government, and . . . I should always have been happy to have assisted in promoting every wish they could reasonably form consistent with that subjection to the supreme authority of the Mother Country, upon which I think their own as well as our welfare and prosperity much depend. I should have been glad to have continued on any footing that would have put it in my power to be of real use, but after having been refused the only thing that in my opinion could have enabled me to be of any service, without the offer of any other method of removing my difficulties, I thought it best to withdraw. . . ."[37]

This letter makes it clear that Dartmouth's friendship for the colonists assumed the existence of "that subjection to the supreme authority of the Mother Country," which the Declaratory Act had affirmed. It is also significant that he informed DeBerdt that he had been "refused the only thing" that would have persuaded him to remain in office—the elevation to a true secretaryship.

Close friends of the family worried about the effect of this resignation upon Dartmouth himself. The Earl of Warwick, for example, regretted the young nobleman's retirement, "because the bringing him out more into the world of business . . . was essential to him and a continuation would be no less so."[38] It was obvious to his contemporaries that Dartmouth would withdraw into the peacefully

---

[36] From Rockingham, 25 July 1766, Hist. Mss. Comm., *15th Report, App., Pt. I,* p. 182. King to Pitt, 25 July 1766, *Correspondence of William Pitt, Earl of Chatham* (W. S. Taylor & J. H. Pringle, eds., London, 1840), II, 463.

[37] To De Berdt, 13 August 1766, in William B. Reed, *Life and Correspondence of Joseph Reed* (Philadelphia, 1847), I, 46-47.

[38] Earl of Warwick to Guilford, 1 August 1766, Ms. North, d.10, f.138.

pious mode of life from which Rockingham and Newcastle had extracted him a year earlier. As a member of the aristocratic minority who ruled the kingdom, Dartmouth had a duty as well as a privilege in assisting the government. And now, added to his uprightness of character, there was a further recommendation in his experience with the problems of the Board of Trade. The Rockingham Whigs expected to return to power and assumed that Dartmouth would have charge of American affairs. Many Americans, particularly Benjamin Franklin, eagerly looked forward to Dartmouth's re-appointment, partly because of the general sympathy which his religious views and philanthropic actions had excited, but more especially because of his association with the repeal of the Stamp Act. It was assumed that Dartmouth would be more lenient than Hillsborough, especially in regard to westward expansion.

Dartmouth's year of "most agreeable employment," then, made it impossible for him to resume his former mode of life forever. The Rockinghams failed to return to power until 1782, but when "brother North" called upon him for support in 1772, Dartmouth could not refuse. The personal tie which bound him in almost every important decision would bring him back into an active political office, at a time when the problems would be overwhelming.

Chapter VI

YEARS OF TRANSITION

ALTHOUGH he held no political office between 1766 and 1772, these were important years in Dartmouth's life. He was deeply involved with a number of personal problems, as we have seen: Lady Huntingdon's illness in 1767, work with the English trustees of Wheelock's Indian School, worry about his sons' education. Politically, this period of his life is significant, too. At the beginning he was working closely with the Rockingham Whigs, but before the end of 1772 he would become a member of North's ministry. It is temptingly simple to say that he left the Whig Party and joined the Tories, but this would be highly inaccurate. The circumstances surrounding Dartmouth's gradual separation from the Old Whig faction and his acceptance of North's invitation require detailed description.

When Parliament met in the autumn of 1766, William Pitt, the erstwhile Great Commoner, made his debut in unfamiliar ermine, as Earl of Chatham. In spite of Chatham's earlier rudeness, Dartmouth bore him no grudge, nor did he oppose the new administration's policies with regard to the embargo on corn. He was disappointed with Chatham's maiden speech, which he thought inaudible and repetitious. He was more annoyed by the tactics of the opposition speakers, Lords Temple and Suffolk.[1] After December, 1766, when illness forced Chatham into retirement, Charles Townshend began to dominate the ministry. In view of difficulties later occasioned by the duties which he introduced, it may be well to note the attitude of the Old Whigs toward their passage. Rockingham himself was "emphatic that he stood by the Declaratory Act and the 'dependency' of America."[2] So few members of either House opposed the Townshend duties,[3] that it would be unreasonable to suppose that Dartmouth did so.

When the ministry undertook the regulation of the East India Company, the Rockingham group rose to its defense. The Duke of Grafton, on whose inadequate shoulders rested the mantle of Chatham, introduced a bill to restrict the Company's dividends to ten per cent. The Rockingham Whigs opposed this measure on the age-

---

[1] To Guilford, 13 November 1766, Ms. North, d.10, ff.198-9. B. D. Bargar, "Chatham's First Debate in the House of Lords," *Journal of Modern History,* XXIX (December, 1957), 361-2.

[2] Feiling, *Second Tory Party,* 94.

[3] *Ibid.,* 93. Grafton's *Autobiography,* 127.

old grounds that it interfered with the property rights of a chartered company.[4] Similarly, when Grafton introduced another bill regulating the East India Company the following year, Dartmouth not only spoke against the bill but also joined other Old Whigs in signing the protest in the House of Lords.[5] Opposition tactics in 1767 injured the ministry less than Chatham's incapacity and the administration's internal divisions. In July Grafton, seeking additional support, opened complicated negotiations with opposition leaders.[6] For a brief period it looked as though the Old Whig faction might return to office. Newcastle, acting his customary part in the drama of ministry-making, drew up several lists of supporters and appropriate appointments. In the previous March the old Duke had enumerated the "persons named by my Lord Rockingham to be the friends without whom he would take no step."[7] Dartmouth's name appeared in third place, but even more significant is the list of three points upon which Rockingham was to insist. One of them was: "to give the whole care of the West Indies and North America to my Lord Dartmouth, with the seals as third Secretary of State."

If the negotiations had been successful, Dartmouth would have returned to office in 1767 in charge of colonial affairs, but not as a mere First Lord of Trade. By contrast with the political negotiations in 1765, Dartmouth was informed of the steps in these negotiations, including a long report from Rockingham on their failure.[8] In his reply, Dartmouth expressed sympathy for Rockingham's disappointment, but no regret at his own failure to return to office.[9]

Continuing his affiliation with the Old Whig group, Dartmouth visited Rockingham on his autumn trip to Woodsome. The immediate object of his Yorkshire visit was to inspect the timber on his property. He had been unwilling to cut any of it until 1767, but now assumed that it would become an annual event, so he made arrangements for planting replacement seedlings. Woodsome could never take the place of Sandwell in his affections, however; the latter was "every day putting on new charms and doing all

---

[4] Harlow, *Second British Empire*, I, 187.

[5] Grafton to the King, 5 February 1768, Fortescue, ed., *Correspondence of George III*, II, 10. *Parl. Hist.*, XVI, 405. James E. Thorold Rogers, *A Complete Collection of the Protests of the Lords* (Oxford, 1875), II, 96 *et seq.*

[6] A summary will be found in Ritcheson, *British Politics*, Chap. 4; the details are in John Brooke, *The Chatham Administration, 1766-1768* (London, 1956), Chap. 5.

[7] "Persons named by Ld. Rockingham to be Friends without whom he would take no step," 31 March 1767, Add. Mss. 32,980, f.450.

[8] From Lady Rockingham [15 June 1767], Dartmouth Manuscripts, 263. From Rockingham, 15 August 1767, *ibid.*, 266. Compare these and other letters in the Dartmouth Manuscripts with the small parcel of memoranda in the Rockingham Manuscripts (Sheffield) labelled R. 9.

[9] To Rockingham, 17 August 1767, Rockingham Manuscripts, R. 1, f.548.

she can to make herself agreeable. . . ."[10] With so many personal
and proprietary attachments, perhaps Dartmouth was relieved at the
failure of the negotiations with the Grafton ministry. Spared the
necessity of listening to the call of duty, he could devote himself to
his private concerns. There can be no doubt of his attachment to
the Rockingham faction at this particular period. Calling at Wentworth House on his way to Woodsome, he had breakfast with Lady
Rockingham and was persuaded by her to remain until the Marquess
returned from the Doncaster races that evening. Dartmouth admitted
that he could not resist the opportunity for a little political conversation, especially since Dowdeswell and Burke were members of the
party. In his mildly humorous report to his stepfather he said that
it was "near three in the morning before the state of the nation could
be perfectly adjusted and settled. . . ."[11]

Meanwhile, the government was recovering its strength without the
Rockingham alliance. After the nadir of July 1767, Grafton's situation improved, especially when Lord North agreed to accept the
Chancellorship of the Exchequer in September.[12] The Bedford
Whigs, more eager for the comforts of office than for membership in
Rockingham's union of the opposition, acceded to the administration
at the end of 1767.[13] North and Dartmouth had never served in the
same administration and occasionally they had voted on opposite
sides in specific divisions. Their personal ties nevertheless remained
strong and intimate, transcending political differences. Dartmouth
congratulated North on his appointment, saying in complete sincerity
and with perhaps a memory of his own disappointments, "I heartily
wish Lord North all the credit and satisfaction in his post that it can
afford him; if he has little of the latter, I am sure he will have much
of the former."[14] Now that his stepbrother was an important member
of the ministry (and would soon become its leader), Dartmouth had
to reconsider his relationship with the Rockingham faction. The Old
Whigs were organizing for opposition, with the intention of over-
throwing or at least weakening the administration in order that they
might return to power as a group. Since the King was the real head
of His Majesty's Government, this kind of systematic opposition
might be contaminated with the suspicion of disloyalty. Dartmouth's
political inclinations were passive at best; Rockingham ought not to
expect him to bestir himself in opposition to his stepbrother.

Throughout 1768 and 1769 Dartmouth continued to act with the
Rockingham group, especially when American affairs were under

---

10 To Guilford, 7 October 1767, Ms. North, d.11, ff.68-9.
11 *Ibid.*
12 Grafton's *Autobiography,* 166-174.
13 Brooke, *Chatham Administration,* Chap. 8.
14 To Guilford, 17 October 1767, Ms. North, d.11, ff.74-5.

consideration. In December, 1768, the new American Secretary, Lord Hillsborough, presented papers concerning the colonists' reception of the Townshend Duties together with a series of strongly worded resolutions designed to enforce parliamentary supremacy. Rockingham knew that his following was in the minority, but he urged Dartmouth to attend the Lords' debate and lend whatever support he could to the opposition: "The part your lordship took, the principles you supported [in the Rockingham administration] may want the assistance of your abilities and it may appear odd that you should be absent."[15] Dartmouth's reply indicated that he still regarded himself as an Old Whig, but the numerous reasons he listed for his absence should have warned Rockingham that his principal spokesman on American affairs was drifting into a position of neutrality:

> I confess there was ground enough to encourage you to beset me in this almost but not quite irresistible manner. My zeal for the welfare and prosperity of the Americans, and in them of this country, the indignation I feel against those, who upon partial and unfair representations of a prejudiced and heated Governor, would drive them to despair and above all, the value I set upon your Lordship's friendship inclines me to wish myself now in consultation with you upon the proper means to resist the resolutions that are to be produced on Thursday. At the same time, the shortness of the time to prepare myself for such an event, together with the distance that I am at (which your lordship's imagination has passed over much quicker than, I am afraid, my person could), the snow that is in the air and will fall before tomorrow morning, and a variety of family reasons constrain me to lament that administration will bring on their measures at a time when they are not only sure of carrying them (which I am afraid they would do at any time), but when many of those who do not probably entertain exactly the same ideas with themselves are not in the way to declare their disapprobation. My comfort is that it will be resolutely done by those who are present, and that my absence will be of no more consequence than the loss of one ineffectual voice from the number of the dissidents.[16]

Dartmouth was sufficiently interested in the American problem to preserve both a petition from the New York Assembly to the House of Lords objecting to the Townshend Duties, and also the resolutions which Hillsborough introduced in December and which

---

15 From Rockingham, 12 December 1768, Dartmouth Manuscripts, 294.

16 To Rockingham, 13 December 1768, Rockingham Manuscripts, R. 75, f.59.

were approved in February, 1769.[17] In March Dartmouth lent his voice to the opposition in the debate on the address, but Grafton's majority was substantially larger than the opposition's vote.[18] Dartmouth's reputation as an opposition speaker was probably less widespread than his sympathetic and conciliatory nature where American grievances were concerned. In the autumn of 1769, a London merchant engaged in the West Indian trade approached him with a plan for reconciling Britain's differences with the colonies. Dartmouth was favorably impressed by the proposal. He recommended it to Rockingham's consideration, saying, "It is evident that something of this sort must be attempted [in] the next session, and therefore, he will be under the necessity of offering his plan to the present administration; but he wishes that the execution of it might fall to the lot of some other set of men. . . ."[19]

The proposed solution to the American problem included the establishment of a new constitution which would grant America a lord lieutenant, appointed by the King as in Ireland, a Council of at least twenty-four "independent . . . men of fortune," appointed for life, and a House of Commons, elected by the colonial assemblies. This parliament for all America would apportion the requisitions of the Crown, while the legislature at Westminster would exercise supremacy in all matters of imperial policy except taxation and internal affairs.[20] Rockingham replied that he was willing to discuss the plan, but he disapproved of establishing a united parliament for the American colonies. Referring to the Stamp Act, Rockingham declared that he had always regarded it as a "fundamental error in policy . . . because it united *them* . . . to *resist*."[21] Besides increasing the colonists' potential for resistance to the trade laws, an American parliament would also increase the revenue of the Crown, uncontrolled by Britain's legislature. No true Whig could agree to such a measure, least of all one who had sponsored the Declaratory Act. Americans, then and since, who have regarded the Rockingham faction as friends of the colonies have usually overlooked this attachment to the principles of parliamentary supremacy and mercantilism.

Although Dartmouth generally supported Rockingham's group, albeit passively at times, he took exception to the tactics which they employed in 1769. Deciding to embrace John Wilkes's grievances against the government which denied him a seat in Parliament, Rock-

---

[17] Dartmouth Manuscripts, 296, 297, 304 & 305.

[18] Grafton to the King, 2 March 1769, Fortescue, ed., *Correspondence of George III,* II, 85.

[19] To Rockingham, 21 October 1769, Rockingham Manuscripts, R. 1, f.688.

[20] Dr. James Smith's "Thoughts on the Dispute," n.d., Dartmouth Manuscripts, 1084.

[21] From Rockingham, 8 November 1769, *ibid.,* 312. A copy of this letter, undated, also appears in the Rockingham Manuscripts, R. 1, 1217-102.

ingham utilized the device of petitioning which had worked so successfully in the Stamp Act repeal. Dartmouth had little use for
Wilkes, who represented the radicalism of the London mob. When
Rockingham asked for his approval of the petition concocted in
Yorkshire, Dartmouth replied that it smelt of "faction"—a word
with unpleasant connotations—and emphasized his opinion with
underscoring and hyphenization. He objected to the petitioning
movement, Dartmouth explained, because it "is more likely to increase than compose the distractions and distresses which we seem
to be running ourselves into. I should perhaps have had a better
opinion of the measure than I have . . . if it had originally sprung
from those whom I esteem and admire, but as I looked upon it at
the first to be the result of intemperate heat and *f-a-c-t-i-o-u-s* zeal,
rather than the sad and sober offspring of the necessity of the time,
I was sorry to hear that those whom I believed to be the true friends
to this country and its constitution had been persuaded to concur
in and adopt it. . . . I cannot help lamenting that certain people
should add their weight and influence . . . to give a sanction to the
violence of any turbulent individual, however great, or association
of individuals, however numerous."[22]

This disagreement over tactics was the thin edge of the wedge
between Dartmouth and the Rockingham faction. During 1770, the
Marquess continued to consult the Earl, but the old enthusiasm that
had once kept them up until three in the morning discussing politics
was absent. In February Rockingham considered entering another
protest on the records of the House of Lords. Dartmouth apparently
demurred, for Rockingham begged him to attend a meeting of the
party leaders, where he proposed to explain to the reluctant Earl
"the necessity of our being *Firm.*"[23] In April the Rockinghams were
considering an attempt to repeal the tea duty, but there is no evidence that Dartmouth was interested in assisting them.[24] Finally, on
November 12th, Rockingham wrote to invite Dartmouth to attend
a meeting of the party leaders in the House of Lords.[25] Whether he
attended or not, we do not know, but this is the last in a series of
letters between Dartmouth and Rockingham which began with the
latter's invitation to join the ministry five and one-half years earlier.
In January, 1771, Lord North asked his stepbrother to enter the
cabinet. Even though Dartmouth refused to do so at that time,
Rockingham apparently abandoned all hope of persuading him to
support the opposition to the North administration.

---

22 Dartmouth kept a copy of his letter to Rockingham, 20 November 1769,
Dartmouth Manuscripts, 312.

23 From Rockingham, 4 February 1770, *ibid.,* 317. From Rockingham, 5
February 1770, *ibid.,* Rockingham's italics.

24 From Rockingham, 9 April 1770, *ibid.,* 322.

25 From Rockingham, 12 November 1770, *ibid.,* 328.

Throughout the period when Dartmouth was out of office and a member of the Rockingham group, he had never lost his intimate relationship with the North family. He continued to correspond with his stepfather, Lord Guilford, and to visit back and forth with that thrice-married old gentleman's various offspring. These letters largely concerned family and personal matters, although politics was occasionally included. There was no deep, dividing difference of political principle between Dartmouth and North; to call one a Whig and the other a Tory would be misleading. Party labels are less significant in a period when the principal goal is to gain office and avoid being ejected from it. Dartmouth had resigned in 1766, while North had entered Chatham's mosaic ministry as paymaster, but there was no ill will between them. If Dartmouth resented North's new position, it was only because North became too busy to repay family calls. Using a bantering tone acceptable only in families on the best of terms, Dartmouth told his stepfather, "Pray tell that perfidious swain Lord North that we are not at all obliged to him for the concise and peremptory letter he sent us the other day, instead of bringing himself and Lady North to see us."[26] The next year the Norths visited Sandwell just before Dartmouth's trip to Yorkshire and his midnight conversation with Rockingham and Burke. In 1769, the Dartmouths stayed at North's Dillington property and, later, both families called upon Lord Guilford.[27] Dartmouth was particularly happy in these family gatherings and correspondingly saddened by the inevitable parting: "I did not recover my spirits the whole day, not even when I saw my dear boys in [good] health at Stratford. . . ."[28]

The deep, genuine affection which he felt for his stepfather extended to other members of the family as well. His half brother, Brownlow North, progressing through various episcopal appointments to become, successively, Bishop of Lichfield, Worcester, and Winchester, also exchanged correspondence and visits with Dartmouth.[29] His two true sisters and his half sister rounded out the family circle, especially after their respective marriages began to produce an assortment of nieces and nephews, but no one of Dartmouth's contemporaries occupied the same high place in his affection as Lord North. After one of his frequent visits to Lord Guilford,

[26] To Guilford, 22 August 1766, Ms. North, d.10, ff.171-2.

[27] To Guilford, 7 October 1767, *ibid.*, d.11, ff.68-9. Lady North to Guilford, 24 May 1769, *ibid.*, d.24, ff.62-3. F. Burgoyne to Guilford, 30 May 1769, *ibid.*, d.12, f.86.

[28] To Guilford, 31 July 1769, *ibid.*, f.117.

[29] Brownlow North to Guilford, 3 July 1770, *ibid.*, d.24, ff.96-7, refers to dining at Blackheath (Dartmouth's residence) and receiving the Dartmouths "on Saturday." To Guilford, 6 October 1770, *ibid.*, d.13, f.99, congratulations are extended to Brother Brownlow on his appointment to deanery of Canterbury.

Dartmouth emphasized his regret at having to leave the old gentleman by adding: "pray tell Lord North that missing him was one . . . of many ingredients of which the lump was composed that rose in my throat when the coach came round to the door. Nobody can more sincerely wish him well, because nobody can be more sensible of his deserts than I am. . . ."[30] This personal affection was reenforced in Dartmouth's mind by a growing respect for North as an administrator. His handling of foreign affairs, when there was a possibility of war with Spain, excited Dartmouth's admiration. Writing from Woodsome Manor to his stepfather, Dartmouth said, "I hope Lord North's spirit and activity have prevented the war which seemed to threaten us. He has got great credit, and with reason, on this occasion. . . ."[31]

The affair of John Wilkes undoubtedly drew more of Dartmouth's sympathy for North. Wilkes had been elected by large majorities on three different occasions. Yet, by one means or another, the House of Commons had denied him any right to be seated. Many contemporaries were ardent supporters of Wilkes, though for various reasons. American radicals thought he was leading a crusade for freedom, when in reality he seems to have been more interested in lining his pockets. Although he was the darling of the London mob, aristocrats like Rockingham embraced his cause because it provided a lever against the administration. We have already noticed that Dartmouth took exception to Old Whig strategy on this issue. He was by heritage and inclination an aristocrat, accustomed to social intercourse with the ruling minority; Wilkes and the London mob represented a threat to the orderly way of life he loved. Furthermore, the pious Lord Dartmouth could not be expected to admire the coarse, vulgar author of the *Essay on Woman*. Crowning all other reasons for antipathy between the two was the fact that North, as leader of the King's government, became the protagonist in the struggle against Wilkes. Addressing his stepfather, Dartmouth revealed his feelings on this issue in terms so filled with hyperbole that only an intimate, thoroughly familiar with his strong attachment to his stepbrother, could avoid taking his derogatory remarks at face value: "I hope you are duly sensible of your obligations to your friend and countryman Mr. Sawbridge for overriding Mr. Wilkes's motion to direct an impeachment of Lord North. It is well that he has some friends that will stand up for him upon proper occasions. For my own part, I am very well convinced that he is the wickedest of all the wicked ministers that this poor country has been governed by for several years past, that he has been the adviser not only of all the wicked steps that have been taken in regard to the Middlesex election, but of all

---

[30] To Guilford, 17 July 1771, *ibid.*, d.14, ff.58-9.
[31] To Guilford, 6 October 1770, *ibid.*, d.13, f.100.

the bad measures that have been pursued ever since he was born and long before, and that the plague and the war and every other calamity that threatens us, if they come, will all be his doing, and in short, that he ought to be hanged without farther ceremony, but I see that the vilest miscreant will always find some to screen them from public justice."[32] In a more serious vein, Dartmouth once confessed that he was "very much shocked at the insolence of Mr. Wilkes, and really alarmed at the madness of the mob about him. Let who will call him patriot, I can consider him in no other light than as a desperate incendiary, whose plain object is to excite tumult and confusion in this country. . . . [Wilkes] is alderman of Farington for the same reason that he became member for Middlesex, because no body dares vote against him."[33]

North's clever handling of the Wilkes affair helped to break up the opposition, for he succeeded in attracting a number of conservatives away from Chatham, Grenville and Rockingham.[34] Apparently, Dartmouth was among those who admired North for his success at the difficult task assigned to him by the King, to run the government in spite of internal divisions and external attacks.[35] The real test of loyalty came, however, in January 1771. The Falkland Islands dispute was causing North serious difficulty and, without additional support, the cabinet might have fallen. Some members of the cabinet were in favor of a war with Spain, in order to maintain the British outpost in the Falkland Islands. North, however, did not regard the islands worth fighting for and was prepared to make great concessions to the Spanish ambassador. Peace was preserved, but several cabinet posts had to be reshuffled. Lord Weymouth, who had been outspokenly in favor of a war, resigned from his post as Secretary of State. After considering several possibilities, North asked Dartmouth to fill the vacancy left by Weymouth's resignation.[36] This invitation surprised Dartmouth as much as Rockingham's nearly six years earlier, and his reaction was the same: he asked for "a short time to consider of a step which he looks upon as so important to him."[37]

North believed that the hesitation implied a later refusal, but the King, like Newcastle on a previous occasion, tried to apply a touch of flattery. He told North: "It gives me much pleasure that Lord

---

[32] To Guilford, 5 November 1770, *ibid.,* ff.132-3. It might help to explain Dartmouth's rather exaggerated humor, which this letter reveals, to realize that it was written on Guy Fawkes Day.

[33] To Guilford [6 January 1769], *ibid.,* d.12, ff.47-8.

[34] William Baring Pemberton, *Lord North* (London, 1938), 116 *et seq.*

[35] J. D. Griffith Davies, *George the Third: A Record of a King's Reign* (London, 1936), 142.

[36] Harlow, *Second British Empire,* 22-32. King to North, 16 January 1771, Fortescue, ed., *Corres. of George III,* II, 208.

[37] North to King, 16 January 1771, *ibid.*

Dartmouth has desired time to consider whether he will accept the seals of the Secretary of State, as it shows that inclination to my service that gives me personal satisfaction when it comes from a man of his excellent character."[38] When North showed his stepbrother this flattering reference, the Earl was complimented but still could not bring himself to accept the office. His reasons for declining were acceptable to North, although he told the King that he could "not do justice to Lord Dartmouth's sentiments in the compass of a note."[39] Thus, we can only conjecture that the principal reason was probably Dartmouth's natural preference for a private life as opposed to the responsibilities of political office. His past associations with the Rockingham group would not, taken by themselves, be sufficient to account for his refusal.

The King expressed his sorrow at Dartmouth's decision, but as soon as Lord Halifax accepted the vacant secretaryship, the crisis passed and North could relax. Not so his father, however. Lord Guilford was so upset by his stepson's actions that he reprimanded him in a letter, the tone of which was especially severe, contrasting sharply with the placid and affectionate nature of the previous correspondence. "The more I reflect upon your refusal yesterday [Guilford wrote] the more I am vexed. To have you appear to the world wanting in duty and regard to the King, love to your country, friendship to Lord North, and affection to me, is what I thought I should never live to see. I am too much hurt to talk upon the subject, and hope we shall never name it, as I cannot help being, Your affectionate, G."[40] Dartmouth was so stunned that he exaggerated the strength of Guilford's rebuke into a determination never to forgive him. He excused himself from an expected call upon his stepfather by saying that "while I feel myself under the mortifying circumstances of having taken a step which your lordship tells me you can never forgive, I am afraid I shall not be in spirit to appear in a company where everyone will feel so differently from myself."[41]

This little storm within the North family circle abated as rapidly as it arose. Guilford replied immediately that he wanted Dartmouth to attend the party he had planned, that he could not remember using "so strong an expression as that I never could forgive the step you had taken," but if he had used it, it was only in the heat of the moment. "As I am not apt to be warm [Guilford continued], my late

---

[38] King to North, 17 January 1771, *ibid.,* 209.

[39] North to King, 17 January 1771, *ibid.,* 210.

[40] From Guilford, 18 January 1771, Dartmouth Manuscripts, 336.

[41] Draft reply to Guilford, 20 January 1771, *ibid.* Compare, Hist. Mss. Comm., *14th Report, App. Pt. X,* p. 77, which errs in printing the summary of this letter. Lord Rockingham's name appears nowhere in the original. The first line of the printed reply should read: "Having taken a step contrary to Lord Guilford's opinion, etc."

warmth may have surprised you, but I hope you will impute it [to] the true cause: the agony of mind I have felt from the idea of having had reason to take any thing unkindly of one I love so tenderly as I do your lordship."[42] The full significance of the exchange of letters is not that Dartmouth was forgiven, but rather that he had felt the disapproval of one he regarded as a father. This rebuke must have burned deeply into so sensitive a soul and, on the next occasion when North asked him to join the cabinet, he would be virtually bound to accept. North might forgive him if he refused, but his stepfather would be greatly upset. If his refusal were to prolong a government crisis, possibly endangering North's position, then the whole family would be furious with him. Dartmouth's refusal to enter the cabinet in 1771 produced a paradox, for he was unable to refuse the offer of the American Secretaryship in 1772.

---

[42] From Guilford [20 January 1771], Dartmouth Manuscripts, 336.

Chapter VII

THE AMERICAN SECRETARYSHIP

IN AUGUST, 1772, Lord North found himself in the midst of a political crisis. When he appealed to his stepbrother for support, Dartmouth entered the cabinet as Secretary of State for the Colonies and that particular crisis passed. But why did North need Dartmouth? He was not particularly active in politics in these years. He was neither a borough patron nor the leader of a parliamentary faction, commanding votes in the House of Commons. His only experience in administration so far was the single year at the Board of Trade. The only support he could give North was of a personal nature, which is exactly what his stepbrother needed at this particular time.

North was Chancellor of the Exchequer and First Lord of the Treasury, although he would have objected to the title "prime minister." He was not the leader of a political party, nor even a "faction," and he professed no set of principles that would resemble a modern party platform. He had gradually developed his position of leadership after accepting Grafton's offer of the chancellorship in 1767. The Duke's subsequent resignation in 1770 had left a vacancy at the Treasury which the King invited North to fill. He maintained his position for the next dozen years, because he enjoyed the confidence of the King and because he demonstrated a remarkable ability both at the Treasury and in the House of Commons. As a result, the King's Friends, led by Charles Jenkinson, gave him their support. At the same time, a series of coincidences weakened the opposition. The death of George Grenville in 1770 removed a powerful debater from the Commons. His followers were easily persuaded to support the government, especially after Lord Suffolk and Alexander Wedderburn accepted offices in it. The Wilkes affair had driven many conservatives from their allegiance to Rockingham into support of the administration, so that the remainder of the opposition was weak and divided between a few Old Whigs and Chathamites.[1]

One of the most powerful of the traditional Whig factions was the Bedford group, also called the "Bloomsbury Gang." The leaders of this group were already in the government when North became the leading minister in 1770, but he could not always rely upon their support nor upon the votes of their followers. Sandwich, Weymouth

---

[1] Pemberton, *North*, 132-3. Fitzmaurice, *Shelburne*, I, 418-19.

and Gower were eagerly looking forward to the day when North would resign. Then they could take over the government in full force, controlling the patronage in order to make provision for their numerous adherents.[2] These various cabinet ministers were not united by principle so much as by "the most recent friendship and the most recent enmity."[3]

Of all the members of the cabinet, Lord Hillsborough was North's closest friend.[4] He had occupied the office of colonial secretary since its creation in 1768, but now found himself the target of the Bedford group. They had little reason to object to his colonial policy, but they hoped to force North into resigning with him. When Hillsborough recommended rejecting the petition of the Ohio Company, and a plan to establish a new colony in the interior of North America, the Privy Council voted against his recommendation. Rather than assume responsibility for inaugurating the new colony, Hillsborough decided to resign. North found that he was going to lose a firm friend from the cabinet. The situation was worse than the previous crisis in 1771. Rather than abandon the leadership to the Bedfordites, North appealed to Dartmouth to save the ministry by lending him personal support. Perhaps North wished to prevent the Bedfordites from controlling colonial policy, but this was only a secondary consideration.

"It is impossible within the compass of a letter [North wrote] to explain to you the nature, or to give you a clear history of these transactions. Suffice it to say that my attempts to keep things as they are have been ineffectual and that Lord Hillsborough, after many conversations I have had with him, persists in his resolution . . . to retire, so that I shall lose one of the best and firmest friends I have in the cabinet. Will you permit me to mention you to the King as his successor? I can venture to assure you that His Majesty's sentiments towards you are such as will make him accept the proposal with joy. You know the nature of the American Department much better than I do, and that it is upon the footing where you formerly wished to see it. You can not, I think, doubt of my earnest wish to have you within the service of the Crown, in a situation becoming your rank, abilities, and character, and you must be sensible how much I stand in need of your friendship and assistance upon the present occasion. . . . [If] you decline my proposition, you will certainly distress [me], if not the public service. . . . Let me con-

2 Feiling, *Second Tory Party,* 112-16.

3 Pares, "George III and the Politicians," *Transactions of R. Hist. Soc.* (1951), I, 142.

4 Lady North to Guilford, 25 May 1771, Ms. North, d.24, f.111, illustrates the close social bonds between North and Hillsborough.

jure you not to send me a refusal, til you have seen me, and considered what I have to say."[5]

This letter interrupted Dartmouth's holiday at Eastbourne. His conference with North took place sometime between August 4th and 10th. The temptation to remain at leisure must have been strong, yet Dartmouth could hardly refuse the office which North proffered him. He would have incurred his stepfather's wrath. Furthermore, a negative answer would have been inconsistent with Dartmouth's earlier actions, when he left the Board of Trade on the grounds that Chatham had denied him "the only thing" that would have made his continuation useful. Searching for advice, Dartmouth wrote to an old friend of the family, Frederick Montagu, suggesting that he might assist the Earl as a junior lord of trade. Montague's reply indicated how widely separated Dartmouth had become from the Rockingham group, for he said: "You are perfectly right to accept the seals of the American Department. . . . But I am brought into Parliament by Lord Rockingham; I love him for a thousand good qualities, I have always acted with his party, and I have taken an active part in almost every question of opposition in the House of Commons. If, therefore, a seat at the Board of Trade was offered me, I could not accept it unless Lord Rockingham wished me to accept it, which you know would never be the case."[6]

As the result of these pressures—North's urgings, Guilford's anger with his earlier refusal, Montague's re-assurance—Dartmouth finally overcame his temptation to remain a private citizen and cast his lot with the administration. He accepted the seals of the office of Secretary of State for the Colonies on August 14th. Later, he told his stepfather that his greatest concern was whether he would be able to "bring either that strength or credit to Lord North which I most sincerely wish him on all occasions."[7] He need not have worried. Except for the Bedfordites who had failed to undermine North, there was almost universal rejoicing at Dartmouth's appointment. Lord North and Lord Guilford received congratulations from all the members of the family and their friends. Mrs. Delany, for example, wrote that Dartmouth's new office must "give pleasure to all his friends and does honour to those who distinguish his merit."[8] Benjamin Franklin

---

[5] From North, 3 August 1772, Dartmouth Manuscripts, 373. Burke fully appreciated North's need for personal support in counteracting the schemes of the Bedfords within the cabinet; see his letter to DeLancey, 20 August 1772, *Corres.* (Sutherland, ed.), II, 326-27.

[6] From Montagu, 10 August 1772, Dartmouth Manuscripts, 378.

[7] To Guilford, 12 October 1772, Ms. North, d.14, ff.239-40. According to P.R.O., CO 5/241, f.426, Hillsborough resigned on 13 August and Dartmouth accepted the seals of office on the 14th. The "Oath of Secretary of State," 14 August 1772, Dartmouth Manuscripts, 382.

[8] Mrs. Delany to Viscountess Andover, 16 August 1772, *Mrs. Delany's Corres.*, IV, 447.

had often suffered humiliation and insult from Lord Hillsborough, but now he expected that his work as the agent for Massachusetts would become much easier in the new Secretary's administration.[9] The colonists were generally pleased with the resignation of Hillsborough, whose policy was "firmness," and the appointment of Dartmouth, whom they regarded as conciliatory and sympathetic. Even the New England provinces looked forward to "the full enjoyment of civil and religious liberty" under the new Secretary.[10] How ironic that the American Revolution should begin before Dartmouth had served three years!

Among Dartmouth's many well-wishers was the Earl of Warwick, who wrote from France to congratulate Lord Guilford on the occasion of "your other son, good Lord Dartmouth, being again put at the head of the Board of Trade. . . ."[11] Possibly Warwick had not heard the full account, that Dartmouth had become instead Secretary of State. More likely, he labored under the common misconception at the time, that the American secretaryship was merely an enlarged Board of Trade and not a true secretarial office at all. It is true that Dartmouth became First Lord of Trade again in 1772, but only because the colonial secretary occupied the position *ex officio*. The confusion had arisen in the latter part of 1768, when Lord Hillsborough first resigned from the Board of Trade to take the secretarial seals and then a few months later regained the presidency of the Board. Although the greater office absorbed the lesser, Hillsborough's enemies always maintained that he was merely a First Lord of Trade with seals and a cabinet seat.[12] Dartmouth was to encounter similar difficulties arising from this jealousy.

As Secretary of State for the Colonies, Dartmouth also presided at the Board of Trade, but he did not convene it very often. As a matter of fact, in one year (1774) the Board met on the average of only twice a month, "the lowest figure that it ever reached."[13] Dartmouth preferred to rely upon the staff in the American Department for gathering information, with the result that the Lords of Trade complained. They told the First Lord that if they had no other business but signing papers, there was no reason to attend meetings.[14] Compared to earlier boards, this one had neither the quantity nor the variety of business to attend to. Yet, it would be a mistake to assume

---

[9] Benjamin Franklin to his son, 17 and 19 August 1772, *Franklin's Works* (J. Sparks, ed., London, 1882), VIII, 10-11, 14.

[10] From Thomas Wooldridge, 24 November 1772, Dartmouth Manuscripts, 462.

[11] Warwick to Guilford, 22 August 1772, Ms. North, d.14, ff.203-4.

[12] Basye, *Board of Trade*, 171.

[13] Clarke, "Board of Trade at Work," *A.H.R.*, XVII, 21, n.27.

[14] From C. Grenville, 13 July 1774, Pub. Archs. Can., Dartmouth Manuscripts, VII, 2368.

that members did nothing. The struggling colony of Georgia required a great deal of their attention, particularly in regard to the Indian problem. Whereas Hillsborough had ignored Governor Wright's proposals, Dartmouth's board drafted a formal representation to the King endorsing the plan to purchase land from the Cherokees and the Creeks, sell it to settlers, and then use the proceeds to pay the Indians' debts to white traders and for defense.[15] Governor Tryon of New York caused the Board of Trade to deliberate at length when he granted land, contrary to instructions, in territory reserved to the Indians and also in the area disputed by New Hampshire. This complex of problems required a great deal of correspondence and eventually the Governor's recall to England for personal explanations of his conduct.[16] The dispute between Peter Livius and Governor Wentworth of New Hampshire caused the Board to devote much of their time to hearing evidence and assessing the conflicting reports in the matter. Their report was finally presented to the Privy Council, only to be rejected and the charges against the Governor dismissed.[17] Finally, a dispute with the Dutch over African trade occupied much of the Board's attention during the year 1773.[18]

If the quantity of the Board's work is not very impressive, they nevertheless contributed an unusual monument to their quality. The Board had a standing obligation to collect information about the colonies, but seldom bothered to perform this function in a systematic manner. In July of 1773, however, Dartmouth sent out a circular letter to all the governors, containing a score of specific questions about their respective colonies. It required more than two years for some governors to reply, but the answers eventually provided an interesting picture of the colonies on the eve of the Revolution. Dartmouth and his colleagues on the Board sought information on a wide range of topics. First of all, each governor must supply some basic geographical facts about his province: location, boundaries, proportion of cultivated and uncultivated land, rivers and harbors. The sixth point inquired, "What is the Constitution of the Government?" The answers in this instance revealed the wide disparity in British colonial practice, from chartered colonies like Rhode Island and Connecticut to royal colonies like Virginia and the

[15] Minutes of the Board of Trade, 9, 12, 16 & 18 November 1772, Dartmouth Manuscripts, 107. Representation to the King, 9 November 1772, *ibid.*, 457.

[16] Correspondence between Tryon and the Board of Trade will be found in *New York Colonial Documents,* VIII, and Dartmouth Manuscripts, *e.g.,* 465.

[17] From Pownall, 26 August 1773, Dartmouth Manuscripts, 876. There are many papers in the Dartmouth collection referring to Livius and Wentworth, *e.g.,* 584.

[18] From Pownall, 12 October 1773, Dartmouth Manuscripts, 895. To Suffolk, 23 January 1773, P.R.O., CO 5/138, Part II, ff.759-60.

Carolinas, and including the remaining proprietaries in Pennsylvania and Maryland. No other empire in the Eighteenth-Century permitted such a wide variation in local self-government.

Naturally the Board of Trade was interested in certain economic matters. The governors were to supply statistics about trade and shipping, imports and exports, including specifically foreign commerce, methods of preventing illegal trade and the value of the natural products of each colony. Two demographic questions constituted the last census taken in the Thirteen Colonies. Each governor was expected to supply the number of inhabitants, white and black, in his province and, furthermore, to explain whether the numbers were increasing or decreasing, together with the reasons why. The Board next wanted to know about the military situation. How was the militia constituted? What was the number and condition of colonial forts? How many Indians lived in the province and, even more important, how friendly were they? With respect to military matters, the Governor of West Florida had a special question addressed to him: what was the effect upon his territory of the close proximity of French and Spanish settlements on the Mississippi?

The last three questions in the census concerned revenue matters. How did each colony appropriate its revenue? What were the expenses of the colony? Lastly, "What are the establishments civil and military within your government; and by what authority do the officers hold their places? What is the annual value of each office, civil or military? How are they respectively appointed? And who are the present possessors?"[19] All in all, these points of inquiry represented a very comprehensive summary of colonial statistics. It is not surprising that some governors failed to reply. Of course, much of this information was already in the Board of Trade's files, particularly the different colonial constitutions, but this systematic collection of details was much easier and convenient. These tasks which the Board of Trade undertook, however, could just as easily have been assigned to a staff of expert clerks, who would have drawn smaller salaries than the Lords of Trade. In Dartmouth's term, the Board was not inefficient, but it was expensive. When the reformers abolished it in 1782, they were able to use the argument of greater economy, even though their primary aim was to reduce the influence of the Crown.[20]

---

[19] Sir Henry Strachey Papers, William L. Clements Library, Ann Arbor. Strachey was secretary to Lord Howe and his brother, as peace commissioners in 1776. He copied the information found in Dartmouth's letter to all the governors, 5 July 1773, and the available replies about 1776. Some governors, like South Carolina's, never replied, but those who did followed the outline provided in Dartmouth's "Heads of Enquiry."

[20] Andrews, *Guide*, I, 99.

If Dartmouth appeared to neglect the Board of Trade, it was because his other office was so much more important and so much busier during the period 1772 to 1775. As Secretary of State, he was a member of the innermost circle of royal advisers. The composition of the cabinet varied from time to time, but there was never more than nine in North's administration. Dartmouth was consistently one of this group after 1772. The seals of the office which he held were not as old as those of the Lord Chancellor nor of the Treasury commissioners, for the Secretary of State had not become prominent until the Tudor period.[21] It is one of the conventions of the British constitution that the office is indivisible, no matter how many Secretaries might hold the seals at any given time. In recent years there have been as many as eight Secretaries of State. In theory, each one is competent to do the work of the other seven. In the Eighteenth-Century, there were usually two Secretaries. Their offices were known as the Northern and Southern Departments because of the geographical division in foreign affairs. The Northern Department had charge of the embassies in roughly the northern half of Europe, while the other Secretary corresponded with southern European states. Since there was no Home Office, both secretaries were responsible for internal matters. Usually the senior Secretary dominated the other, but the Southern Department, whether occupied by a new or veteran Secretary, took charge of the colonial affairs throughout most of the century.[22]

The appointment of a third Secretary of State was regarded as unusual, although there was a precedent in the office of Secretary of State for Scotland which existed intermittently between 1709 and 1746. When the Rockingham government had considered appointing Charles Townshend third secretary in charge of the colonies, Newcastle declared that this would be a "new office" in terms of an act passed in Queen Anne's reign. Townshend would have had to resign his seat in the House of Commons. The appointment of a peer, however, would not raise this issue. Dartmouth fulfilled this latter qualification, but he failed to obtain a secretarial office in 1766 for reasons we have already seen.

By the time the American Department was established by Grafton in 1768, it was already long overdue. The British constitution pro-

---

[21] Edward R. Turner, *The Cabinet Council of England . . . 1622-1784* (Baltimore, 1932), II, 350-2. Various "Cabinet Minutes" appear in the Dartmouth Manuscripts, *passim*.

[22] Detailed accounts of the evolution of the secretary's office will be found in: Mark A. Thomson, *The Secretaries of State, 1681-1782* (Oxford, 1932); Sir H. Nicholas, ed., *Proceedings and Ordinances of the Privy Council of England* (London, 1837), VI; Sir William Holdsworth, *History of English Law* (London, 1938), Sixth Edition), IV; and Margaret M. Spector, *The American Department of the British Government* (New York, 1940).

vided for no office with exclusive jurisdiction over the colonies until seven years before losing thirteen of them. Such an office would have been a logical step at any time after 1660, but when colonial policy became so important in the 1760's a centralized American Department was essential. One of the first to urge the erection of a separate and distinct department for colonial affairs was Thomas Pownall, a former governor of Massachusetts, South Carolina and New Jersey. Governor Pownall, "one of the fairest and most discerning Englishmen,"[23] wrote a book entitled *Administration of the Colonies,* in which he argued his case. First published in 1764, the volume had several editions. In all of them before 1768, Pownall demonstrated the inefficiency of British colonial administration. He pointed out that military officers in the colonies corresponded with, and accepted their instructions from, a Secretary of State. Civilian authorities divided their correspondence between the Secretary of State and the Board of Trade. Naval officers corresponded with the Admiralty "in matters not merely naval," and engineers took their orders from the Board of Ordnance, while revenue officers communicated with the Treasury. These officials did not receive their instructions from a single department "which has, or ought to have, the general direction and administration" over all the colonies.[24] The result of this multiple supervision was that no one department in the government had collected all the information necessary to conduct the affairs of a large empire. Pownall not only believed that there should be such an office, but stressed that it *"must be a secretary of state's office in itself."*[25] Many others agreed in principle with Pownall's suggestions, including one of Shelburne's correspondents who outlined a similar plan in 1762 or 1763.[26] Hillsborough, as we have already noted, urged Dartmouth to press for full secretarial powers in 1765, while Newcastle worked toward the same end by pointing out to General Conway that "no one man can have time to do the duty of Secretary of State and attend the King every day and give attention to the settlement and government of our colonies which . . . they will require."[27]

In spite of so many excellent reasons for creating a department in charge of colonial affairs, the eventual erection of the American

[23] Leonard W. Labaree, *Royal Government in America* (New Haven, 1930), 43.

[24] Pownall, *Administration of the Colonies* (second edition), 14.

[25] *Ibid.,* 15, Pownall's italics. He reiterated the same point in the fourth edition (1768).

[26] Fitzmaurice, *Shelburne,* I, 174-5.

[27] Newcastle to Conway, 7 May 1766, Add. Mss., 32,975, f.104-5. (L.C. Trans.) Newcastle, of course, referred to the non-colonial duties of a Secretary of State for the Southern Department, which were already extensive and onerous.

Department was contaminated with suspicions of jobbery. The urgings of disinterested Englishmen, the pleas of experienced administrators, the fears concerning the overloading of the Southern Department were all unavailing. But when the Duke of Grafton needed additional support from the Bedford faction in 1768, it was a surprisingly easy matter to establish a separate colonial office. When the Bedford faction agreed to support Grafton's administration, they not only demanded several "jobs" but also insisted that colonial affairs be removed from Shelburne's supervision. Grafton's solution was to divide the business of the Southern Department, but he refused to entrust the colonies to a Bedfordite. He actually offered the new department to Shelburne, but the latter preferred to retain the Southern Secretary's seals. Grafton then offered the post to Hillsborough, a courtier unconnected to any faction, who would remain loyal to the "present system." Although they did not gain control of colonial matters, the Bedfords were satisfied with this arrangement.[28]

Grafton believed, or professed to believe, that Shelburne was overworked in the complex business of the Southern Department, paying him the somewhat dubious compliment of comparing him first to a horse and then to King Solomon: "A horse, my Lord, could not go through the business of your office properly. . . . Were a Solomon in the situation, I should not be of opinion that he could go through it. When General Conway had that department . . . I was then of opinion that it ought to be separated, and was the strongest for Lord Dartmouth's being made a third secretary. . . ."[29] At the time, Shelburne had no alternative but to acquiesce in Grafton's plan and the long-overdue American Department was established. Some of Hillsborough's colleagues, however, preferred to regard him merely as an exalted First Lord of Trade.[30] His commission might be construed as limiting him to colonial affairs, rather than empowering him to act in the broad sphere of secretarial business. The older Secretaries of State were especially contemptuous of this new office and did their utmost to restrict and undermine the American secretariat.[31]

The American Department occupied a set of rooms in the old Treasury Building, Whitehall, not far from the Board of Trade.[32] One of the few contemporary references to its location placed undersecretary Pownall's office in what was formerly the Duke of

28 Basye, *Board of Trade*, 146-7, 166-9. Fitzmaurice, *Shelburne*, I, 326-7. Grafton's *Autobiography*, 172-4 & Chapter V.
29 Interview of 11 December 1767 in Fitzmaurice, *Shelburne*, I, 327-8.
30 Horace Walpole reflects this prejudice in his *Memoirs*, III, 153.
31 William Knox's Memorandum of November, 1775, Hist. Mss. Comm., *Report on Various Collections*, VI (1909), 256. Hereafter called *Knox Mss*.
32 Spector, *American Department*, 33.

Monmouth's bedroom.[33] Besides the Secretary and the two under-secretaries, the staff included: one first clerk, two senior clerks, two ordinary clerks, one chamber keeper, his deputy and a "necessary woman."[34] Unlike the other two Secretaries' offices, this staff was virtually permanent. Dartmouth established a precedent by retaining his predecessor's appointees, with the result that many of his subordinates were still holding office when the American Department was abolished in 1782.[35] This department was always smaller in numbers than the other secretarial departments. Even during the Revolutionary War, the staff did not increase in proportion to its duties and responsibilities.[36]

The two most important members of Dartmouth's staff were certainly the undersecretaries, Pownall and Knox. John Pownall, the senior undersecretary, was especially helpful at the beginning of Dartmouth's term of office. He forwarded papers and advice to Sandwell Park, keeping the new Secretary informed of events that required his attention and reminding him of vacancies which lay within his patronage to fill.[37] Pownall's experience with colonial policy had begun with his appointment as secretary to the Board of Trade in 1753 and continued until his dismissal by Dartmouth's successor, Lord George Germain, in 1776.[38] A second undersecretary, William Knox, had already gained a considerable reputation as a pamphleteer. His efforts to defend government policy included four pamphlets published between 1765 and 1774.[39] The last one, entitled "The Interest of the Merchants and Manufacturers of Great Britain," was an able defense of the mercantilist system. In it Knox stressed the advantages of bounties and other forms of protection to the colonies, and pointed out that English merchants ought to support parliamentary supremacy, rather than colonial protests, since only

[33] P. O. Hutchinson, ed., *The Diary and Letters of His Excellency, Thomas Huchinson* (London, 1883), I, 309.

[34] Spector, *American Department,* 34-35.

[35] *Ibid.,* 35.

[36] *Ibid.,* 34. The Southern Department averaged 10 clerks and the Northern Department 8, while there were only 5 clerks in the Colonial Office as late as 1775. For the customary practice of removing and promoting personnel in other departments, see Thomson, *Secretaries of State,* 130-31.

[37] There are numerous letters from Pownall in the Dartmouth Manuscripts, *passim.* B. D. Bargar, "Lord Dartmouth's Patronage, 1772-1775," *William and Mary Quarterly,* Third Series, XV (April, 1958), 191 *et seq.*

[38] Andrews, *Guide,* I, 86. From Germain, 23 January 1776, Dartmouth Manuscripts, 1654.

[39] Knox was the author of the following pamphlets: "The Claims of the Colonies to exemption from taxation by authority of Parliament examined," 1765; "The American Controversy Revived," 1768; "The Defense of the Quebec Act," 1774; "The Interest of the Merchants and Manufacturers in the present contest with the colonies considered," 1774. See his letter to Dartmouth, written sometime in 1777, *ibid.,* 1817.

Parliament could protect the Englishman's credit and property overseas.[40]

It was wise of Dartmouth to retain the services of Hillsborough's undersecretaries. The department was still young in 1772 and they preserved some continuity in procedure. In retaining them, however, Dartmouth ignored an anonymous warning that Pownall and Knox would "insidiously labour to possess your Lordship with their private prejudices and resentments."[41] In view of their experience with colonial affairs and their known principles and prejudices, it is quite possible that they attempted to exercise some influence in the formulation of colonial policy. Certainly, early in Dartmouth's term of office, they were better informed than he was with respect to the forms and procedures of the department. Since both had very decided views on every issue from the filling of vacant offices to the role of parliament in the imperial constitution, the extent of their influence would depend upon their ability to persuade Dartmouth to adopt their ideas. In the instance of parliamentary supremacy, their influence was negligible, for Dartmouth took his stand on the principle of the Declaratory Act of 1766. In other matters, he usually took his lead from the cabinet, where Lord North and the other two Secretaries of State often discussed colonial problems. Pownall and Knox, in fact, often complained that their suggestions were ignored in favor of policies originating in North's, Rochford's, or Suffolk's offices.[42]

Relationships between the new American Department on the one hand and the two older divisions of the secretariat on the other were especially critical at the beginning of Dartmouth's administration. The King, who had apparently grown weary of the constant bickering among his principal Secretaries of State, had suggested some special regulations to "prevent jarrings."[43] Although Dartmouth was willing to comply with these orders, his undersecretaries were determined to preserve the American Department from any encroachment. An issue arose in the autumn of 1772 respecting the transfer of regiments which renewed the interdepartmental strife. The established procedure for rotating regiments among the various stations in Ire-

[40] Knox's name does not appear on the title-page of the printed pamphlet, but his correspondence with Dartmouth makes his authorship clear.

[41] From "A Londoner," October 1772, Dartmouth Manuscripts, 448.

[42] Pownall to Knox, 10 October 1775, *Knox Mss.* (Hist. Mss. Comm.), 122. The late Prof. Chester Martin was convinced that Knox was extremely influential in determining colonial policy, but this thesis has not been generally adopted by other historians; *Empire and Commonwealth: Studies in Governance and Self-Government in Canada* (Oxford, 1929), especially Chapter III on the Quebec Act. Mrs. Spector raised the same question, independently and in a milder form, in her *American Department,* 37-38.

[43] King to North, 4 August 1772, Fortescue, *Corres. of George III,* I, 376.

land, the West Indies, and North America was designed to give each group a fair share of duty at home. It was a reasonable arrangement, but the amount of correspondence involved was great, for the Secretary at War, the Admiralty, the Commander-in-Chief, all had to be notified. The office of Secretary of State, as the principal channel of communications from the King, would naturally undertake this correspondence, but it was still an open question in 1772 as to the extent of the American Department's participation in the process.

Early in October, Pownall drafted what he considered to be a routine order regarding the transfer of troops from Ireland to the West Indies. Since Dartmouth was at Sandwell, he submitted the papers to Rochford to be signed "in Lord Dartmouth's absence." Rochford not only objected to this phrase but insisted that only one of the two older secretaries could issue orders to the Admiralty and War Office.[44] The faithful undersecretary recited a series of precedents from Hillsborough's administration and secured Rochford's signature. When Lord Suffolk also objected to the phrase "in Lord Dartmouth's absence," in a subsequent letter, Pownall secured his signature by similar arguments.[45] The victory was only temporary, for the American Department's authority was challenged again in 1773 when Dartmouth attempted to arrange for the transportation of relief regiments from Ireland to the colonies.[46] To summarize this tedious dispute, a compromise was arranged whereby the Southern Department was charged with arranging the transport of troops to the colonies and the reception of troops returning to Britain, while the American Department was responsible for the reception of troops in the colonies and the transport of relieved regiments to home duty.[47] This cumbersome arrangement satisfied Dartmouth, although it disappointed his undersecretaries. During the remainder of his term of office, Dartmouth enjoyed far more cordial relations with his cabinet colleagues than did the respective undersecretaries. Knox especially disliked William Eden, Suffolk's undersecretary in the Northern Department. Knox said that Eden "possessed a most insinuating, gentle manner, which covered a deeply intriguing and ambitious spirit."[48] Pownall's opinion of Sir Stanier Porten, his counterpart in Rochford's office, was equally mistrustful.[49] Perhaps these personal feelings of jealousy explain some of the undersecre-

[44] From Pownall, 8 October 1772, Dartmouth Manuscripts, 429.

[45] "Precedents," an undated memorandum, ibid., 430. Suffolk to Barrington, 2 October 1772, P.R.O., CO 5/167, #9, uses the phrase, "in Lord Dartmouth's absence," when ordering the embarkation of troops for the West Indies.

[46] To Barrington, 8 February 1773, Dartmouth Manuscripts, 555.

[47] "Arrangement . . . concerning troops to be transported. . . ." [February 1772], ibid., 573. Thomson, Secretaries of State, 85.

[48] Knox Mss. (Hist. Mss. Comm.), 266.

[49] From Pownall, 7 September 1772, Dartmouth Manuscripts, 413.

taries' frequent complaints about the loss of departmental business or prestige.

During Dartmouth's term as colonial Secretary, he encountered many problems. One basic difficulty remained constant throughout these years: he held the secretarials seals in order to give his personal support to Lord North. His conciliatory nature may have constituted an additional recommendation, but it would be incorrect to assume that he was appointed to change Hillsborough's policy. The office which he held proved to be less than satisfactory, owing to the jealousy of the two older Secretaries. But Dartmouth's first year in office would have been an extremely difficult one in any case. Three serious problems arose to plague him. All three had originated in the months before he entered the cabinet. Although he had to deal with them almost simultaneously, the petition of the Ohio Company, the *Gaspée* incident, and the petitions from Massachusetts, will be considered separately.

Chapter VIII

WESTERN EXPANSION

THE FIRST serious problem to concern the new Colonial Secretary was the question of whether to permit Americans to move west of the Appalachians. The Ohio Company had earlier petitioned for a grant of land. What would Dartmouth's attitude be in this question and what policy would the ministry adopt? Official policy before 1772 had followed the Proclamation of 1763 which established a western boundary at the Appalachian divide. This so-called "Proclamation Line" was intended to be temporary and did not preclude the establishment of new governments in the west, but the changes in the ministries during the 1760's had operated to prevent any modification. Meanwhile, colonists continued to migrate west of the Line, causing friction with the Indians and confusion among various colonies, such as Pennsylvania and Virginia, which claimed western lands.[1]

Lord Hillsborough had been especially intransigent in his refusal to sanction any colonization west of the Appalachians.[2] He opposed the Ohio Company's project, but when Samuel Wharton, Benjamin Franklin, and other members presented their petition, his refusal was indirect. They requested a private land grant of 2,000,000 acres, offering to pay £10,700 for it. Instead of replying with an outright negative, Hillsborough actually suggested that they ask for more land and a colonial government: "enough to make a province." He apparently thought that the Company would be unable to afford the larger tract, but the Treasury agreed that they might have ten times as much land at the original price, much to the Colonial Secretary's surprise.[3] Hillsborough was worried by the resistance of the seaboard colonies and the de-population of his Irish estates. Knowing that other members of the government supported, and held stock in, the Ohio Company, he deliberately delayed his report to the Privy Council as long as possible. When forced to do so, he submitted a

---

[1] For details, see Harlow, *Second British Empire*, I, 175-196.

[2] Alvord considered Hillsborough a "moderate expansionist" until 1770, *Mississippi Valley*, II, 120-130.

[3] *Knox Mss.* (Hist. Mss. Comm.), 253-5. J. Munro, ed., *Acts of the Privy Council of England (Colonial Series)*, (London, 1912), V, 202-3. Franklin to his Son, 14 July 1773, *Life of Benjamin Franklin, written by himself* (John Bigelow, ed., Philadelphia, 1916), II, 156.

report opposing the new grant, citing arguments from an earlier report, the letters of General Gage and the Governor of Georgia.[4]

When the Privy Council rejected Hillsborough's negative report, as he had anticipated, he resigned rather than execute their new policy.[5] North regarded Hillsborough as his "best and firmest friend" in the cabinet[6] without whom he would have to yield to the Bedfordites. At this point he turned to his stepbrother and, as we have seen, replaced Hillsborough with another true friend. Dartmouth's appointment to the colonial office depended in the first instance upon his close relationship with North and the fact that his stepbrother needed his support. It was only co-incidentally significant that he was experienced in American policy and that he was known to favor regulated expansionism.

Although Rochford, Suffolk, Gower and other Bedfordites hoping to overthrow North may have been disappointed, Benjamin Franklin and the members of the Ohio Company were immensely pleased with Dartmouth's return to office. Franklin had described Hillsborough as "proud, supercilious, extremely conceited . . ."[7] and very difficult to work with. The change in personnel was most welcome, especially in view of Dartmouth's interest in American land. As early as 1770, Dartmouth had acquired a grant of 100,000 acres in East Florida.[8] During the years of his secretaryship (1772-1775), he attempted to promote the surveying and settling of his tract in approximately the area of modern Miami.[9] As late as 1784, he was still paying surveying fees for this land, although his plans for settling it had proven unsuccessful.[10] His interest in acquiring land was so well known that friends and strangers alike offered to help him in his speculations. His kinsman, Governor Legge, advised him to apply for grants of 20,000 acres in Nova Scotia for each of his sons. Lieutenant-Colonel Desbrisay offered to sell him a portion of St. John's Island. Dennis de Berdt and his brother-in-law, Joseph Reed, tried to interest him in buying shares in the Jersey Society.[11] Dartmouth did not participate in any of these tempting schemes, but it is significant that the offers were made. They indicate his interest in such propositions. No wonder the Ohio Company was encouraged by his appointment!

---

[4] Alvord, *Mississippi Valley*, II, 129-31.

[5] *Acts of the Privy Council*, V, 208-9.

[6] From North, 3 August 1772, Dartmouth Manuscripts, 373.

[7] Franklin to Cushing, 10 June 1771, P.R.O., CO 5/118, f.61.

[8] *Acts of the Privy Council*, V, 593.

[9] "DeBrahm's Survey," British Museum, King's Manuscripts, 211, pp. 281 & 306-7.

[10] "An Account from the Surveyor-General of East Florida," 29 November 1784, Dartmouth Manuscripts, 1351.

[11] From Legge, 18 August 1775, Pub. Archs. Can., Dartmouth Manuscripts, XI, 2507. From Desbrisay, 4 September 1773, Dartmouth Manuscripts, 699. From DeBerdt, 14 August 1773, *ibid.*, 682. From Reed, 23 July 1773, *ibid.*, 870.

Dartmouth's only reservation regarding expansionism was his sincere concern for the Indians. His new position greatly increased his natural interest in their welfare. As a private citizen, he had supported the Indian Charity School of Dartmouth College. Now, as a minister of the Crown, he had a further responsibility to protect all Indians and their hunting grounds, as defined in several solemn treaties. Permitting unregulated migration west of the Proclamation Line would surely provoke them into massacres and wars. Dartmouth, accepting the idea of the *noble savage,* believed them to be "more rational than ourselves."[12] But he realized that westward migration was an irresistible process. One witness had testified before the Privy Council that there were already 30,000 persons west of the Line. This was probably an exaggeration in 1772, but it convinced the ministry that some form of government was necessary for so many squatters in Indian country. Dartmouth hoped that a new colony in the interior would restrain the whites and protect the Indians, although he confessed to Superintendent Stuart that he doubted "whether that dangerous spirit of unlicensed emigration into the interior parts of America can be effectively restrained by any authority whatever."[13]

There were a number of possible objections to the establishment of a new colony. Opponents of the plan, who preferred to remain anonymous, urged Dartmouth to continue Hillsborough's policy. Such a remote colony could not supply men in an emergency, but would have a contrary effect in depopulating older settlements. The empire's commerce would not benefit from the produce of the interior, owing to the lack of water transportation to the coast. Cut off from British manufactures by the mountain barrier, the inhabitants would begin to manufacture for themselves, thus competing with the mother country. Finally, it was argued, if these people are the type who would do evil if no government were placed over them, why remedy one evil with a greater one?[14] Other objections, on military grounds, came from General Gage who regretted Hillsborough's resignation and worked to prevent the Ohio Grant during his leave in England in 1773.[15]

In spite of these objections, Dartmouth proceeded to execute the new policy adopted by the Privy Council in their order in council of August 14. His first action was to inquire of Sir William Johnson

---

12 To Lt. Col. Legge, 17 March 1773, *ibid.,* 848.

13 To Stuart, 3 March 1773, P.R.O., CO 5/74, f.63, cited in Alvord, *Mississippi Valley,* II, 141.

14 Two anonymous letters, 18 August 1772 and October 1772, Dartmouth Manuscripts, 385 & 449.

15 Gage to Hillsborough, 5 November 1772, *Correspondence of General Thomas Gage* (C. E. Carter, ed., New Haven, 1931 & 1953), I, 339. John R. Alden, *General Gage in America* (Baton Rouge, 1948), 149.

whether the Indians of the Six Nations would object to a new colony. The Iroquois League had no objections, although it was suspicious of the type of people who settled new grants. Johnson described the frontiersmen as a "lawless set of people, as fond of independency as [the Indians themselves], and more regardless of government owing to ignorance, prejudice, democratical principles and their remote situation."[16] The Indians, reported Johnson, hoped that an organized colony would act as a restraining influence upon these irresistible settlers.[17] Dartmouth had no way of knowing that Johnson was something less than ingenuous in this matter. The superintendent was materially involved with the land speculators and had received some stock in the Ohio Company for his co-operation.[18] If the Iroquois were willing to have a new colony established in the interior, then Dartmouth had no further reservations about promoting the grant to the company. He was free to organize a new colony west of the Line.

Although Dartmouth endeavored to hurry the necessary papers through the bureaucratic process, the opponents of the plan adopted delaying tactics which prevented success. Bamber Gascoyne, who represented Hillsborough's viewpoint at the Board of Trade, succeeded in postponing action on the petition from November, 1772, until April, 1773. During this same period, it will be remembered, the American Department itself was under attack from the two older departments. Still, Dartmouth was optimistic about the results. In the middle of March, he made an offer of the governorship of the new colony to his kinsman, Francis Legge.[19] Legge wisely accepted instead an appointment as Governor of Nova Scotia in May, rather than wait for the completion of the Ohio project. Nevertheless, considerable progress was made before obstructionism again halted the plan. During the month of April (1773), the Board of Trade, under Dartmouth's direction, considered the Ohio Company's petition, interviewed Samuel Wharton, drafted a representation to the Privy Council and, finally, signed it in May.[20]

The Board's report of 6 May 1773, in response to the order in council of 14 August 1772, dealt with the double problem of granting land to a group of private persons and also establishing a government for the area. The proposed colony was designated *Vandalia* and its boundaries were to embrace an area west of the Proclamation Line, between the Ohio River and the western limits of Virginia and North

---

[16] From Sir William Johnson, 4 November 1772, *N.Y. Col. Docs.*, VIII, 315-16.

[17] From Johnson, 22 September 1773, *ibid.*, 396.

[18] Sosin, *Whitehall and the Wilderness*, 142 & 173.

[19] To Lt. Col. Legge, 17 March 1773, Dartmouth Manuscripts, 848.

[20] *Journal of the Board of Trade*, 1 April to 6 May 1773, XIII, 351-6.

Carolina. The usual form of royal government was to be constituted, including an appointed governor and council, assisted by an elected assembly. The Church of England was to be established, although dissenters were given full toleration. The usual courts were to be erected, with ultimate appeal to the Privy Council; minor officials and their salaries were stipulated. Within this proposed colony, in the approximate location of present-day West Virginia, the Ohio Company was to receive a large grant of land, for which they must pay £10,000 immediately, quit-rents of two shillings per acre in the future, and also provide for the Governor's house and the support of the Church. To pacify the Colony of Virginia, 200,000 acres were specifically reserved for colonial officers of the French and Indian War.[21]

Two months after receiving this report, the Privy Council ordered the Attorney General and the Solicitor General to prepare a draft of a grant based on the Board of Trade's recommendations.[22] Here again further delay occurred. The law officers of the Crown, Thurlow and Wedderburn, rarely agreed with each other prior to 1774. Now both raised objections to the Board's report, instead of proceeding directly to the drafting of an instrument for the Great Seal. They objected first to the terms of the grant to the Ohio Company, since it would cause the land to accumulate in the hands of the last survivor. They found the methods of collecting quit-rents not in accordance with custom, and finally they objected to the boundaries as too vaguely described. Since Dartmouth was absent on his usual holiday, Lord Rochford sent him the law officers' reply together with his opinion of it. Rochford, materially interested in the Ohio Company, was prepared to overlook any jealousy he might have felt toward the third secretaryship and to work with Dartmouth in the promotion of Vandalia. He and Dartmouth agreed that the joint tenancy might be altered to the benefit of individual heirs of the Ohio Company, and that the quit-rents should be collected according to custom. The question of the boundaries, however, was a different matter. Rochford had consulted Pownall, who expressed great surprise at this objection, for the description followed both the precedent established in the case of Georgia and also the maps deposited in the Council's office. Dartmouth also believed the boundaries to be "as clearly and distinctly ascertained as [possible]."[23]

The law officers knew that the Privy Council could overrule their objections, but this action would require further delay. Dartmouth

[21] Board of Trade to the King, 6 May 1773, Dartmouth Manuscripts, 609.

[22] *Acts of the Privy Council*, V, 210.

[23] From Rochford, 7 September 1773, enclosing Thurlow and Wedderburn to the Lords of the Committee for Plantation Affairs, 16 July 1773, Dartmouth Manuscripts, 702. Dartmouth's draft reply, 9 September 1773, *ibid*.

and Rochford were prepared to press the issue. The latter drafted an order in council for Dartmouth's approval, directing the law officers to alter the provisions for joint tenancy and quit-rents, but to incorporate the boundaries unchanged.[24] Attorney General Thurlow remarked to Pownall at this same time that he considered the proposed colony, with its provisions for new royal appointments, as "an infamous job. . . ."[25] Whether for this reason or some other one, the law officers managed to delay their amended report until the end of October. Further postponements of the decision, owing to technicalities and necessary paper work, prevented the conclusion of the project until after the return of the tea ships in January, 1774, with their alarming news from Boston. This crisis produced a new set of problems and policies in which there was no room for the still-born Colony of Vandalia. The outbreak of war removed the problem of westward expansion from imperial officials and gave it instead to the new Republic.

Dartmouth's policy for the west is worth considering, in spite of its failure. His attitude was both more realistic and more statesmanlike than his predecessor's. Hillsborough regarded the Proclamation Line as a permanent boundary and consistently overruled such governors as Lord Dunmore of Virginia, who attempted to grant land in the western extremities of their colonies. Dartmouth, on the other hand, recognized the inevitability of westward expansion, in spite of proclamations and lines to the contrary. Unregulated expansion would provoke the noble savages and destroy their confidence in the King's pledges to protect them, but the establishment of new governments in the interior seemed a logical solution. Hillsborough's advice to Franklin and his associates to ask for a province was facetious and Machiavellian. Dartmouth's policy was to incorporate the land grant in a larger area to be governed as a royal colony. Thus, Dartmouth was following in Shelburne's footsteps. The Proclamation Line was never intended to be permanent, but migration into the interior was to be orderly and regular. When Dunmore asserted the authority of the Crown over some settlers on the upper Ohio, Dartmouth congratulated him for "the steps you have taken to introduce order and government amongst those settlers. . . ."[26] Although this contrasted favorably with Hillsborough's policy, it was too late to pursue it to a successful conclusion. The opponents of expansionism were strong enough to delay, if not prevent, the new policy, until events in Boston cancelled Dartmouth's well-laid plans completely.

---

[24] From Rochford, 23 September 1773, *ibid.,* 708.
[25] From Pownall, 22 September 1773, *ibid.,* 882.
[26] To Dunmore, 1 June 1774, P.R.O., CO 5/1352, f.67 (L.C. Trans.).

Chapter IX

THE GASPEE INCIDENT

DURING the same months when Dartmouth was trying to hasten the establishment of the new Colony of Vandalia, another serious problem required some of his attention. The *Gaspée* incident had taken place two months before this appointment to the secretaryship, but over a year elapsed before the special commission concluded its investigation of the affair. Their report was both inconclusive and unsatisfactory, from the Ministry's point of view, but the immediate consequences of the *Gaspée* affair stimulated a revival of the revolutionary spirit among the colonists.

The people of New England have been traditionally famous for their skill as shipbuilders and for their success in maritime commerce. The Rhode Islanders were no exception to this tradition; but much of their mercantile activity was contrary to the laws of trade and navigation. Colonial governors were supposed to enforce Britain's policy of mercantilism, but Rhode Island's exceptionally democratic constitution provided for the popular election of colonial officers, including the governor. Customs officials were, of course, appointed by the Crown, but during most of the Eighteenth-Century the appointed officials preferred to remain in England, collecting their salaries in comfort while underpaid deputies performed their duties. This neglect proved most salutary for the colonists. They were quite willing to supplement the meager incomes of customs officials with private contributions from their own pockets in exchange for laxity in enforcing the Navigation Acts. While the government paid out £8,000 annually to maintain the service, its officials collected a mere £2,000 in colonial customs duties.[1]

This state of affairs could not endure indefinitely. It was especially unseemly in view of the tremendous debt which Great Britain had incurred as a result of the Seven Years' War. The interest alone was £5,000,000 a year.[2] The taxpayer at home naturally expected the American colonist, who had benefited by the removal of the French menace, to bear a just share of the cost of imperial defense afterwards. First Grenville, and later Townshend, attempted to enforce this policy upon the colonists. The government sought to prevent bribery by ordering customs officials to go to America and to perform their duties personally. In order to reduce the amount of smuggling

[1] Miller, *Origins of the American Revolution*, 83.
[2] *Ibid.*, 89.

and evasion of the laws of trade, the navy stationed ships in American waters for the purpose of patrol.

The appearance of the patrol ships on the coasts of the colonies aroused deep resentment and hostility among the residents. The people of Rhode Island were particularly incensed by this attempt to curtail their lucrative and sometimes illegal trade. The *Gaspée* incident came as a climax to a series of lawless actions. The people of Newport first took the law into their own hands in 1764 when they attacked the schooner *St. John*. At a later date, one of the boats belonging to the patrol ship *Maidstone* was captured and taken to Newport Common, where it was burned amid great rejoicing. The sloop *Liberty* also came to grief while attempting to enforce the unpopular acts in Rhode Island waters. In 1769 she was cut adrift, her masts cut down, her armament thrown overboard, and then she was set afire by the angry mob.[3]

The people of Rhode Island did not welcome any vessel which the Royal Navy assigned to patrol their coasts. Lieutenant Dudingston, in command of the schooner *Gaspée,* made himself and his ship especially obnoxious to the colonists. He stopped every ship that came within sight, even small market vessels and packets. He carried out a thorough search which proved inconvenient and often embarrassing to the captain when contraband was found on board. Since Dudingston had not observed the formality of showing his commission to the Governor and being duly sworn in,[4] the Rhode Islanders regarded these seizures as illegal.

A protest from the Governor to Admiral Montagu was ineffective. Dudingston continued to make seizures and to send them to Boston for trial. His zeal proved to be his undoing, for on June 9th the *Gaspée* ran aground while giving chase to a sloop near Providence. Apparently, the patrol ship suffered no great damage, for the order to abandon ship was not given. The commander retired for the night, confident that the high tide would free his schooner from the sand bar on which she rested. Shortly after sunset, however, the *Gaspée* was surrounded by several boat-loads of armed men. Dudingston, aroused by the watch, appeared on deck, where he received some

---

[3] P.R.O., CO 5/145, #27, a-f. John R. Bartlett, *A History of the Destruction of His Britannic Majesty's Schooner Gaspée* (Providence, 1861), 6-7. David S. Lovejoy, *Rhode Island Politics and the American Revolution, 1760-1776* (Providence, 1958), 158-166, deals with the *Gaspée* incident, showing how impossible it was to obtain an impartial jury of the vicinage. William R. Leslie, "The Gaspee Affair: A Study of Its Constitutional Significance," *Mississippi Valley Historical Review*, XXXIX (Sept., 1952), 233-56.

[4] Darius Sessions to Gov. Wanton, 21 March 1772, Bartlett, *History of the Gaspée*, 8-9.

choice New England profanity and a shot in the abdomen.[5] The boarding party easily captured the ship after this piece of violence. They treated the Lieutenant's wound, transported him and his crew to the shore, and then burned the offensive *Gaspée* to the water line.

News of the deed spread rapidly throughout the colonies. The Governor of Rhode Island issued a proclamation a few days later, referring to the attack as "an atrocious crime" and offering a reward of £100 for information leading to a conviction.[6] When Governor Hutchinson of Massachusetts Bay heard of the incident he wrote to undersecretary Pownall to urge an official inquiry. If the affair "is passed over without full inquiry and due resentment, our liberty people will think they may with impunity commit any acts of violence. . . ."[7] At the same time, Admiral Montagu sent all available information to Lord Hillsborough at the Colonial Office.[8] Later the Admiral assured Hutchinson that the Ministry intended to take strong measures. Some members of the government would not be content with mere punishment of the actual culprits. Rhode Island's charter was in jeopardy, if Lord Sandwich of the Admiralty were to have his way. Montagu reported that Sandwich "will never leave pursuing the colony, until it is disfranchised."[9]

Hillsborough's term of office was about to come to an end. When he reported the business to the Cabinet at the end of July, it was agreed to obtain an opinion from the Attorney and Solicitor General.[10] Several days elapsed before the law officers made their report, so Hillsborough prepared a letter to the Governor and Company of Rhode Island, instructing them to "exert themselves most actively for the discovery of the offenders."[11] Within the next few days the legal authorities decided that the burning of the *Gaspée* was not merely a violation of the recent act of Parliament for the preservation of the King's dockyards, but was actually high treason, or levying war against the King.[12] At this point Hillsborough resigned on the

[5] *Ibid.*, 18-19, contains the "Narrative" of Ephraim Bowen, who took part in the attack. See also, *Documents relating to the Colonial History of the State of New Jersey* (F. W. Ricord and W. Nelson, eds., Newark, N. J., 1886), First Series, X, 375-6.

[6] Printed in Bartlett, *History of the Gaspée*, 29.

[7] Gov. Hutchinson to Pownall, 29 August 1772, *ibid.*, 50n.

[8] Montagu to Hillsborough, 11 July 1772, Dartmouth Manuscripts, 369.

[9] Hutchinson to Samuel Hood, 2 September 1772, Bartlett, *History of the Gaspée*, 51n.

[10] Cabinet Minute, 30 July 1772, Dartmouth Manuscripts, 372.

[11] Hillsborough to the Governor and Company of Rhode Island, 7 August 1772, *ibid.*, 376. This dispatch was recalled.

[12] Thurlow and Wedderburn to Hillsborough, 10 August 1772, *ibid.*, 379 and also P.R.O., CO 5/159, #93. Clements Library, Ann Arbor, also owns a set of these legal reports: Wedderburn Papers, Vol. I.

question of the Ohio Grant, leaving this difficult problem to his successor.

Lord Dartmouth's policy in the *Gaspée* affair was cautious and moderate. Certainly, he did not share the viewpoint of the Bedford faction in the Ministry nor, like Sandwich, advocate the suppression of Rhode Island's democratic constitution. On the other hand, his temperament and outlook were essentially conservative, and he could not condone mob violence and the destruction of property. Therefore, in taking over the business from Hillsborough he naturally formulated his policy on the basis of the law officers' opinion.

Dartmouth took office in August and since important officials of the period seldom remained in London during hot weather, the undersecretary, John Pownall, handled most of the details. He prepared all the necessary papers and forwarded them to Sandwell for his chief's approval and signature. Pownall believed this business was very important. If the new Colonial Secretary encountered any difficulties in understanding the dispatches, Pownall begged Dartmouth to return to the office. Apparently, he suspected a plot against the colonial office, for he warned his superior that "I am convinced that this proceeding is meant to pledge the American minister in coercive measures and your lordship will judge what other people will think of this proceeding when I tell you that the Attorney General said to me himself this morning that he thought it five times the magnitude of the Stamp Act [crisis]."[13]

As a result of the legal authorities' report, it was decided to appoint a commission of inquiry, consisting of the Governor of Rhode Island, the Chief Justices of Massachusetts, New York, and New Jersey and the Judge of the Admiralty Court at Boston.[14] This commission was intended to be independent of the control of the people of Rhode Island. They were given stringent instructions to discover the culprits, have them apprehended and sent to England for trial.[15] Dartmouth agreed to the principle of sending a Commission of Inquiry, and he signed the necessary papers to assist them in carrying out their duties. For example, when he wrote to General Gage, the Commander-in-Chief of the King's Forces in America, he called the *Gaspée* incident a "daring Act of violence." He instructed Gage to hold himself "in readiness to send into the said Colony of Rhode Island, whenever you shall be called upon by the Commissioners, such a part of the Troops under your command," as might be necessary to suppress a riot or insurrection.[16]

---

13 From Pownall, 29 August 1772, Dartmouth Manuscripts, 400.
14 Copy of a Commission, 2 September 1772, *ibid.*, 405.
15 Copy of the King's Instructions, 4 September 1772, *ibid.*, 410.
16 To Gage, 4 September 1772, *Gage Corres.* (Carter, ed.), II, 149.

At the same time, Dartmouth did not agree with the members of the government who had insisted that the accused colonists should be brought to England for trial. He told an acquaintance of Admiral Keppel that he was determined "not to allow of any orders to issue from his office for bringing home for trial one of the prisoners accused of riot in Rhode Island; [and] that he conceives it legal for the person to take his trial in the country where the offence was committed: . . . ."[17] Dartmouth's position on this issue was a difficult one. The instructions to the Commission of Inquiry were quite sufficient to authorize the transportation to England for trial of any prisoners they might have apprehended. Once the names of some suspects were known, the Secretary of State might have written additional letters to colonial governors, directing them to hand over the prisoners to one of His Majesty's ships.[18] A certain amount of correspondence with the Admiralty, providing for the transportation of the prisoners to England, might have been necessary. Still, it does not appear that Dartmouth could have prevented this step, if the commission had had the slightest success in uncovering information in Rhode Island. He was already committed to the principle of transportation for trial. It is just possible that he might have resigned in protest over the action, but the person who informed Keppel of the Earl's intentions thought that this course was unlikely. His resignation so soon after his appointment would have caused irreparable harm to his stepbrother's Ministry—and this was a step which Dartmouth could never bring himself to take.

It was very fortunate for Lord Dartmouth that the crisis never occurred. Although the Commission of Inquiry held two sessions in Providence, in January and May of 1773, they were unable to unearth a single piece of valuable evidence or to find one reliable witness. Charles Dudley, the Collector of Customs in Rhode Island, prophesied the ultimate failure of the commission early in 1773. He noted in a letter which was subsequently forwarded to Dartmouth: "The offenders are not only safe from detection but ridicule the measures taken to punish them."[19] Chief Justice Smyth, one of the commissioners, reported that Dudingston was so universally hated that no one would give any useful information about the attack, although "hundreds of the inhabitants of the Colony" must have known one or more of the participants.[20] In their official report the commissioners censured the civil magistrates of Rhode Island

---

[17] Keppel to Rockingham, September 1772, Thomas Keppel, *Life of Augustus Viscount Keppel* . . . (London, 1842), I, 409.

[18] Leslie, "Gaspee Affair," *Miss. V.H.R.*, XXXIX, 240.

[19] Dudley to Reeve, 19 January 1773, enclosed in a communication from Reeve, February 1773, Dartmouth Manuscripts, 572.

[20] From Chief Justice Smyth, 8 February 1773, *ibid.*, 559. Also *New Jersey Archives*, X, 396.

for their lack of cooperation during the course of their investigations.[21] In fact, all that they were able to discover was the information supplied by a colored servant named Aaron. Both Chief Justice Smyth and Chief Justice Horsmanden regarded his testimony as unreliable.[22] Consequently, the commission was forced to confess complete failure in their efforts to discover the culprits. No one was charged with treason; no one was taken into custody to be sent to England for trial. A convenient attack of mass amnesia in Rhode Island made it unnecessary for Lord Dartmouth to stand by his resolution to prevent transportation for trial.

The ultimate consequences of the *Gaspée* affair were very important to the history of the period. It provided a strong stimulus for the revolutionary movement in the colonies by providing a new grievance for the radical leaders. The radical movement had declined greatly in popularity after the repeal of all but one of the Townshend duties.[23] The quarrel between the colonies and the mother country quieted down in the early years of the 1770's. Importation of all kinds of British goods, including even tea, took place, as the colonists doffed their homespun and returned to older ways of life. Instead of maintaining a united front against British policy, the colonists were beginning to engage in serious disputes with one another. The present area of Vermont became the scene of great contention between New Hampshire and Massachusetts settlers on the one hand and those claiming to exercise the authority of New York on the other. In the South, the "Regulators" of Carolina rose in rebellion against the Tidewater aristocrats who dominated the Colonial Assembly. Serious rifts were appearing in colonial unity before the *Gaspée* incident.

In Great Britain, too, the radical movement was entering upon a decline, owing to the quarrel between John Wilkes and Horne Tooke. What was needed, of course, was a new issue upon which contending factions could unite. All the grievances of the past had become too stale and uninteresting to be of value for propaganda purposes. The appearance of the *Gaspée* Commission of Inquiry, then, provided a much needed issue for the radicals to put to their own use. Dudingston's determination to stamp out smuggling had made him extremely unpopular; "in a Word, his Behaviour was so *piratical* and provoking

---

[21] Report of the Commissioners to the King, 22 June 1773, Bartlett, *History of the Gaspée,* 130. See also, P.R.O., CO 5/1285, ff.218 *et seq.* (L.C. Microfilm).

[22] From Chief Justice Horsmanden, 20 February 1773, *N.Y. Col.Docs.,* VIII, 351-2. For Smyth's letter, see note 20 above.

[23] Miller, *Origins of the American Revolution,* Chapter XII. Compare, Leslie, "Gaspee Affair," *Miss V.H.R.,* XXXIX, 234 note 2, which corrects some inaccurate details.

that Englishmen could not patiently bear it."[24] The destruction of the *Gaspée* a few months later was regarded as a test case by the Sons of Liberty, for "if the British government passed this 'attrocious offence,' it would lose all title to respect in British America."[25] The appointment of the Commission of Inquiry, on the other hand, provided the opposition elements in the colonies with a splendid example of "tyranny," and they lost no time in denouncing this "Court of Inquisition." They compared its procedure to that of the Star Chamber, and especially condemned its inhuman instructions to send the prisoners abroad for trial.[26]

So skillfully did the radicals ring the changes on this old theme of British tyranny and unconstitutional procedure, that even the moderate elements began to take alarm. One of Dartmouth's unofficial correspondents, Thomas Wooldridge, described "the apprehensions of the judicious of this country as to what may be the result of the execution of a commission to examine into the affair of the 'Gaspee' schooner."[27] The most important result of the *Gaspée* incident, however, was the strong impetus toward colonial union which it provided. The proceedings of the commission and their instructions to deprive the prisoners of a trial by a jury of the vicinage were represented as attacks upon the liberties of all the colonies, not just Rhode Island. Once this point was perceived, a storm of protest rose in the other parts of America. The Virginia House of Burgesses expressed its alarm in a series of formal resolutions on March 12. They suggested the establishment of interprovincial committees of correspondence, patterned after those in Massachusetts.[28]

Several of the men who took it upon themselves to advise the Colonial Office of sentiment in America noted this rebirth of revolutionary spirit. One Charles Smith described himself as a merchant who travelled to New England and the Middle Colonies every two or three years in order to collect debts. He observed a "disposition which savours too much of rebellion." He also informed Dartmouth that the American newspapers were full of "rebellious sentiments," and expressed his fears that the colonists were about "to throw off their dependence." Smith suggested that there was a great need "to cool and quiet the present tumults in New England and to choose the wisest men for governors of the different provinces."[29] Another correspondent told Dartmouth of the rapid establishment of Com-

[24] Miller, *Origins*, 326. Leslie identifies the newspaper which Miller quotes, as the Providence *Gazette*, 9 January 1773 (*Miss. V.H.R.*, XXXIX, 235, n.11).
[25] Miller, *Origins*, 327.
[26] Leslie, "Gaspee Affair," *Miss. V.H.R.*, XXXIX, 245.
[27] From Thomas Wooldridge, 4 January 1773, Dartmouth Manuscripts, 522.
[28] Merrill Jensen, ed., *English Historical Documents* (Vol. IX): *American Colonial Documents to 1776* (New York, 1955), pp. 763-5.
[29] From Charles Smith, March 1773, Dartmouth Manuscripts, 592.

mittees of Correspondence throughout all the colonies. "Affairs are altering visibly and the people are almost universally determined to support an independent government unless Great Britain will confirm their liberties."[30]

The colonists frequently expressed their idea of remedying the situation by suggesting that the government "should take things back as far as possible to the state they were in at his Majesty's accession."[31] This proposal involved a complete reversal of George III's colonial policy and would have been beyond the power of a man like Dartmouth, in the face of the opposition which the Bedfords and the Grenvilles would have aroused. Dartmouth tried to ride out the storm, in hopes that it would all blow over in time. At best, this could have only a temporary effect, for until basic grievances could be settled there was nothing to guarantee that a new and more violent storm might not appear in the sky.

Some of the colonists appreciated the tact with which Dartmouth handled the situation. It was a welcome relief from the blustering of Lord Hillsborough. After the failure of the Commission of Inquiry became apparent, an American clergyman congratulated Dartmouth on "having escaped the difficulties that must have followed had a discovery been made by the court of inquiry at Rhode Island of any concerned in the burning of the *Gaspée*." Any attempt to take the accused to Great Britain for trial would have "set the continent into a fresh flame."[32] This should have given Dartmouth ample indication of the seriousness of the situation, if he was not already fully aware of it. The *Gaspée* incident marks both a turning point in Anglo-American relations and an inauspicious beginning for Dartmouth's term of office in the colonial secretaryship. The issue was seized upon by the radicals, in order to stimulate colonial union and a rebirth of the revolutionary spirit. The Virginia Resolves set in motion the continental organization of Committees of Correspondence. This efficient propaganda machinery continued to operate effectively throughout the course of Dartmouth's unhappy term of office as a Secretary of State.

---

30 From Joseph Ward, 8 May 1773, *ibid.*, 613.
31 From the Rev. W. Gordon, 16 June 1773, *ibid.*, 637.
32 *Ibid.*

Chapter X

PETITIONS FROM MASSACHUSETTS

D URING Dartmouth's first year in the American Department, a third problem arose in the form of petitions from Massachusetts. At the same time that he faced the frustrations of the Vandalia problem, and long before he knew of the results of the *Gaspée* inquiry, he had to consider the grievances of Massachusetts and petitions for their redress. Some of the colonists had convinced themselves that the ministry aimed to enslave them, whereas their worst intention was to collect a fair share of the cost of imperial defense. Americans revolted against assumed oppression at a time when they had more liberties than any other colonial population.[1] Grievances, especially in Massachusetts, were exacerbated by two factors: The vacillation of British policy and the apparent success of violent protests as contrasted with the utter failure of peaceful petitioning. By the time Dartmouth assumed office the pattern of events had already become quite clear and the most effective means of resistance were well known to the colonists. British policy had wavered from the firmness of Grenville to the conciliation of Rockingham; later, Shelburne's broad-minded policy was overruled by Charles Townshend's ill-fated program of indirect taxation of colonial imports. Petitions against the unfavorable developments in colonial policy were either ignored or treated with contempt. Only when the colonists resorted to extra-constitutional measures like the Stamp Act Congress, or more violent behavior which harmed British trade, did the mother country take remedial action. The repeal of the Stamp Act and the removal of all but one of the Townshend duties merely provided the more radical elements with object lessons in the usefulness of violence.

The resignation of Hillsborough was generally believed to mark another change in colonial policy. The keynote of Hillsborough's policy had been "firmness," as he himself once told Dr. Franklin.[2] As one application of this policy, the Secretary had refused to recognize Franklin as the legal agent of the Massachusetts Assembly, on the grounds that the Governor had not consented to the appointment.

---

[1] C. H. Van Tyne, *The Causes of the War of Independence* (New York, 1922) final chapter discusses the relative advantages of British colonists over those of France, Spain, Portugal and the Dutch.

[2] Interview of 16 January 1771, *The Complete Works of Benjamin Franklin* (John Bigelow, ed., New York, 1888), II, 78.

He treated Franklin very rudely, compelling him to cool his heels in the outer office for as long as four hours on one occasion and sending word that he was not in his office on another.[3] Little wonder that Franklin rejoiced at Hillsborough's resignation and the appointment of a man with a reputation for conciliation. He fully expected to be able to "obtain more in favor of our colonies upon occasion, than I could for some time past."[4]

Franklin's expectations seemed to be justified by the results of his first meeting with the new Secretary of State. When Dartmouth returned to London at the end of October, he held the customary "levee" or morning reception. Franklin attended and found Dartmouth's attitude pleasant and their conversation satisfactory. He made no objection to Franklin's agency and seemed unconcerned when Franklin told him that he would deliver a petition from the Massachusetts Assembly within a few days. This petition protested the payment of the Governor's salary by the Crown. The Assembly resented this. They claimed that it endangered the colonial constitution, since naturally they would prefer to retain control of executive salaries.[5]

Dartmouth reacted to this petition for redress of grievances with cautious hesitation. After a lengthy consideration of the matter, he summoned Franklin to his office and requested him to withdraw it for the present. Pressing the grievance would only offend the King and possibly move Parliament to reprimand the Assembly. In Dartmouth's opinion, heated tempers on both sides of the Atlantic were beginning to cool and delay would be the best course of action. Franklin assumed that the petition was being rejected and warned the Secretary of the dangerous consequences of denying a legal vent for the airing of grievances. Colonial petitions were no longer sent to Parliament, because of the cavalier treatment which had been accorded them in the past. It had become the practice to address the King directly, but if this channel for the redress of grievances became blocked as well, only violence and unconstitutional procedure could result. Dartmouth reassured him, however, that delay was all he requested. Franklin readily agreed to this, justifying his actions to the Speaker of the Assembly by pointing out that the decision to pay the Governor from Crown revenues had been taken in Hillsborough's administration while "the present Minister was our friend in the

[3] Franklin to Samuel Cooper, 5 February 1771, *ibid.*, 75 *et seq.*
[4] Franklin to his Son, 17 August 1772, *ibid.*, 114.
[5] Franklin to Thomas Cushing, 4 November 1772, *Franklin's Works* (Sparks, ed.), VIII, 22. Same to same, 3 September 1772, *The Writings of Benjamin Franklin* (Albert H. Smyth, ed., New York, 1905-7), V, 435. Carl Van Doren, *Benjamin Franklin* (New York, 1938), 442.

Repeal of the Stamp Act. . . ."[6] He asked for further instructions from the Assembly.

Dartmouth's request that the Massachusetts petition to the King be temporarily withdrawn was more than mere procrastination on his part. It is true that he had only recently entered upon his difficult duties, but it was not lack of familiarity with American affairs and British politics that caused him to ask Franklin to postpone the crisis. Dartmouth judged the time to be inopportune and hoped that the American problem would clear up of its own accord, if given sufficient time to cool. There is some evidence that his confidence was justified, for as one of his friends observed about the Americans, "they are evidently returning to their old sentiments of loyalty and the spirit of Boston don't seem to communicate any heat into the country."[7] Unfortunately, events were taking place which militated against the policy of delay.

Although the issue of the Governor's salary was the first grievance which Dartmouth encountered in a formal petition, it was not the only problem which required his attention. If he was not already aware of these grievances, his correspondence soon informed him of their nature. One letter in particular, from the Reverend Mr. Gordon, summarized the outstanding issues rather conveniently. He recommended several steps that might be taken to restore good feelings in the colonies and, in effect, return them to the "state in which they were before the Stamp Act."[8] First, remove the troops from Boston; second, restore Castle William to the control of the provincial government; third, instruct the Governor to sign all money bills; and, fourth, return the appropriation of the judge's salaries to the colonial assembly. Dartmouth already knew that "Acts of Parliament raising a revenue in America without our consent"[9] was high on the list of complaints. The appropriation of this revenue for the support of the Governor was alleged to have destroyed "the mutual dependence between him [and the] people, established by Charter." Similarly, royal salaries created an undue dependence of the judges upon the Crown. The needless multiplication of revenue officers was held to be both an innovation and an embarrassment to trade. The extension of the authority of admiralty courts deprived the inhabitants of their right to trial by jury. The list of New England grievances also included the instruction to the Governor of Massachusetts restraining him from consenting to the payment of the colonial agent in Britain.

---

[6] Franklin to Cushing, 2 December 1772, *Franklin's Writings* (Smyth, ed.), V, 450.

[7] From Major General Phineas Lyman, 8 December 1772, Dartmouth Manuscripts, 471.

[8] From Rev. William Gordon, 24 October 1772, *ibid.*, 442.

[9] "List of New England Grievances," undated, *ibid.*, 625.

What did Dartmouth do about these grievances? For the most part, there was little that he could do. In his view of the constitution, the doctrine of parliamentary supremacy was essential; therefore, laws passed by Parliament had to be obeyed, whether they provided for colonial revenue or something else. The Governor and the judiciary ought to be free of local pressure, in order to be able to enforce the laws. Thus, his belief in the principles of the Declaratory Act prevented Dartmouth from giving the colonists the satisfaction they demanded.

Nevertheless, he was willing to interpret these principles in the broadest and most favorable manner. With respect to salaries, Dartmouth drafted an instruction to Hutchinson in June, 1773, that whenever the Assembly "think fit to establish permanently competent salaries for the Judges, His Majesty will withdraw the allowances at present made and will grant their commissions during good behaviour, and further that His Majesty will be also graciously pleased to permit his Governor to receive his salary from the province in the usual manner, provided that such salary be not less than 2000 per annum and that the house allotted for his residence be kept in constant and proper repair."[10] While this may have been a concession of form, it was not a change of policy, for the assembly would not have controlled the salaries of independent executive and judicial officials, as in the past. In any event, the offer was definitely withdrawn a year later, when General Gage succeeded Hutchinson. Dartmouth instructed the new governor that the judges' salaries were to be paid by royal warrant, over which the Colonial Legislature would have no control, rather than an appropriation from the Assembly.[11] Thus, even the one small concession he was prepared to make failed to promote conciliation.

Dartmouth had placed great reliance upon the healing powers of time and at the close of 1772 it looked as though he might succeed. Early in 1773, however, an event in Massachusetts renewed the argument and greatly complicated Dartmouth's administration. Governor Hutchinson opened the session of the General Court with a speech, in which he attempted to show "that the colonies were settled as parts of the British dominions, and, consequently, as subject to the supreme legislative authority thereof." The portion of the speech which especially antagonized the legislators included the statement: "I know of no line that can be drawn between the supreme authority of Parliament and the total independence of the colonies. . . ."[12] This was a serious challenge to the patriot viewpoint which, in 1773,

---

[10] To Governor Hutchinson [2 June 1773], *ibid.*, 625.

[11] To Gage, 8 September 1774, *Gage Correspondence* (Carter, ed.), II, 172.

[12] Hutchinson, *History of Massachusetts* (Mayo, ed.), III, 266. J. K. Hosmer, *Life of Thomas Hutchinson* (Boston, 1896), App. B, p. 367.

demanded rights of local autonomy but denied that they were aiming at independence. The Council was quick to reply to the Governor's address. Disclaiming any desire for separation from the empire, they nevertheless insisted that the authority of Parliament was limited by the provisions of the Charter, which had given the power of taxation to the people's representatives.[13] The Assembly's reply, both longer and later than the Council's, asserted that "the free and full exercise of the liberties and immunities granted by the charter" would not endanger "that just sense of allegiance which they owe to the 'crown'. . . ."[14] The Governor had hoped to settle the issue once and for all by forcing an acknowledgment of parliamentary supremacy, but the two houses of the legislature had side-stepped the central argument while at the same time defending the charter as the constitution of the colony. Colonial assemblies were coming to regard themselves as miniature parliaments, omnicompetent within their respective provinces.

When news of the altercation reached Great Britain, Dartmouth was greatly dismayed, for it seemed to speed the end of the cooling-off period. Franklin reported that even Hutchinson's friends were inclined to doubt the wisdom of his action, and that they were "apprehensive of some ill consequences from his forcing the assembly into that dispute. . . ."[15] While the British government groped for a solution, Franklin observed that there was "some alarm at the discontents in New England, and some appearance of softening in the disposition of government on the idea that matters have been carried too far there."[16] Although he could hope for a more conciliatory attitude, the shrewd old agent criticized the ministry's lack of forthright policy: "all depends upon circumstances and events. We govern from hand to mouth. There seems to be no wise regular plan."[17]

Hutchinson had made his disturbing speech in January; first reports of it reached England in April; but in May Dartmouth had still not evolved any "wise regular plan." On May 5th he voiced many of his uncertainties to Franklin, which the latter reported to Speaker Cushing. Concerning Hutchinson, Dartmouth exclaimed, "What difficulties that gentleman has brought us all into by his imprudence!" He told Franklin that it was not possible for Parliament to ignore the Massachusetts Assembly's assertion of their independent authority. When the Agent assured the Secretary that "Force would do no

---

[13] Hutchinson, *History of Massachusetts,* III, 268. Hosmer, *Life of Hutchinson,* App. B, p. 379.

[14] *Ibid.,* 380 *et seq.* Hutchinson, *History of Massachusetts,* III, 270.

[15] Franklin to Cushing, 3 April 1773, *Franklin's Writings* (Smyth, ed.), VI, 29-30.

[16] Franklin to his Son, 6 April 1773, *ibid.,* 31.

[17] *Ibid.*

good," Dartmouth replied: "I do not know that force would be thought of; but perhaps an act may pass to lay them under some inconveniences, till they rescind that declaration." Dartmouth's suggested solution to the immediate problem was that the Assembly should be persuaded to withdraw their replies to the Governor's speech. Franklin was too tactful to tell the Secretary that this suggestion was neither very constructive nor realistic, but he did point out that the addresses had each been passed by unanimous vote and that the circumstances required the Governor to withdraw his speech first, "which . . . would be an awkward operation."[18]

In spite of Hutchinson's "imprudent" action, the government supported him officially. Dartmouth was far more disturbed by the dangerous doctrines employed by the Assembly in its reply, for he had formerly considered these to be held by only a small but desperate faction in the colony. "After so public an avowal in the representative body of the people of doctrines subversive of every principle of the constitutional dependence of the colonies upon this kingdom, it is vain to hope that they will be induced by argument and persuasion to yield due obedience to the laws of Parliament and to acquiesce in those arrangements which the King, consulting the welfare and the happiness of his subjects, has thought fit to adopt."[19] Consequently, the Secretary instructed the Governor to "avoid any further discussion whatever upon those questions." He did not, however, order the addresses to be withdrawn upon pain of dissolution, as his predecessor would in all likelihood have done. In 1768, when the Massachusetts Assembly had issued a circular letter of protest against the Townshend Duties, Hillsborough had instructed Governor Bernard to dissolve the Assembly if they refused to withdraw the offending letter.[20] In justifying this order later, Hillsborough adopted a very high-handed tone: "The colonies are our subjects; as such they are bound by our laws; and I trust that we shall never use the language of supplication, to beg that our subjects will condescendingly yield obedience to our inherent pre-eminence."[21] By contrast with this attitude, Dartmouth merely recommended that Hutchinson "avoid any further discussion" and that he use his own discretion whether to prorogue or dissolve the General Court. The Governor willingly accepted these instructions, for he later admitted that the consequences of his speech had been "disagreeable."[22]

---

[18] Interview of 5 May 1773, reported in Franklin to Cushing, 6 May 1773, *Franklin's Writings* (Smyth, ed.), VI, 48. Compare, P.R.O., CO 5/118, ff. 113-4.

[19] To Hutchinson, 10 April 1773, Dartmouth Manuscripts, 596.

[20] *Dict. Nat. Biog.*, IV, 380-1. Fitzmaurice, *Shelburne*, I, 385-6.

[21] *Parl. Hist.*, XVI, 1019 (Debate of 18 May 1770). See also Hillsborough to the Governors, 21 April 1768, *N. Y. Col. Docs.*, VIII, 58-9.

[22] Hutchinson, *History of Massachusetts*, III, 276-7.

In the meantime, the situation continued to deteriorate. In February, the Massachusetts Assembly had denounced the payment of judges by the Crown as a measure designed "totally to subvert the constitution, and to introduce an arbitrary government into the province. . . ."[23] They drew up a new petition to the King, praying for the redress of this grievance, as well as the problem of the governor's salary, complained of the previous year. When he delivered this second petition to Dartmouth in May, Franklin also submitted the older petition, which he had temporarily withdrawn at the Secretary's request. He had kept faith with Dartmouth, for he had withheld the original petition while the Assembly reconsidered the problem. Since the only change of sentiment in Massachusetts had been in favor of more, rather than less, resistance, further delay seemed pointless. Dartmouth accepted both petitions and promised to lay them before the King.[24]

The royal reply was neither wholly unexpected nor very satisfactory to Massachusetts.

When Franklin wrote a report to Speaker Cushing, he underscored certain words for emphasis and irony: "His Majesty has well weighed the subject-matter and the expressions contained in those petitions; and . . . as he will ever attend to the humble petitions of his subjects and be forward to redress every real grievance, so he is determined to support the constitution and resist with firmness every attempt to derogate from the authority of the supreme legislature."[25]

The agent correctly interpreted this reply to mean that the petitions were not sufficiently humble in tone, that the grievances were not considered real and that George III regarded parliamentary supremacy as an essential part of the constitution. The use of the word "firmness" was unpleasantly reminiscent of Hillsborough's language. Franklin began to doubt whether the change in the colonial secretaryship meant a change in policy, as he had at first thought. He confided his misgivings to his son in July. "Lord Dartmouth," he wrote, "is truly a good man, and wishes sincerely a good understanding with the colonies, but does not seem to have the strength equal to his wishes. Between you and me [Franklin continued] the late measures have been, I suspect, very much the King's own, and he has in some cases a great share of what his friends call firmness."[26]

---

[23] "Message to the House," 12 February 1773, *ibid.*, 277-8.

[24] Franklin to Cushing, 2 June 1773, *Franklin's Writings* (Smyth, ed.), VI, 55-6.

[25] Same to same, 7 July 1773, *ibid.*, 74.

[26] Franklin to his Son, 14 July 1773, *Franklin's Works* (Bigelow, ed.), II, 154.

Another example of Dartmouth's sincere desire for a "good understanding with the colonies," is the letter which he wrote to Thomas Cushing, the Speaker of the Massachusetts House of Representatives.[27] This unprecedented step, which by-passed the Governor, caused great alarm among the more conservative Americans, especially the friends of former Governor Bernard. They regarded it as "beneath the dignity of a Secretary of State to correspond with the speaker of a petty provincial assembly."[28] Dartmouth's letter was supposed to be a private communication, thanking the Massachusetts House for their congratulations upon his taking office. The letter bears the address of Dartmouth's house in St. James's Square, rather than his office in Whitehall, but a comparison of the original manuscript with the final draft reveals several interesting details. The handwriting of one of the clerks in the American Department is easily discernible, so this letter is more than just a private matter. Furthermore, the corrections in Dartmouth's own hand indicate that he worked very diligently in selecting his words, rather than depending upon formal phrases of gratitude.

Dartmouth insisted that he wrote to Cushing "not in the discharge of my duty as a minister of the Crown . . ., but only as a simple individual according to the dictates of my own private judgment and opinion." After thanking the Assembly for their congratulations, the Earl proceeded to denounce their constitutional principles as "wild and extravagant doctrines . . . which appear to me so utterly inconsistent with any pretension to a share in the privileges and advantages of British subjects, that I could never subscribe to them. . . ." He very clearly stated his own belief in the right of Parliament to supremacy over all parts of the Empire, a power which was "inherent in and inseparable from the supreme authority of the State." Dartmouth distinguished, however, between the theoretical possession of this power and its exercise. In the most heavily corrected portion of his letter, he told Cushing that "if my wishes and sentiments could have any weight with a British Parliament, the exercise of that right . . . should be suspended and lie dormant till some occasion should arise . . . in which the expediency and necessity of such exercise should be obvious. . . ."[29] Returning to the specific problem at hand, however, Dartmouth suggested to Cushing that the assembly withdraw their reply to Governor Hutchinson's speech. Although Franklin had assured him earlier that this was highly im-

---

[27] B. F. Stevens, *Facsimiles of MSS in European Archives relating to America, 1773-1783* (London, 1889-98), #2025. Compare the draft letter with corrections in Dartmouth's hand in Dartmouth Manuscripts, 641.

[28] From Gordon, 18 September 1773, *ibid.*, 705.

[29] To Cushing, 19 June 1773, *ibid.*, 641. Dartmouth's first choice of phraseology stated that the right of parliamentary supremacy should "for ever be relinquished, except in cases which should justify their own expediency."

probable, Dartmouth vainly hoped for a co-operative attitude in Massachusetts.

Unfortunately for Dartmouth's hopes, a new crisis appeared. Franklin had acquired several letters written by Hutchinson and Lieutenant-Governor Oliver to friends in England; and the revelation of the letters caused further deterioration in Anglo-American relations. How he acquired them is not known for certain, and his motives for sending them to the Massachusetts radicals are even more dubious.[30] Although he instructed his correspondents not to publish the letters, they leapt at the chance to discredit the "oligarchs." The letters were read to the General Court and then published in a carefully "edited" version. It is not within the scope of the present study to determine the morality of Franklin's actions, nor to decide whether he intended to allay or to increase American suspicions of British motives. He claimed that he wanted to demonstrate that the most obnoxious acts of the Ministry had been "projected, proposed, and solicited by some of the principal and best esteemed" men in Massachusetts.[31]

Whatever his intentions may have been, the letters were skillfully used by the radicals to stir up resentment against the Governor and Lieutenant-Governor. They were branded as "enemies of the constitution," because of views which they had expressed in private letters several years earlier. Actually, some of these ideas, such as Hutchinson's preference for an appointed council, were already well-known.[32] Nevertheless, the secrecy enshrouding the letters, and the way in which sentences were lifted from their context, served to make the whole affair appear much more sinister than it actually was. After a secret session in which the letters were read, the Council and the Assembly solemnly advised Dartmouth that the "original causes of the interruption in the union that formerly subsisted between Great Britain and her colonies may probably be found in the letters sent from hence to Administration and to other gentlemen of influence in Parliament. . . ."[33] Their recommended remedy was the now familiar suggestion to turn the clock back to 1763.

When the General Court's petition for the removal of Hutchinson and Oliver arrived in England, Dartmouth had gone into the country for the customary summer holiday. Franklin forwarded it to Staffordshire, with assurances that the colonists' opinion of Great Britain

---

[30] Hutchinson, *History of Massachusetts*, III, 383 *et seq.* Van Doren, *Franklin*, 443 *et seq.*

[31] Franklin to Galloway, 18 February 1774, *Franklin's Works* (Bigelow, ed.), II, 238e and also Chap. VII, *passim.*

[32] Hutchinson, *History of Massachusetts*, III, 295-6. James T. Adams, *Revolutionary New England, 1691-1776* (Boston, 1923), 384.

[33] From the Massachusetts Council and Assembly, 29 June 1773, Dartmouth Manuscripts, 689, enclosed in a letter from Bollan and Franklin, 20 August 1773.

had greatly improved since they had learned that some of their own number were responsible for advising the Ministry to attack their liberties. He also suggested that a favorable answer to the petition would produce even happier results.[34] Dartmouth's reply, following in just five days, was quite cordial. He promised to lay the petition before the King and ventured to hope that "every ground of uneasiness will cease," and be replaced by "the most perfect tranquillity and happiness."[35] Action on the petition, however, must wait until the Privy Councillors returned to London in the autumn, he said.

In the meantime, news and rumors circulated rapidly. Some colonists planned to demand an "equivalent to the bill of rights."[36] A newspaper published a letter, signed "an American," calling upon Dartmouth to resign, since "moral honesty" was no substitute for "political virtue."[37] The rumor, that Dartmouth would resign over the question of whether to remove Hutchinson, reached the ears of Samuel Adams.[38]

It was not until December that the Privy Council was prepared to receive the petition and then the Christmas holidays prevented any action until almost the end of January, 1774. By this time, the part which Franklin had played in transmitting the Hutchinson-Oliver letters to Boston was common knowledge. Instead of considering the petition on its merits, Alexander Wedderburn, the Solicitor General, conducted a personal attack upon the Agent from Massachusetts. With scurrilous language and vicious innuendo, Wedderburn branded Franklin a thief, saying no gentleman would feel secure in his presence in the future, but would lock up his desk and conceal his private papers. The Solicitor General concluded his attack by fashioning a not-so-subtle pun upon Franklin's distinction as a "man of letters." According to one account, Franklin never again wore the clothes in which he was dressed that black day, until the signing of the Peace of Paris in 1783. But Wedderburn had won the immediate victory. With the bearer of the petition completely discredited, the Privy Council lightly dismissed the request for Hutchinson's and Oliver's recall.[39]

---

[34] Hutchinson, *History of Massachusetts,* III, 297.

[35] To Franklin, 25 August 1773, *Franklin's Writings* (Smyth, ed.), VI, 281.

[36] From Gordon, 28 August 1773, Dartmouth Manuscripts, 694.

[37] Clipping from the *Public Ledger* (number 4243, Saturday, ? August 1773), enclosed in a letter signed "Fact," 2 August 1773, *ibid.,* 672. "Fact" identifies "An American" as Mr. Temple, Lt.-Gov. of New Hampshire.

[38] Samuel Adams to Joseph Warren, 28 December 1773, *Warren-Adams Letters: Being chiefly a correspondence among John Adams, Samuel Adams, and James Warren* (Massachusetts Historical Society, 1917), I, 21.

[39] *Acts of the Privy Council (Colonial Series),* V, 385-8. Petition received 10 December 1773; rejected by unanimous vote, 7 February 1774. For Wedderburn's conduct, see *Franklin's Writings* (Smyth, ed.), X, 270 and Hutchinson, *History of Massachusetts,* III, 298-9n. Miller, *Origins of the American Revolution,* 333.

Whatever Dartmouth may have thought of Wedderburn's intemperate attack, he agreed with the report of the Council. By unanimous vote, including Dartmouth's, they rejected the petition. Later he wrote to Joseph Reed of Philadelphia: "I am sorry that the case of Dr. Franklin should have contributed to the discontent of the minds of any people in America. Whatever respect I may have for that gentleman on other accounts, I cannot applaud his conduct on the occasion of Mr. Hutchinson's letters."[40] Dartmouth also told Reed that many persons who did not think especially high of the Governor of Massachusetts were ashamed of the way in which the letters had been used against him. He was personally surprised that they could have been considered the grounds of serious accusation. If Dartmouth had once been annoyed by Hutchinson's speech to the General Court, he nevertheless supported him. He officially approved the Governor's administration of a rebellious colony, telling him just before Hutchinson's departure for England that there was "no room to hope for the restoration of order and regular government till the sentiments of those who see the necessity of a due acknowledgment of the supreme power of the whole empire, and the absurdity of a contrary doctrine, shall become the prevailing and ruling principle of the province."[41] After Hutchinson reached England in 1774, Dartmouth found that they shared many similar views in both religion and politics. The Secretary frequently consulted the now-unemployed Governor on American questions and treated him with cordial consideration. He once offered to request a baronetcy for Hutchinson as a reward for his services to the Crown.[42]

Dartmouth considered the doctrine of parliamentary supremacy as the keystone of the imperial arch; without it the empire would disintegrate. From his point of view, a colonial legislature must either acknowledge a subordinate position or else it would become entirely independent. It was illogical and unreasonable, he believed, for a provincial assembly to claim a divided sovereignty. The possible solutions to the problem, a federal empire or a system of responsible government, were equally foreign to the constitutional principles of the Eighteenth-Century. The King was still too directly concerned with the details of administration. Not until the monarchy was divorced from practical politics in the early Nineteenth-Century would the King become a symbol of unity.[43] The issues which eventually

---

[40] To Joseph Reed, 11 July 1773, *Reed's Corres.*, I, 74.

[41] To Hutchinson, 9 April 1774, Dartmouth Manuscripts, 887 and also *Proceedings* of the Mass. Hist. Soc., First Series, XIII (December, 1873), 175-6.

[42] "Conversation between the King, Lord Dartmouth and Mr. Hutchinson, 1 July 1774," Dartmouth Manuscripts, 918, and also *Proceedings* of the Mass. Hist. Soc., First Series, XV (October, 1877), 33. Hosmer, *Hutchinson*, 334.

[43] Namier, *England in the Age of the American Revolution*, 33.

produced responsible government did not involve the doctrine of parliamentary supremacy. Sam Adams and the American radicals directly challenged the right of Parliament to legislate for the colonies, thus making a compromise impossible in the constitutional atmosphere of the time. When Joseph Howe and the Canadian reformers attacked the vested interests of local oligarchies some seventy-five years later, it was possible to find a solution without raising the issue of parliamentary supremacy. The English cabinet had by that time developed into a completely responsible institution.

In the 1770's, however, the colonists refused to accept the principle of parliamentary supremacy, and were understandably reluctant to trust Parliament with an emergency power of such great proportions. Some Americans continued to hope that their petitions would be successful, but the advocates of peaceful resistance lost support for their views with each rejection.[44] The terms of the petitions appeared to British officials to be constitutionally preposterous and therefore no compromise was reached that might prevent war. Franklin accurately forecast the course of events in his conversation with Dartmouth in 1773, when he remarked that: "As to an act of Parliament, laying that country [Massachusetts] under inconveniences, it is likely that it will only put them as heretofore on some method of incommoding this country till the act is repealed; and so we shall go on injuring and provoking each other, instead of cultivating that good will and harmony, so necessary to the general welfare."[45]

By contrast with its auspicious beginning, the conclusion of Dartmouth's first year in the American Department presents a discouraging picture. Failure and disappointment characterize the major aspects of his policy. He favored regular and orderly expansion of the settled areas of America, but the delaying tactics of the law officers and the violence of the Bostonians had prevented him from reversing Hillsborough's anti-expansionist policy. Dartmouth had insisted that he would issue no orders for bringing the men responsible for the burning of the *Gaspée* to England for trial, yet it would have been impossible for him to prevent this action, if the commissioners had been successful in Rhode Island. It is ironic that the organization of the revolutionary propaganda machine, the committees of correspondence, began in the first year of the conciliatory Dartmouth's administration and as a result of the unsuccessful *Gaspée* inquiry. Finally, Dartmouth's efforts to restore peace and harmony were not attended with success in the matter of specific grievances. He was willing to accept Franklin as a colonial agent,

---

[44] Pauline Maier, "John Wilkes and American Disillusionment with Britain," *William and Mary Quarterly*, XX (July, 1963), 373-395.

[45] Interview of 5 May 1773, reported in Franklin to Cushing, 6 May 1773, P.R.O., CO 5/118, ff.113-14.

receiving his petitions with expressions of cordiality quite unlike Hillsborough, but he was unable to secure redress of any of the grievances. Thus, his policy of delay, in order to allow tempers to cool, proved ineffective. At the end of his first year in office, Britain and her colonies were as far from accommodation and compromise as they had been under Hillsborough's administration.

Chapter XI

A MOST UNWARRANTABLE INSULT

WHILE A few clouds gathered during Dartmouth's first year in the American Department, the real storm did not break until the middle of his second year. The problems which had arisen in 1772 and early 1773 were difficult and perplexing for him, but even so, in the autumn of 1773 he might have looked back with some degree of optimism. His western policy had encountered delay, but he could still afford to hope for success. The *Gaspée* incident still appeared to be an isolated case without any serious consequences. The principal result of that crisis, the formation of Committees of Correspondence in all the colonies, had not yet reached dangerous proportions. For example, the Assembly of South Carolina did not approve the Virginia Resolutions of March 12th until the summer of 1773. Official notification of their actions did not reach Dartmouth's office in Whitehall until September 6th, just a little over a year after he first accepted the secretarial seals.[1] The problem of petitions from Massachusetts remained unresolved, but Dartmouth still hoped for cooler tempers and a spirit of accommodation in that area. Lacking the gift of prophecy, Dartmouth entered upon his second year in the American Department with a general sense of satisfaction.

Anglo-American relations had begun to assume a more peaceful appearance with the repeal of all but one of the Townshend Duties in 1770. In the colonies, dangerous crises like the Boston "Massacre" had passed and the radicals were losing control of the situation. The moderates had been satisfied with the repeal of the Townshend duties, even if the right to tax remained. In this period, Governor Hutchinson noticed "a great disposition in government . . . to gratify the colonies in every thing they desired. . . ."[2] In Great Britain, moreover, the affairs of the East India Company required so much of the government's time that colonial business tended to fall into the background. Only routine dispatches from overseas arrived in the American Department during Dartmouth's long holiday between August and November 1773. He was free to tend his estates

---

[1] From Lt.-Gov. Bull, 24 July 1773, P.R.O. Transcripts (South Carolina Archives) XXXIII, 288.

[2] Hutchinson, *Hist. of Mass.*, III, 297. See also: Fitzmaurice, *Shelburne*, I, 465; C. M. Andrews, *The Colonial Background of the American Revolution* (New Haven, 1948, revised edition), 156.

in Staffordshire and Yorkshire with only occasional interruptions from his undersecretaries, Pownall and Knox. Yet, the most serious crisis of Dartmouth's administration was brewing during this period of apparent calm.

To understand the Boston Tea Party, it is necessary to go back to the time of the repeal of all but one of the Townshend duties. Lord North told the House of Commons in 1770 that he favored total repeal, on the grounds that the duties were interfering with the empire's commerce. Since the colonists might misinterpret the repeal of all the duties, North proposed to retain the tax on tea, in order to maintain Parliament's "just right . . . of taxing the Americans."[3] One unforeseen result of this policy was that Dutch tea sold cheaper than English tea in some of the colonies. Smuggling became highly profitable in New York and Philadelphia, although merchants in other ports paid the duty without protest. The East India Company soon found that its warehouses were overstocked with unsalable tea. By the spring of 1773 the situation required some sort of remedial action. The simplest expedient of repealing the tea tax was impossible, from North's viewpoint, but something had to be done about the smugglers. North's solution was to grant the East India Company a monopoly of the American market and to permit it to sell tea there through its own agents. Previously, the law had required the company to sell tea at public auction in England. The new Tea Act thus freed the company from the expenses incidental to the mercantilistic regulations in England, while retaining the threepence per pound duty. The elimination of the incidental expenses reduced the price of a pound of tea. Many people, both at the time and later, assumed that the East India Company's tea would undersell Dutch tea. Recent research reveals that this was not true, but the smugglers would have found their margin of profit greatly reduced.[4]

Although North's new policy produced the most serious consequences in America, Dartmouth's office was not consulted in the matter. The Treasury regarded the measure as primarily a revenue bill designed to rescue the East India Company from bankruptcy. As the eldest son of a peer who was still living, North sat in the House of Commons. Furthermore, he was the only member of the cabinet between 1771 and 1775 to sit in the House where money bills are traditionally introduced. These facts may have operated to exclude Dartmouth from management of the business. North expected no ill consequences and it is doubtful whether anyone in the Colonial Office would have been able to foresee the disastrous

---

[3] *Parl. Hist.*, XVI, 852 *et seq.* Debate of 5 March 1770.

[4] B. W. Labaree, *The Boston Tea Party* (New York, 1964), 76-77, & 284 n. 57.

results of this Tea Act, since similar duties on wine and molasses were already in operation.[5]

Benjamin Franklin understood the reaction of the colonists very well when he summarized North's policy for Thomas Cushing: "It was thought at the beginning of the session, that the American duty on tea would be taken off. But now the wise scheme is to take off so much duty here, as will make tea cheaper in America than foreigners can supply us, and to confine the duty there to keep up the exercise of the right. They have no idea that any people can act from any other principle but that of interest; and they believe that 3d in a pound of tea is sufficient to overcome all the patriotism of an American."[6] When news of the measure reached the colonists in September, the reactions were varied. The official view, represented by the commissioner of customs for Boston, was that it was "well calculated to establish the authority of Parliament in America. . . ."[7] Radicals like Sam Adams, however, were pleased for a different reason: "The ministry could not have devised a more effectual measure to unite the colonies. . . . Old Jealousies are removed and perfect harmony subsists between them."[8]

British officials and colonial radicals were both over-optimistic. The actual removal of old jealousies and the establishment of a united opposition was neither so immediate as Adams indicated nor so free from self-interest as Franklin believed. The first opposition to the measure came from the merchants who had already bought large quantities of Dutch tea. They could not compete with the new consignments, but they said their chief objection was the monopolistic role assumed by the East India Company. "Taxation without representation" became a useful slogan for uniting this group of moderate merchants with the radical element, whom they had forsaken after the repeal of the Townshend duties.[9] Hutchinson believed that the original objection to the Tea Act was based upon the idea of a monopoly and actually blamed the opposition parties in England for suggesting that taxation without representation was involved.[10] Governor Tryon of New York reported to Dartmouth that, while some opposition was certain, the precise grounds were still undetermined as late as November, for the New Yorkers were "fluctuating

---

[5] J. T. Adams, *Revolutionary New England, 1691-1776* (Boston, 1923), 394.

[6] Franklin to Cushing, 4 June 1773, *Franklin's Writings* (Smyth, ed.), VI, 57.

[7] Benjamin Hallowell to Pownall, 29 September 1773, Stevens' *Facsimiles*, #2029.

[8] Adams to Warren, 28 December 1773, *Warren-Adams Letters,* I, 20-21.

[9] J. T. Adams, *Revolutionary New England,* 389. A. M. Schlesinger, *The Colonial Merchants and the American Revolution, 1763-1776* (New York, 1919), 265 *et seq.*

[10] Hutchinson, *Hist. of Mass.,* III, 303.

in a variety of opinions."[11] General Haldimand, commanding the royal troops in Gage's absence, was in New York during the crisis. He observed that the opposition became united in their "determination not to pay any new duties or taxes laid by the Parliament" after the Tea Party had occurred in Boston. He concluded that "the fear of the introduction of a monopoly in this country had induced the mercantile part of its inhabitants to be very industrious in opposing this step of the . . . East India Company . . . and added strength to a spirit of independence already too prevalent."[12] Officers of the Crown tended to emphasize the spirit of factionalism and the lack of unity in the opposition, but Dartmouth was also warned unofficially that any action which the government might take against one colony would meet united resistance.[13] The possibility of a united opposition was not mentioned in the official communications which reached Dartmouth's office, but events proved the significance of this warning.

It is ironic that the first of the tea ships to reach Boston should be named the *Dartmouth*. When the disguised "Indians" boarded her they not only ruined her cargo of tea but also spoiled any chance her namesake might have had for conciliation. The famous Boston Tea Party marks the turning-point in Dartmouth's political career. It is easy to blame Hutchinson for preventing the departure of the tea ships without unloading. He had once said, "I will live and die by the law."[14] His conduct in December, 1773, is characterized by a scrupulous observance of the letter of the law, with little appreciation of the crisis he was provoking—or, at least, aiding Sam Adams to provoke. According to the law, all ships entering the harbor must unload their cargoes and pay the required duties before receiving their clearance papers. If a ship remained in the harbor for more than twenty days without unloading, its cargo was liable to confiscation for non-payment of duties.[15] Thus, when the radicals demanded that the tea ships leave without landing their cargo, Hutchinson took his stand on a legal technicality, refusing to issue clearance papers until the duties had been paid. The first ship had arrived on November 27th. The twenty days had almost expired when the mob took matters into their own hands and threw 340 chests of tea overboard on the night of December 16th. In reporting the event to Dartmouth, Hutchinson called it a "high-handed riot" and an "unhappy affair," but he defended his own course of action: "Had the same method been taken, which was afterwards taken at Philadelphia and

---

[11] From Tryon, 3 November 1773, *N. Y. Col. Docs.,* VIII, 400-1.

[12] From Haldimand, 28 December 1773, Pub. Archs. Can., Haldimand Papers, 35:54-5.

[13] From Gordon, 11 December 1773, Dartmouth Manuscripts, 754.

[14] Adams, *Revolutionary New England*, 371.

[15] *Ibid.,* 390.

New York, and the ship been ordered back to London without entering at the custom-house, the difficulty to which the Governor was subjected, by refusing his permit, would have been avoided; but the greatest part of the goods, for the supply of New England that winter, was on board the ship arrived, and the other ships expected: and the merchants would never have submitted to the disappointment and loss."[16]

The immediate effect of the Boston affair was to unify the opposition elements in other colonies and strengthen their determination to resist. Sam Adams, Governor Tryon and General Haldimand were all in agreement about the conduct of New York. The arrival of Paul Revere with news of the Tea Party ended the divided counsels of the opposition. Before they knew what the Bostonians had done, many had wanted to store the tea in New York. "But immediately they became united and determined that it should not be landed."[17] The Governor reported that "the better sort" of people opposed violence, but ever since the arrival of the Boston courier, united opposition to both the monopoly and the import duty had grown to such proportions that public opinion would no longer permit the unloading and storing of the tea. Even if unloaded under the protection of bayonet and cannon, the tea would never be purchased.[18] Haldimand noted similar developments and prophesied that Tryon would have to allow the tea to be sent back to England, in order to "prevent dangerous extremities."[19]

In his reply, Dartmouth professed to believe that those who attempted "to spread alarm and to create fresh disturbances" were impelled by "self-interested motives," and he hoped that their efforts might "prove abortive."[20] In this extremely dangerous situation, the Colonial Secretary ordered the General to assist the civil authorities in the event of violence. But New York was spared the disorders of Boston. During the long delay before the tea ship's arrival, Haldimand reported that all was quiet. When the ship finally arrived in mid-April, a committee of citizens "persuaded" the master to leave port without unloading. Twenty chests of tea, which another ship carried on the master's own account, however, joined their Boston counterparts in salt water.[21] In spite of this event, the general conduct of New York was calmer and cooler than Boston's.

---

[16] From Hutchinson, 17 December 1773, *Proceedings* of the Mass. Hist. Soc., XIII (December 1873), 172-3. Labaree finds Hutchinson's account "erroneous" and says that the Governor wanted to force a "showdown." *Tea Party*, 128-132.

[17] Adams to Warren, 28 December 1773, *Warren-Adams Letters*, I, 20.

[18] From Tryon, 3 January 1774, *N. Y. Col. Docs.*, VIII, 407-8.

[19] From Haldimand, 28 December 1773, Pub. Archs. Can., Haldimand Papers, 35:54-5.

[20] To Haldimand, 8 January 1774, *ibid.*, 35:64.

[21] From Haldimand, 2 February & 4 May 1774, *ibid.*, 35:81, 111-12.

The ministry in England depended upon its officials in the colonies for information upon which to base policy. These representatives of authority were far more likely to attribute resistance to the mob than they were to search for deeper motives. Although Philadelphia's conduct on the arrival of a tea ship was even more peaceful than New York's, Haldimand still reported that the ship failed to unload, because it had been "ordered by the mob of that town to depart. . . ."[22] A different picture of the crisis emerged from the correspondence of private citizens. Joseph Reed of Philadelphia tried to establish grounds for conciliation at this period, although he later became a leading "patriot." Because he believed that officials in the colonies misrepresented the situation to their superiors at home, he undertook a private correspondence with Dartmouth in order to keep him informed of the "true" state of affairs. Describing his own correspondence with the Colonial Secretary, Reed said, "if it does not tell him what he wishes to know yet it tells him what he ought to know."[23]

In his first letters, written during the tea crisis, Reed told Dartmouth a number of things he thought he ought to know about Pennsylvania. The partial repeal of the Townshend duties was regarded there as a particularly harsh measure, for the government gave up the revenue in order to keep the tax. Throughout this correspondence, which lasted a little over a year, Reed stressed the unanimity of thought and action in the colonies. He probably exaggerated this aspect, but his error in favor of unity was no greater than the officials' emphasis upon factiousness. Referring specifically to the reception of the tea in Philadelphia, Reed emphasized the peaceful, determined and unanimous nature of the resistance. He wanted Dartmouth to understand that the best people opposed the tea tax and that there were "no mobs, no insults to individuals, no injury to private property. . . ."[24] Nevertheless, the spirit of the people was rising and Reed ventured to prophesy that any attempt to enforce North's Tea Act would lead to bloodshed.

An agent of the East India Company confirmed Reed's account when he reported that not one Philadelphian "in an hundred was to be met with who approved of the sending of the tea, while the duty was to be paid here. . . ." The same un-named agent estimated that between 600 and 700 "respectable" inhabitants, "many of the first rank," were active in the resistance movement.[25] Whether by accident or design, these reports of unanimous and "respectable"

---

[22] From Haldimand, 5 January 1774, *ibid.*, 35:60.

[23] Joseph Reed to Dennys De Berdt, 24 December 1774, *Reed's Corres.*, I. 89.

[24] From Reed, 22 December & 27 December 1773, *ibid.*, 55.

[25] Extract dated 30 October 1773, enclosed in a letter from the Chairman of the East India Company, 24 December 1773, P.R.O., CO 5/133, p. 49 (L.C. Trans.)

opposition neglected to mention the formation of a "Committee for Tarring and Feathering" in Philadelphia.[26] Did the "best people" approve of the Committee's threatening the owner of the tea ship *Polly* with "ten gallons of liquid tar" and "the feathers of a dozen wild geese"? Whether Dartmouth knew of such activity or not, he preferred to accept the information contained in his official correspondence. He believed that a lawless minority threatened the peace of the empire.

The first word which Dartmouth received from the Crown's representative in South Carolina came after the event. Lieutenant-Governor Bull was a South Carolina planter, substituting for the absent English Governor. His dispatches during the summer and autumn of 1773 dealt with a variety of provincial business, but contained no mention of tea. Nor did he mention the growth of opposition, much less indicate that it was unanimous. On Christmas eve, however, he informed Dartmouth of the arrival of the tea ship on the 2nd of December and the conduct of the people of Charles Town. Like other officials, he stressed the differences of opinions. Letters from Boston had encouraged several meetings of the populace, in order to consider similar measures, "but though the warmth of some was great, many were cool and some differed in the reasonableness and utility" of resistance. They succeeded in persuading the agents of the East India Company to resign by a combination of "threats and flatterys." Declarations against the landing of the tea were posted, so Captain Curling held the tea on board his ship. Since there were no agents of the company to accept the cargo, he had little alternative, but he received anonymous threats against his ship. As the twenty-day time limit was about to expire, Bull ordered the sheriff to support the collector of customs in transferring the tea to safe storage. No one appeared to oppose this procedure and Bull even ventured to suggest that all would have gone according to the government's plan, had it not been for the correspondence from northern radicals.[27]

---

[26] Labaree, *Tea Party,* 101 & 159. Gov. Penn sent Dartmouth neither warning nor information about the reception Philadelphia was preparing for the tea ship until after the "Tea Party." When Dartmouth expressed his surprise at this silence, he suggested that perhaps Penn's dispatches had been lost at sea. Penn manfully admitted that he had never sent any dispatches on the subject of tea, but he rather lamely accounted for his conduct by saying that: (1) he had had no idea of what the Philadelphians were going to do; (2) customs officers had not requested his assistance; and (3) he had regarded the tea ship *Polly* as a private matter relating to the East India Company, rather than government business. See letter from John Penn, 3 May 1774, P.R.O. CO 5/1285, f. 34 (L.C. Microfilm).

[27] From Lt.-Gov. Bull, 24 December 1773, P.R.O. Transcripts (South Carolina Archives), XXXIII, 350 *et seq.* Council Journal (S. C. Archives), XXXVIII, under the date 31 December 1773, which is probably a slip of the pen where the 13th was intended.

Dartmouth responded that Charles Town's conduct did "not equal in criminality" that of Boston, but even so the affair constituted a "most unwarrantable insult to the authority of this Kingdom." Bull had acted correctly in seizing the tea for protection, but additional measures would be necessary to secure "the dependence of the colonies."[28]

Only in Halifax was the tea accepted and ultimately sold to the inhabitants. The high-handed actions of Governor Legge may explain why this port proved to be an exception. When he heard of an attempt to organize a protest meeting, Legge summoned his council, declared such meetings illegal, and dismissed two magistrates who had encouraged it. As a result, "the inhabitants in general have behaved with due decorum. The East India Company's tea has been disposed of, purchased, and dispersed" throughout Nova Scotia.[29] The special commendation which Dartmouth sent his kinsman reflected his attitude toward tea parties in general: "I see with concern and regret any appearance in the colony under your government of that spirit of disobedience and resistance to the laws which has erected so much mischief in the other colonies. The efforts, however, which were made to induce the people to commit themselves in acts of violence were weak and contemptible, and the King approves the steps you took to convince the authors and abettors of those proceedings that such a conduct would not be passed over with impunity."[30] Apparently, Reed's letters, telling Dartmouth what he ought to know, had less effect than other reports.

When they had time for second thoughts, many persons, even in Massachusetts, began to lose some of their enthusiasm for resistance. Unanimity, if it ever existed, began to dissolve. The value of the first consignment of tea was more than £9,000. Furthermore, it was private property belonging to the East India Company; the government's interest in the tea was confined to the nominal tax of threepence per pound. General Haldimand reported in January, 1774, that there was wide-spread disapproval of Boston's actions and a growing desire that the town should pay for the tea.[31] A few days later, another of Dartmouth's correspondents informed him that the Bostonians were trying to raise a sum of money for compensation, because they were afraid of the "consequences of their late frantic

---

28 To Bull, 5 February 1774, P.R.O. Transcripts (South Carolina Archives), XXXIV, 5.

29 From Legge, 20 September & 18 October 1774, Pub. Archs. Can., Nova Scotia Papers, A.91, 19 & 56 *et seq.*

30 To Legge, 7 January 1775, *ibid.*, 75-6.

31 From Haldimand, 5 January 1774, Pub. Archs. Can., Haldimand Papers, 35:60.

behaviour."[32] Benjamin Franklin, who was among the first to receive definite news of the latest crisis, shared this same reaction. He was dismayed by the account which Thomas Cushing, Sam Adams, John Hancock and William Phillips sent him, even though they naturally represented their actions in the most favorable light. He hastened to point out to them in reply that "the India Company . . . are not our adversaries, and the offensive measure of sending their teas did not arise with them, but was an expedient of the ministry to serve them and yet avoid a repeal of the old act. . . ."[33] In spite of his treatment by Wedderburn at the Council, he was unwilling to see violence destroy the imperial connection. He urged Cushing to persuade the Assembly to volunteer reparations to the Company, reminding his correspondents that there were a number of precedents for legislative compensation for the destruction of private property by "persons unknown."[34]

According to the information sent to Dartmouth, Boston assumed a more peaceful aspect in the opening months of 1774. Matthew Brickdale, for example, reported that Boston was very quiet and that "contrition seemed to have succeeded violence."[35] Even Haldimand permitted himself to take a more optimistic view. He wrote in mid-May that many New Yorkers expected the Bostonians to pay for the tea and regain the King's favor by "a proper submission."[36] The rapid progress of the government's policy of coercion, however, removed all hope for this easy solution. If the moderate elements had paid for the tea more swiftly, and if the ministry had not acted so hastily to punish the entire Province of Massachusetts, a peaceful settlement might have been possible. The time-element involved in trans-Atlantic communication must also be considered. In this modern age of almost instantaneous exchange of news and messages, it is necessary to remind ourselves of the weeks and months required for colonial reports to reach England. Additional time passed before the decision and the reply could return. There are many examples of this factor, but to cite only one: Lieutenant-Governor Bull wrote from South Carolina on 11 February 1774, to say that he was still waiting for the return of the packet which had departed in the middle

---

[32] From Lt. Col. Dalrymple, 29 January 1774, Dartmouth Manuscripts, 801.

[33] Franklin to Cushing et al., 2 February 1774, Franklin's Writings (Smyth, ed.), VI, 179.

[34] Franklin's Autobiography (Bigelow, ed.), II, 238.

[35] From Brickdale, 4 April 1774, Dartmouth Manuscripts, 878. Brickdale was M.P. for Bristol, where many ships from New England called. In this letter, he relays information carried by the John, the ship on which Governor Hutchinson had intended to sail, until delayed by Lt.-Gov. Oliver's indisposition.

[36] From Haldimand, 15 May 1774, Pub. Archs. Can., Haldimand Papers, 35:115.

of the previous November. This dispatch, sent by merchant ship, did not reach Dartmouth's office for nearly two months.[37]

The ministry may have acted over-hastily in this matter, but they obviously believed that it was facing emergency conditions. They could not afford to wait two or three months, in order to learn whether Boston had peacefully accepted the first of their coercive acts. This first measure, the Port Bill, produced little effect one way or the other. "The sober part of the people" continued to believe it only right to pay for the tea and to petition for the repeal of the bill at the same time. At least, this was the report of a Philadelphia customs-officer in the middle of May.[38] As Parliament passed additional measures, however, the radicals declared that they would never consent to compensation while under coercion, and the moderates abandoned hope of ever raising enough money.[39] Thus, the coercive policy antagonized the very elements who might have been able to secure a reconciliation in the colonies.

---

[37] From Bull, 11 February 1774, P.R.O. Transcripts (South Carolina Archives), XXXIV, 7.

[38] Extract of a letter from Philadelphia, 15 May 1774, enclosed in a letter from Richard Reeve, 17 June 1774, Dartmouth Manuscripts, 810.

[39] Hutchinson, *Hist. of Mass.*, III, 328-30. After writing this chapter, I read Dean Labaree's excellent account of the Tea Party and was able to change one or two details, as noted above, 4 & 16. I also accept his conclusion that it was the tax and not the monopoly which aroused the greatest opposition in the colonies. My reason for not changing this part of the chapter, is that the officials who advised Dartmouth *thought* that the monopoly was the greater issue.

Chapter XII

SECURING COLONIAL DEPENDENCE

D URING the first half of 1774 the imperial Parliament passed a series of measures,[1] which taken together constitute a policy of coercion. The ministry did not submit all of these bills at the same time, nor did they have the later ones in mind when they drafted the first one. They first presented the Boston Port Bill, which became law on March 31st. Then, to assist the enforcement of this and other imperial statutes, they asked Parliament to change the Massachusetts Charter and to regulate that colony's administration of justice. Both of these measures received royal assent on May 20th. During the debate on these supporting measures for the Port Act, the Secretary at War, Lord Barrington, asked for a new Quartering Act, which he obtained on June 2nd. The development of this policy seemed perfectly logical to the majority of the members of Parliament. Each succeeding measure strengthened the previous ones. To the colonists, however, this series of punitive statutes appeared to pass with undue haste. They branded the coercive acts as "intolerable" and usually included a fifth measure, the Quebec Act, in this category.

Lord Dartmouth had earned a reputation as a conciliatory friend of the colonies at the time of the repeal of the Stamp Act. Unfortunately, this reputation was somewhat inflated, especially where the doctrine of parliamentary sovereignty was involved. From Dartmouth's point of view, the colonial situation had changed completely on the night the Boston "Indians" destroyed the tea. Instead of a rather tedious debate about the right of Parliament to legislate for all parts of the empire, the case now involved direct resistance to lawful authority. As he phrased it in a letter to Joseph Reed: "The question then is whether these laws are to be submitted to? If the people of America say no, they say in effect that they will no longer be a part of the British Empire. . . ."[2] Although the history of the following century was to prove that the empire could be held together without parliamentary supremacy, officials of Dartmouth's day saw

---

[1] Texts in Peter Force, *American Archives, Fourth Series* (Washington, 1839), I; extracts in Merrill Jensen, ed., *American Colonial Documents to 1776* (David C. Douglas, general editor, *English Historical Documents*, Vol. IX), 779-785.

[2] To Reed, 11 July 1774, *Reed's Corres.*, I, 73.

the issue in simple black-and-white contrasts: either a colony acknowledged Parliament's right to make laws for all Englishmen or
else it became an independent state.

The Tea Party proved to be a turning point in Dartmouth's administration of the American Department. It was no longer possible to
postpone action on the assumption that tempers were cooling. As
soon as word reached England, Dartmouth's office became a hive
of activity, as the inevitable collection of papers and reports began
to accumulate. A clear picture of the event emerges from the numerous extracts of letters received by the East India Company, résumés
of the cargo sent in each ship, and accounts of the several conferences between the Company's officials and the Colonial Secretary.[3]
An examination of these papers clarifies Dartmouth's attitude in
this new crisis. He obviously felt that Boston deserved punishment
for the destruction of private property and for the resistance to law.
Therefore, he endorsed the coercive policy in principle. A question
soon arose in his mind as to the nature and degree of that punishment. He opposed the extreme measures advocated by his more
belligerent colleagues in the privacy of cabinet meetings. His loyalty
to Lord North prevented him from publicly displaying this opposition, but the coercive policy might have been even more stringent if
executed by someone like Hillsborough or Sandwich.

He informed the colonial governors that the King was firmly re-
solved, "upon the unanimous advice of his confidential servants,"
to adopt effective measures for "securing the dependence of the
colonies upon this kingdom."[4] A dispatch to General Haldimand
confirmed the fact that the principle of coercion was adopted by the
"unanimous advice" of the ministers.[5] When it came to drafting
specific pieces of legislation for the application of the policy, differences of opinion would arise, but not at this early stage. Dartmouth
told John Thornton, an associate on the Indian School Board of
Trustees, that the people of Massachusetts must realize "how fatally
and effectually they have now shut the door against all possibility
of present relief for any of the things they complain of, and how
utterly vain it must be to expect that Parliament will ever give it to
them till there appears to be a change in their temper and conduct."
He went on to say that only a mad man would recommend the repeal
of the tea duty in the present circumstances, although he hoped that
the tax would eventually be repealed. In fact, the repeal might have
been introduced this session, if the tea had not been destroyed. Dartmouth concluded, however, that "if it is meant to drive this country

---

[3] P.R.O., CO 5/133, *passim* (L.C. Trans.). Dartmouth Manuscripts, 750
et seq.

[4] To Tryon, 5 February 1774, *N.Y. Col. Docs.,* VIII, 409.

[5] To Haldimand, 5 February 1774, Pub. Archs. Can., Haldimand Papers,
35:82.

to extremites, there is an end of all schemes and plans of reconciliation."[6] Evidently, he regarded coercion as a necessary policy at this point and supported it from his own convictions.

There still remained the problem of how to implement the policy which the cabinet had unanimously adopted. Even as late as March 2nd, Dartmouth admitted that "no final resolution has yet been taken upon what has passed in America. . . ."[7] This delay was hardly due to divided opinion, for both the ministry and the opposition parties favored prompt action. Even those who opposed colonial taxation on principle were determined that Boston should pay for the damage done to private property. The Rockingham Whigs generally agreed with the ministry that some punishment must be administered, although they might well disagree with the form of that punishment. Even Chatham considered the "violence committed upon the tea-cargo is certainly criminal. . . . Boston, therefore, appears to me to owe reparation for such a destruction of . . . property. . . ."[8] Colonel Barré, who often opposed the North Administration's measures, told the House of Commons that "Boston ought to be punished."[9]

While the ministry discussed the details and the means of coercion, Dartmouth moved with unusual promptness and firmness in the direction of the new policy. In ordering General Haldimand to put his troops in readiness to march to Boston, if needed, Dartmouth said that "in the present madness of the people there is no answering for events."[10] Not long before, the Colonial Secretary had ordered the General not to use the regular troops to assist the civilian authorities in the quelling of riots, except in extreme cases. The ministry certainly did not underestimate the seriousness of the Tea Party. The application of the unanimously-approved policy to specific pieces of legislation, however, provided the cabinet with some embarrassment. During the debate on the Port Bill, Lord Shelburne noticed a division in the ranks of the government's supporters. Some speakers, he reported, called "what had passed in Boston commotion, [while others called it] open rebellion, a more than disregard to Lord Dartmouth, and somewhat of the same sort towards Lord North."[11] Lord Mansfield, an advocate of extreme punishment, declared that the ministry had crossed the Rubicon and would now execute a much

---

[6] To Thornton, 12 February 1774, Dartmouth Manuscripts, 827.

[7] To Tryon, 2 March 1774, N.Y. Col. Docs., VIII, 413.

[8] Chatham to Shelburne, 20 March 1774, Chatham Corres., IV, 336-7. Feiling, Second Tory Party, 125.

[9] Charles Garth to the Charles Town Committee, 15 March 1774, Letter Book (South Carolina Archives), 167.

[10] To Haldimand, 9 March 1774, Pub. Archs. Can., Haldimand Papers, 35:94.

[11] Shelburne to Chatham, 4 April 1774, Chatham Corres., IV, 339.

firmer policy. By contrast, Dartmouth's speech struck his listeners as softer in tone.[12] Apparently, he felt that the Port Bill contained sufficient punishment and did not envision additional measures.

Dartmouth's position became more uncomfortable after the introduction of the Port Bill. The more belligerent elements, like Mansfield and the Bloomsbury Gang, blamed him for his "softness" in American policy. As an advocate of parliamentary supremacy, however, he had to admonish the colonists to respect the power of Parliament, while hoping Parliament would not go to extremes in punishing them. The difficulties facing Dartmouth at this juncture appear very clearly in a conversation reported by Shelburne. Dartmouth told him, "with great fairness and with very little reserve," that without altering his principles, he was determined "to cover America from the present storm, to the utmost of his power, even to repealing the act. . . ."[13] Since Lord North's conversation at this time was also moderate in tone, Shelburne ventured to hope that additional coercive measures might not be as harsh as expected. Chatham's reply was shrewd to the point of clairvoyance: "I am glad to hear Lord North's tone was of a moderate cast, and I place a degree of hope in the candour and right principles of Lord Dartmouth. But where is the casting voice in this great business?"[14]

Where, indeed, was the casting voice? The Secretary of State for the Colonies was only one member of the government; he could not hope to repeal any act without the unanimous consent of the cabinet, including the two older Secretaries. When the ministers in the House of Lords were pressed to say how far they intended to carry the coercive program, Dartmouth gave his audience the impression that the alteration of the Massachusetts Charter would be the last of the measures. Lord Suffolk, however, "declared very plainly, that *other very determined measures* should be offered, before the end of the session."[15] This accurate prophecy of Suffolk emphasizes Dartmouth's difficulty in reconciling his support of the coercive policy with his desire for a peaceful accommodation. Since he was not exclusively in control of colonial policy, other officers of the government might influence the course of parliamentary legislation.

In discussing the Port Bill with Joseph Reed, Dartmouth described the situation with what seemed to him to be irrefutable logic. As a result of the Tea Party, the people of America were contending that Parliament "has no right to consider them as at all within its juris-

---

[12] Turberville, *House of Lords*, 356. Hosmer, *Hutchinson*, 312.

[13] Shelburne to Chatham, 15 March 1774, *Chatham Corres.*, IV, 335. Compare, Fitzmaurice, *Shelburne*, I, 472. Dartmouth apparently referred to the tea duty. Labaree, *Tea Party*, 182.

[14] Chatham to Shelburne, 20 March 1774, *Chatham Corres.*, IV, 338.

[15] Shelburne to Chatham, 4 April 1774, Fitzmaurice, *Shelburne*, I, 473. Shelburne's italics.

diction." Since Dartmouth could see no compromise between the two positions (supremacy of parliament or independence), he could envision only deadlock. One side should give way. "You observe [he replied to Reed] that if neither Parliament nor America will recede, the most dreadful consequences will ensue. If that were the case, can any reasonable man have a doubt which of them should recede, or at whose door the guilt of those consequences would lie? But I see no occasion for pushing the matter to that issue, I mean as respects the right of taxation. . . . If you suppose, as some have done, that the design of the Boston Port Bill is to obtain an express declaration and acknowledgment of that right, you are very much mistaken. I see no such thing in the act. It requires indeed a submission to the provisions of it; and if the submission be duly paid, things will return into their ancient channel, and peace and harmony be restored to this at present most unhappily divided and distracted empire."[16]

In spite of past events, Dartmouth still entertained the belief that the active power of taxation and the implicit supremacy of Parliament were separable ideas, that the former could lie dormant while the latter continued to operate. Many Americans found it impossible to distinguish between the two powers, especially when British officialdom from the King down regarded the exercising of the taxing power as necessary to maintain the right to tax. Dartmouth's suggestion that submission to the principle alone would restore peace and harmony was naive, to say the least. Reed remarked, after reading this communication: "Such is Lord Dartmouth's confession of faith,—bad enough God knows! But if he thinks thus, what may we expect from Hillsborough and the rest!"[17] Their misunderstanding was mutual. Reed expected that Dartmouth would resign, rather than "dip his hands in blood."[18] He could not understand how Dartmouth could remain a member of a government which had adopted coercion as a policy. Yet, Dartmouth apparently believed that a limited amount of coercion would prevent bloodshed by overwhelming the radical leaders of the mob. At the same time it would strengthen the determination of those elements variously described as the "better sort" or the "right thinking" colonists. To give way before violence would only encourage the radicals to further resistance. Punishment did not mean an end of conciliation, but rather the postponement of healing measures until the respect for law and order returned. Contrary to Reed's expectations, Dartmouth could not resign over the Port Bill nor any other coercive measure, because it would weaken

---

[16] To Reed, 11 July 1774, *Reed's Corres.*, I, 72-4.

[17] Composite quotation from Reed's letter to a kinsman, September 1774, in *Reed's Corres.*, I, 74, and Henry Reed, *Life of Joseph Reed* (Jared Sparks, ed., *Library of American Biography*, Boston, 1864), 255-6.

[18] Reed to De Berdt, 24 December 1774, *Reed's Corres.*, I, 89.

his stepbrother's leadership. To resign over a detail of coercion would not produce a more lenient policy, but on the contrary, it would have removed the last check upon the more determined politicians who advocated even harsher measures. Dartmouth's only possible course of action in 1774 was to remain at his uncomfortable post, trying to prevent the coercive policy from becoming extremist, while at the same time praying for some sign of submission to Parliament on the part of the colonists.

The Boston Port Act was to go into effect on the first day of June, but instead of waiting to see what results it would produce, the government introduced additional measures to punish Massachusetts. The second measure, the Massachusetts Government Act,[19] received royal assent on May 20th, only a few days after General Gage's arrival in Boston with special instructions to enforce the Port Act. While that measure affected only Boston harbor, the Government Act applied to the entire province. Colonial charters had been altered before, but this was the first time that an act of Parliament had done so. When the Stuarts had revoked charters in the Seventeenth Century, they usually issued writs of *quo warranto*. The court proceedings which ensued always conformed to the principle of "due process of law,"[20] and witnesses appeared for both sides of the argument. By the 1770's, however, Parliament had developed into a much more powerful force in the constitution. Regarded by all true Whigs as the best defense against tyranny, Parliament opposed the royal prerogative. The King could do little without his legislature, but the King-in-Parliament was omnicompetent. The Boston Tea Party had not only challenged that power, but it had also produced a crisis which demanded a quick resolution. *Quo warranto* proceedings were long and cumbersome. In the past, Massachusetts had succeeded in ignoring the writ altogether. Since this crisis was immediate, it seemed logical to the ministry to use the undoubted power of Parliament to resolve it.

During the debate on the Massachusetts Government Bill, Sir George Saville, a Rockingham Whig, objected to the ministry's procedure. He claimed that the House of Commons was acting in a judicial capacity and, therefore, ought to hear witnesses on the other side. The ministry refuted this argument. The House was merely "sitting legislatively for the improvement of the government of a part of the British dominions, which was found unequal to maintain

---

[19] "An Act for the Better Regulating the Government of the Province of Massachusetts Bay," Force, comp., *American Archives, Fourth Series*, I, 104-112.

[20] Louise P. Kellogg, "The American Colonial Charters," *Annual Report* of the Amer. Hist. Assoc., 1903, Vol. I, 201.

the just authority of the executive power. . . ."[21] Dowdeswell, another member of Rockingham's faction, spoke in favor of delay, but the bill passed easily with a large majority. The agent for South Carolina, Charles Garth, reported this debate to the Charles Town Committee of Correspondence.[22] He observed that North had not only a large majority in Parliament but also "the Voice of the Nation" behind him. Few Englishmen questioned either the necessity or the wisdom of changing Massachusetts' Charter.

The undersecretaries in the American Department assisted in the drafting of the coercive legislation. Pownall, for example, suggested closing the port of Boston until Massachusetts paid compensation for the tea.[23] Knox, according to his own account, claimed the credit for suggesting "an alteration in the Council" of the province. Dartmouth did not initiate any reforms in the Charter, but when he heard Knox's suggestion about the council, he accepted it.[24] Neither the Secretary nor the undersecretary wished to make any further changes,[25] but once the drafting process began, others contributed specific clauses. Former Governor Bernard, for example, persuaded North to include the provisions pertaining to juries and town meetings in the bill.[26] Again, in Chatham's words, where was the "casting voice" in this affair? Dartmouth did not have exclusive control of colonial policy, but had to incorporate the ideas and pet prejudices of many others in his draft bill. According to Shelburne, Dartmouth wished to "cover the colonies"; it is obvious that he had lost another round to those who agreed with Mansfield and Suffolk. More firmness and determined measures were the order of the day. In this instance, logic was on Governor Bernard's side, for juries and town meetings had caused royal officials more trouble than the council.

When Dartmouth acquiesced in the change in the method of selecting the Council in Massachusetts, he must have thought it a reasonable suggestion, especially from the administrative point of view. The people of Massachusetts regarded this as another attack upon their liberties, but their situation was unique. The Governor of Massachusetts was the only royal executive who was compelled to consult an elected council. This provision of the Charter of 1691 was an exception to the rule which provided for the appointment of councils in all the other royal colonies. According to the official view of the constitution, councils depended for their very existence

---

[21] Charles Garth to the Charles Town Committee, 30 April 1774, Letter Book (South Carolina Archives), 171.

[22] *Ibid.*

[23] "Secret Proceedings respecting America," Hist. Mss. Comm., *Knox Mss.*, 257.

[24] *Ibid.*

[25] *Ibid.*

[26] *Ibid.*

upon a governor's commission and instructions. The colonists might object to this interpretation, but the administrative mind could see many advantages to bringing the Massachusetts council into line with those of other royal governments—quite apart from the spirit of vengeance. In theory, royal prerogative, rather than a written contract or charter, formed the basis for the constitution.[27] It should have been possible, in other words, to change the method of choosing the council in Massachusetts simply by issuing new instructions to the governor.[28] Yet, even Hillsborough had recognized that such an exercise of prerogative would be unwise. He had suggested "an interposition of the authority of Parliament,"[29] to override any opposition.

The council of Massachusetts had long been a source of concern to the authorities. They had failed to support the executive in its struggle with the legislative branch. After 1768, they had adopted the practice of meeting without the governor, assuming executive powers which were not legally theirs. Hillsborough had warned them in unmistakable terms in 1771 to avoid these "unjustifiable and unconstitutional proceedings."[30] The crisis which followed the Tea Party provided the best opportunity for taking action. The civil magistrates had made no attempt to prevent the destruction of private property nor had they supported the royally-appointed Governor. The Tea Party was simply the last in a long succession of events, rather than the sole cause for altering the Council. The additional provisions in the act, suggested by Bernard, were more surprising and disturbing. In the future, sheriffs were to appoint the jurors, instead of allowing their election by the freeholders, and town meetings must secure the consent of the Governor, in order to assemble legally.[31] These provisions represented departures from the accepted way of life not merely in Massachusetts but also in other royal colonies.

How to guarantee unbiased trials was a question still not satisfactorily answered. Although the ministry had incorporated the device of appointed juries into the Government Act, they also introduced the Administration of Justice Act. Both received royal assent on May 20th. This additional measure specifically provided that officials accused of murder could be sent to England for trial, if the Governor or the Lieutenant-Governor believed a colonial jury to

[27] Labaree, *Royal Government in America,* 187.
[28] Hillsborough to Gov. Moore, 12 October 1768, *N. Y. Col. Docs.,* VIII, 100.
[29] Hillsborough to Hutchinson, 31 July 1770, P.R.O., CO 5/765, cited in Labaree, 197.
[30] Instructions to Hutchinson, 1771, P.R.O., CO 5/203, cited in Labaree, 159.
[31] Adams, *Revolutionary New England,* 395-6.

be prejudiced. Dartmouth supported this measure, in spite of his earlier opposition to the principle of transportation for trial, for the sake of ministerial harmony. In transmitting the act to General Gage, the new Governor of Massachusetts, he insisted that "the constitutional authority of this Kingdom over its colonies must be vindicated and its laws obeyed throughout the whole Empire."[32] Nevertheless, he remained true to his personal conviction that there was a distinction between Parliament's abstract right to legislate and the exercise of that right. In his letter Dartmouth expressed the wish that Gage would never find it necessary to use the discretionary authority provided in the act, and that the ordinary civil magistrates would be able to handle all cases.[33]

The colonists classified the Quartering Act, which became law on June 2nd, as a fourth "Intolerable Act." From the official point of view, however, this was merely a precautionary measure, designed to provide suitable barracks for soldiers in Boston itself, where the trouble was, rather than at Castle William on an island three miles away. Dartmouth saw nothing vicious in the act and ventured to prophesy that all would be well in the future. With unwarranted optimism, he wrote to Gage that: "I am willing to suppose that the people will quietly submit to the correction their ill conduct has brought upon them and lay a foundation by their future behaviour for the re-establishment of their commercial privileges."[34] Dartmouth still assumed that "commercial privileges" were the most important issues in the developing struggle, when actually constitutional rights were no less important for the colonists. If the people of Massachusetts had been willing to submit to the various acts of Parliament, the Port Act would have been suspended and the harbor re-opened to commerce.[35] Nothing was said about the possibility of restoring the Charter to its original form.

Constitutional divergence had become the key to the problem. Dartmouth could not accept the colonial viewpoint, because of his adherence to the doctrine of parliamentary supremacy. English officials considered colonial legislatures inferior to the imperial Parliament. But to the American colonists the local legislature was a miniature parliament, exercising sovereignty within the colony. Taxation had become more than a matter of economic advantage. After the tea riots it became a matter of principle. Import taxes had been collected between the repeal of the Townshend duties and the Tea

---

[32] To Gage, 3 June 1774, William Clements Library, Gage Papers, English Series, XXV.

[33] *Ibid.* Compare, *Gage Corres.* (Carter, ed.), II, 166.

[34] To Gage, also 3 June 1774, Gage Papers, English Series, XXV. *Gage Corres.,* II, 167.

[35] To Gage, 9 April 1774, Gage Papers, English Series, XXIV. *Gage Corres.,* II, 159-60.

Party. Never again would this occur, if they were designed to provide revenue rather than regulate trade. To these older issues was
now added the factor of the colonial constitution. To many colonists,
a written contract was the only satisfactory defense against an abu-
sive exercise of the prerogative. This idea conflicted with the official
view that the entire colonial constitution existed by sufferance of the
King and, consequently, could be altered by new instructions to the
governor. With the passage of the Massachusetts Government Act,
the circle of conflict was completed, for the principle of parliamentary
supremacy was now applied directly to the revision of a colonial
constitution. The Charter was as sacred to the people of Massachusetts as the principle of parliamentary supremacy was to British
officialdom. Instead of moving closer to compromise, Britain and
her colonies were heading in opposite directions. Since Dartmouth
and his colleagues in the ministry failed to understand the nature
of the disease, they applied the wrong remedy. Coercion failed to
cure; it led to the death of the first British Empire.

Knowing the disastrous results of the coercive policy, the question
arises how Dartmouth could sponsor and support such legislation.
He believed, sincerely if incorrectly, that a limited amount of punishment would lay the basis for a complete conciliation of differences
between Britain and her misguided colonies. Many of his contemporaries shared this opinion and congratulated him upon his firm
stand in the face of defiance in Massachusetts. In vindicating law
and order, he thought he was giving encouragement to the "better
sort" of people in the colonies. It is true that many colonists agreed
in principle with the Boston Port Act, although royal officials in
America exaggerated both their numbers and their degree of influence. Later coercive measures, however, alienated many of these
moderates. Far from overwhelming the radicals, the coercive policy
as a whole actually united the opposition elements in the colonies.
Considerable time elapsed, however, before this unfortunate result
became apparent.

Congratulatory letters reached Dartmouth from various officials
and personal friends. The Lord Chancellor[36] was one of the first to
support the new policy both in the Cabinet and in private correspondence, but even opposition supporters approved of Dartmouth's
firmness. An old friend of the days when he had associated with
Newcastle and the Rockingham Whigs, the Earl of Hardwicke congratulated Dartmouth upon "so happy a beginning of his American
plan." Hardwicke warned him "against insisting on an express
acknowledgment of the right of taxation," but he believed that "a
general recognition of legislative power is no more than necessary."[37]

---

[36] From Apsley, 6 March 1774, Dartmouth Manuscripts, 849.
[37] From Hardwicke, 3 July 1774, *ibid.*, 919.

Additional encouragement came to Dartmouth from various officials in America. Although Nova Scotia's Governor Legge was some distance from Boston, he ventured the opinion that "this single example, made of the Town of Boston will be a means to convince the Americans that it is their interest as well as duty to be amenable to the laws of Great Britain."[38] General Haldimand in New York agreed that it was wise to make an example of Boston. He was greatly worried by the "rash proceedings of the countrymen blindly led by a few hotheaded and designing men." He congratulated the ministry upon the passage of the Port Act, because its "apparent effect" had been to encourage the loyal to speak their minds and the timid to stand forth and oppose the Bostonians.[39]

Dartmouth's expectations of the policy of limited punishment might have produced harmonious results, if the line had been drawn at the Port Act. This measure gave the moderates pause and created the demand that Boston compensate the East India Company. Governor William Franklin of New Jersey analyzed the consequences of the first coercive act, reporting that "the merchants of Philadelphia and New York at their late meetings were inclined to assist or cooperate with those of Boston in some degree, but not to carry matters so far as to enter into a general Non-Importation and Exportation Agreement, as was proposed to them by the Town of Boston."[40] It was the haste with which the ministry enacted additional measures, rather than the coercive policy itself, which caused the failure of reconciliation. When Hutchinson sailed from Boston on the first day of June, he knew that his successor had been instructed to close the port until the tea had been paid for. He assumed that compensation would be forthcoming. Upon his arrival in England, however, he was dismayed to learn of the passage of the Massachusetts Government Act, for he fully realized that this measure would only encourage the colonists to resort to extra-legal forms of government.[41]

The alteration of a "sacred" charter by act of Parliament had ominous overtones for other colonies besides Massachusetts. It was reported that Connecticut would take up arms and join Massachusetts in defying this act.[42] Connecticut's charter was one of the most

---

[38] Legge to Pownall, 29 May 1774, Pub. Archs. Can., Nova Scotia Papers, A.90, 129.

[39] From Haldimand, 1 June 1774, Pub. Archs. Can., Haldimand Papers, 35:119-20.

[40] From Governor William Franklin, 31 May 1774, *Documents relating to the Colonial History of the State of New Jersey* (F. W. Record & W. Nelson, eds., Newark, New Jersey), *First Series*, X, 457.

[41] Hutchinson, *Hist. of Mass.*, III, 329-30.

[42] Extract of a letter from New York to Gov. Tryon, 5 October 1774, enclosed in a letter from Tryon, 19 November 1774, Dartmouth Manuscripts, 997.

democratic in North America. It had much to lose, if this act represented a new, general policy on the part of the imperial government. Similarly, as additional acts were passed, other colonies became more alarmed for their own liberties. One moderate, who was prepared to accept limited punishment for Massachusetts, reflected this fear when he wrote: "What alarms us is suspicion of the third bill, which we have heard is before the House. Should the import of this bill prove to be what is surmised of it, viz: the sending home those suspected or charged with any act against the Government, to stand trial in *Westminster* Hall, you must not be surprised to find all *America* in flames."[43] The same correspondent continued to say that this bill would make it impossible for the "friends of government" to offer any more arguments for "the proper subordination" of the colonies to England.

Much to Dartmouth's dismay, the passage of additional acts promoted opposition rather than conciliation. His opinion of the spreading resistance is reflected in one of his dispatches to the governor of Virginia: "The information contained in your lordship's letter of the 9th of May of what passed in Virginia, in consequence of the measures pursued in Parliament respecting the Town of Boston has given me the greatest concern. There was reason to hope, from appearances in the other colonies, that the extravagant proposition of the people of Boston would have been everywhere disregarded; but it may now be well doubted whether the extraordinary conduct of the Burgesses of Virginia . . . may not become . . . an example to the other colonies."[44] Dartmouth's fears were well justified in this instance. American opinion had reversed itself as details of the coercive policy became known. The first attitude, that Boston should pay for the tea, had now developed into open sympathy for Massachusetts. Virginia was willing to send delegates to a Continental Congress and other colonies would follow suit. By August, Dartmouth had lost whatever hope he may have had in the effectiveness of coercion. He told Dunmore that: "It remains to be seen whether the measures adopted by Parliament will or will not have the effect to restore peace and harmony between Great Britain and her colonies. The proceedings of the Burgesses of Virginia do not encourage me to hope for a speedy issue to the present disunion and we have seen too much of the prevalence of the example they have set to the other colonies not to be justly alarmed at what may be the result of the unconstitutional meeting they are endeavoring to promote."[45] A Colonial Secre-

---

[43] Extract of a letter to a Gentleman in London, dated New York, June 1774, in Force, *American Archives, Fourth Series,* I, 302. The italics are the original writer's.

[44] To Dunmore, 6 July 1774, P.R.O., CO 5/1352, 125-6 (L.C. Trans.).

[45] To Dunmore, 3 August 1774, *ibid.,* 134.

tary in a modern ministry would probably have resigned before reaching this point of despair. Dartmouth, however, could not desert North, especially over an issue involving the supremacy of Parliament. Although it seems unrealistic, he also continued to work for conciliation. His official correspondence emphasized the division between the factious mob on the one hand and the "better sort" of people on the other. At the same time that coercive acts were reducing the gap between these two groups, Dartmouth was working behind the scenes to conciliate the moderates and re-unite the empire on the basis of parliamentary supremacy. Only when this series of negotiations failed did he insist upon resigning.[46]

---

[46] J. M. Sosin, "The Massachusetts Acts of 1774: Coercive or Preventive?," *Huntington Library Quarterly,* XXVI (1963), 235-252, presents an analysis of the logical and legal procedure with which the ministry prepared the series of acts, which the author believes were preventive in nature. He points out, for example, that the Massachusetts Government Act did not alter the House of Representatives, but was actually quite moderate in intent. This article came to my attention long after writing this chapter.

Chapter XIII

THE QUEBEC ACT

OF ALL THE acts passed during the session of 1774 none aroused greater controversy than the Quebec Act. The controversy began with the Whig opposition in Parliament and the radical elements in the colonies and it has continued to reverberate in modern historiography. The authorities cannot agree whether the Quebec Act resulted from enlightened statesmanship or a Machiavellian plot to destroy colonial liberty.[1] Although it would be impossible to solve this question to everyone's satisfaction, Dartmouth's role in drafting and sponsoring the act is clear. His conduct was perfectly consistent with both principle and honor. He regarded the act as local in application, designed to meet the needs of the French Canadians, and not in any way connected with the punitive measures directed against the colonies to the south.

The Quebec Act received royal assent on June 22nd, at the end of the same session in which the four coercive bills became law. This fact has persuaded many critics of the measure that it was intended as part of the punishment inflicted upon the older colonies. Some have contended that the Quebec business would have been delayed for several more years, except that the colonies needed a lesson in firmness in 1774.[2] On the contrary, the measure passed in June of 1774, because all the complex details had been settled by that date and there was no further reason for delay. The recently conquered French province created a set of difficult problems for British ministries after 1763. The solutions required a decade of consideration, but in 1774 the government was at last prepared to take action.

William Knox, one of the officials interested in finding the answer to the problem of Quebec, admired the arbitrary system of government established by the French. He contrasted it with the "total want of plan or system" in the British empire.[3] This comparison between French uniformity and English diversity was not new in the late Eighteenth-Century. The Stuarts had also attempted to apply the

---

[1] Compare, for example, R. Coupland, *The Quebec Act: A Study in Statesmanship* (Oxford, 1925), and Chester Martin, *Empire and Commonwealth,* Chap. III. V. T. Harlow, *Second British Empire* (London, 1964), II, Chap. X & p. 687 notes.

[2] For example, John Miller, *Origins of the American Revolution,* 375.

[3] Martin, *Empire and Commonwealth,* 49.

system to the colonies, for example in the Dominion of New England, but these planned re-organizations had always failed.[4] One reason for these failures was that the new plan necessitated the reversal of the customs of many decades. The introduction of English institutions into Quebec would also have involved the reversal of long-established customs, held by a people still noted for their conservatism. The same principle would apply to Carleton's Quebec as to Andros' Dominion of New England and the result might have similarly failed. Certainly, it was necessary to tread cautiously in reaching a permanent plan for Quebec, differing as it did from all the other parts of the empire.

When Dartmouth became Secretary of State for the Colonies the policy for Quebec was still undetermined. It is true that the provisions of the bill were completed within the next two years, but the modest Dartmouth would be the last to take the sole credit for that. Many persons expressed opinions and made recommendations for specific provisions. It was Dartmouth's responsibility to introduce the measure into the House of Lords,[5] but the completed bill reflected the need for conciliating the various factions which supported the government of the day.

Soon after taking office, Dartmouth informed Lieutenant-Governor Cramahé of Quebec that the Privy Council was even then considering "everything that concerns the state of Quebec with regard as well to its civil as to its ecclesiastical constitution."[6] He apparently expected definite decisions on these important matters in the near future, for the Board of Trade declined recommending new councillors to fill vacancies in Quebec, pending completion of the new constitution. The government's mill, like that of the proverbial gods, ground slowly, and nothing was produced for many months. When Cramahé reported in June of the following year, he ventured to wish "for the good of the King's service and the happiness of the people that matter may be soon brought to a final conclusion."[7] After further delay, Dartmouth believed that a decision was imminent in December, 1773. He confidently informed Cramahé that, "the arrangements necessary for the adjustment of whatever regards the civil government of the colony are now actually under the immediate consideration of His Majesty's servants and will probably be settled in a very short time."[8] It is significant that this dispatch bears a date

---

[4] Kellogg, "The American Colonial Charters," A.H.A. *Annual Report,* 1903, 223-4. Viola Barnes, *Dominion of New England* (New Haven, 1923 & New York, 1960).

[5] *Lords' Journals,* XXXIV, 154.

[6] To Cramahé, 2 September 1772, Pub. Archs. Can., Q. 12A, 108.

[7] From Cramahé, 22 June 1773, Pub. Archs. Can., Dartmouth Papers, VI, 2317.

[8] To Cramahé, 1 December 1773, Pub. Archs. Can., Q. 12A, 127.

several days earlier than the Boston Tea Party, and several weeks before news of that crisis reached England. No measures of coercion had yet been conceived, but the immediacy in Dartmouth's dispatch indicates that some sort of Quebec bill would have been introduced in the next session of Parliament.

In August, 1773, Lord Chancellor Apsley sent the Colonial Secretary a number of papers relating to Quebec. The purpose of this communication was to "enable his Lordship to form a plan of government for that province fit to be laid before Parliament. . . ."[9] In the same letter, Apsley thanked Dartmouth for his "assurances" that he intended to undertake this business. The Attorney General of Quebec, Francis Masères, was also active in promoting a Quebec bill and was very generous with his advice to Dartmouth during the same summer. After canvassing the opinions of several important officials, Masères informed Dartmouth of the results. Lord North, for one, "seemed fully determined to do something towards the settlement of that province in the next session of Parliament and particularly with respect to the establishment of a revenue and a legislature. His Lordship was clearly of the opinion that this ought to be by a legislative council and not an assembly. . . ."[10] Lord Mansfield and the Lord Chancellor also appeared to be very anxious to settle the provincial constitution, so Masères suggested that Dartmouth might avail himself of the summer's leisure period to prepare a bill for presentation at the beginning of the session. It is obvious that a Quebec bill would have entered the legislative machine in 1774, possibly sooner than it did, if there had been no Tea Party and no coercive policy.

Whether the provisions of the bill which Dartmouth was considering would have been the same as those which eventually passed into law is a matter for speculation. The legislative council became an important feature of the act, but North formed his opinion on that provision several months before the Tea Party. Other persons who were consulted may have been influenced by their knowledge or fear of events in the older colonies. For example, General Gage was in England at this time, very much concerned about the problem of governing settlements west of the Proclamation Line.[11] His discussions with North and Dartmouth undoubtedly contributed to the decision to include these settlements under Quebec's jurisdiction. Similarly, other persons contributed details to the final draft of the act, but probably no one contributed more substantially than General Carleton, the Governor of Quebec. He was in England at the time

---

[9] From Lord Chancellor, 4 or 7 August 1773, Pub. Archs. Can., Dartmouth Papers, VI, 2319.

[10] From Masères, 26 August 1773, *ibid.*, 2322.

[11] Alden, *General Gage in America,* 195.

and he was naturally interested in the framing of the Quebec constitution. Among the few records of his activity there is one remarkable "Memorandum" which indicates a close parallel between Carleton's ideas and the final provisions of the act.[12] His "Memorandum" contained nine specific suggestions. In the first place, he wished to see the Proclamation of 1763 supplanted by a new policy for Quebec. The Proclamation had promised an elective assembly and the whole body of English law to the newly conquered colony. The original intention behind this pledge had been to attract English-speaking settlers to former French territory. Ten years later, it was obvious that the population of Quebec would remain predominantly French. Consequently, Carleton advocated a more realistic policy, re-establishing or maintaining old, familiar institutions wherever possible. The French *habitants* would find an appointed governor and council more agreeable than an elective assembly, especially one dominated by the English minority. English criminal law might be adopted and the French custom of torture abolished, but Carleton declared that the new courts should follow the old form of judicature.

The Quebec Act in its final form contained provisions far more extensive than Carleton's memorandum. It provided for greatly enlarged boundaries and for the virtual establishment of the Roman Catholic Church, as well as for government by governor and council alone and the combination of French civil with English criminal law. No colony had received such an extensive definition of its constitution, embodied in a single document, since the Massachusetts Charter of 1691.[13] It is also significant that, where William III had granted a colonial charter by exercise of the royal prerogative in 1691, George III established the constitution of Quebec by act of Parliament in 1774. When Massachusetts argued against the doctrine of parliamentary supremacy, she was ignoring a factual development in the constitution of Great Britain.

Early drafts of the Quebec Act reveal that the question of boundaries did not cause the ministers much difficulty. It seemed logical to include all the territory north of the Ohio and east of the Mississippi rivers under the same government. The French had once claimed this vast area and had explored it more thoroughly than the English. After the war, however, a new and more restricted boundary for Quebec detached the west from her control. The Proclamation Line prohibited settlers in the western region, until some policy could be formulated for dealing with the Indians. Shelburne, when president of the Board of Trade, had successfully opposed the plan

---

[12] "Memorandum of things necessary for establishing Laws and Government in the Province of Quebec," Pub. Archs. Can., Dartmouth Papers, VII, 2352. I accept Professor Martin's opinion that this is Carleton's handwriting; *Empire and Commonwealth*, 116.

[13] Labaree, *Royal Government*, 7-8.

for erecting a single, military reserve extending along the backs of the settled areas, from the Illinois to the Saguenay rivers. His policy had separated the Ohio valley from the jurisdiction of Quebec, preserving the traditional hunting grounds for the Indians, but permitting all subjects to trade there. Settlement was to be strictly regulated to avoid antagonizing the natives and restricted to areas acquired by public treaty negotiated by the Commander-in-Chief with the Indians.[14] The Quebec Act reversed this policy, for the new boundary embraced the old Northwest, while the Proclamation Line became a permanent boundary between settlement and Indian territory.

Dartmouth accepted this reversal of Shelburne's plan on the grounds that circumstances had changed, requiring a new policy. As he informed Cramahé: "The limits of the colony will also in my judgment make a necessary part of this very extensive consideration. There is no longer any hope of perfecting that plan of policy in respect to the interior country, which was in contemplation when the Proclamation of 1763 was issued; many circumstances with regard to the inhabitancy of parts of that country were then unknown, and there is a variety of considerations that . . . induce a doubt both of the justice and the propriety of restraining the colony to the narrow limits prescribed in that Proclamation."[15] Although he did not specify the other considerations, Dartmouth presumably was concerned about the English merchants in Quebec and Montreal, the fear of mass emigration from the British Isles, and the inevitable conflict between white settlers and Indians. The English merchants had quarreled repeatedly with Governor Carleton. They had demanded an elective assembly, which they hoped to dominate. Typically, the ministry expected that a commercial advantage would counterbalance a constitutional grievance. Dartmouth expressly directed the Governor to remind the "natural born subjects . . . of the attention that has been shown to their interests . . . in opening to the British merchant, by an extension of the province, so many new channels of important commerce."[16] The fear of large scale emigration from the homeland was also influential in the thinking of many British officials. When, for example, 200 Highlanders and 600 Yorkshiremen arrived in Nova Scotia in May, 1774, the Governor reported the fact to the authorities at once. He knew that "the migration of the King's subjects from His Majesty's British dominions is by its increase become a matter of great concern. . . ."[17] Dartmouth

---

14 Fitzmaurice, *Shelburne*, I, 189-91. Sosin, *Whitehall and the Wilderness*, p. 39 and Chapter VI, disputes the usual interpretation of Shelburne's contribution to western policy.

15 To Cramahé, 1 December 1773, Pub. Archs. Can., Q. 12A, 127.

16 To Carleton, 10 December 1774, *ibid.*, 138.

17 From Legge, 10 May 1774, Pub. Archs. Can., Nova Scotia Papers, A. 90, 93.

replied that he appreciated the local advantage to Nova Scotia of such an influx of settlers; nevertheless, "emigration from this Kingdom . . . is a circumstance of very alarming consequence. . . ."[18]

The fear of large scale emigration and consequent depopulation of the home islands played a part in the decision to discourage settlement beyond the Proclamation Line. Even more important than this concern with the quantity of the emigrants, however, was the dark picture which officials painted of the quality of the frontiersmen. Two months before the Tea Party, Dartmouth expressed the hope that "the general tranquillity will be secured and the ill-effects of the licentious conduct of the frontier-inhabitants prevented; at the same time I see with great concern the little attention that is paid in the different colonies to the dangers to which they are exposed by the disorderly conduct of [these] people."[19] Information about the frontiersmen which reached Dartmouth's office was usually uncomplimentary. General Haldimand, for example, reported in November that there was a "constant emigration of families going to settle on the banks of the Ohio," and prophesied that "this spirit of emigration may facilitate the settlements of the lands on the Wabash and seems to threaten [a] great many inconveniences, as without doubt it will irritate the Indians; and such settlements as these, so far remote from all influence of the law, will soon be the asylum of the lawless and the repair of the most licentious inhabitants of His Majesty's already most extensive colonies in America."[20]

English officials who reported to Dartmouth were accustomed to a more settled way of life in the old country. They failed to understand the frontier psychology with its unending quest for greener pastures. Dartmouth apparently agreed with them, at least to the extent of filling the newly acquired territories on the sea coast before allowing westward migration on a large scale. Possibly he was influenced by his own unoccupied real estate in East Florida, but whatever the reason he believed that the "ill consequences that must attend any settlements on the Wabash are obvious," and that they should be prevented.[21] His attitude toward the extension of the Quebec boundary is clearly revealed in an exchange with the former Secretary of State, Lord Hillsborough. Hillsborough objected to the establishment of a civil government, replacing the earlier policy of military rule. The government appeared to him to *"declare* that it is right and proper to *settle* the territories annexed."[22] Dartmouth

18 To Legge, 6 July 1774, *ibid.,* 162-3.

19 To Haldimand, 14 October 1773, Pub. Archs. Can., Haldimand Papers, 35:42.

20 From Haldimand, 3 November 1773, *ibid.,* 46.

21 To Haldimand, 8 January 1774, *ibid.,* 64.

22 "Hillsborough's Objections to the Quebec Act," Pub. Archs. Can., Dartmouth Papers, VII, 2360; presumably once enclosed in a letter from Knox, 30 April 1774, *ibid.,* VI, 2341.

hastened to inform him of the "unanimous opinion" of the cabinet that "the extension of the province to the Ohio and the Mississippi is an essential and very useful part of the bill; it provides for the establishment of civil government over many numerous settlements of French subjects, but does by no means imply an intention of further settling the lands included within this extension, and if it is not wished that British subjects should settle that country nothing can more effectively tend to discourage such attempts, which in the present state of that country, your Lordship knows very well, it is impossible to prevent."[23]

The boundary provisions of the Quebec Act angered colonies with western claims, but Dartmouth had no intention of punishing them when he incorporated these clauses in the act. His policy was based upon the information available to him at the time. Simply stated, the facts were: unlimited emigration from Britain was dangerous; plenty of unoccupied land existed east of the Proclamation Line; the quality of frontier settlers was "licentious" and "lawless"; settlements antagonized the Indians and endangered older, authorized communities. Placing the territory under the civil jurisdiction of Quebec would have two advantages. This step would win the confidence of the French fur traders in the area and at the same time it would discourage British settlers. As long as the military regime had continued on a temporary basis, settlers could hope that one day colonial governments, like Virginia or Pennsylvania, would expand westward. Now, an act of Parliament had established a non-representative jurisdiction west of the Line. Dartmouth admitted to Hillsborough that this provision might not prevent all the dangers of westward migration, but settlers might hesitate to move into an area under the jurisdiction of Quebec.

The form of government was a problem which occupied more of the ministry's time than the boundary question. In the earliest drafts of the act, the council figures more importantly than any of the other provisions which were added later.[24] All officials connected with administration of colonial policy realized that there was a real obstacle which must be cleared away, if Quebec was to have a governor and council, without an assembly. Every royal colony in the empire had an elected assembly. This policy had operated so strongly in the middle of the Eighteenth-Century that Governor Lawrence of Nova Scotia had been specifically ordered to summon that colony's first assembly, contrary to his own strongly-held opinions.[25] The Proclamation of 1763 had assumed that this policy was firmly estab-

---

[23] To Hillsborough, 1 May 1774, *ibid.*, 2343.

[24] Cf. *ibid.*, 2344-2350.

[25] Board of Trade to Lawrence, 25 March 1756, Pub. Archs. Can., Nova Scotia Papers, I, 712-15. Labaree, *Royal Government*, 176-7.

lished, for it contained the promise that an assembly would eventually be elected in Quebec. In the decade after the Proclamation, however, special problems in the newly acquired province rendered the promise more and more impracticable. Not even Nova Scotia, with its large Acadian population, had presented quite the same difficulty. It was patently impossible to expel all the French Canadian inhabitants from the St. Lawrence Valley. Furthermore, it was obvious that English settlers would not come there in large numbers. The practice of granting elective assemblies had been followed without exception, but exceptional circumstances in Quebec required a new policy. One early draft of the bill limited the governor and council to only temporary powers of legislation, with a view to fulfilling the promises of the Proclamation when later developments permitted.[26] This was only a transitional stage, however; all subsequent drafts, including the final one, omitted the elective assembly.

The problem of the legal system was closely related to the type of government. The Proclamation of 1763 had promised that the whole body of English common law would be introduced, replacing the customary law of Paris. If this promise were literally fulfilled, great inconvenience and uncertainty would result for the French Canadians, especially with respect to ownership and transfers of property. The voluble English minority, however, would be certain to resent any attempt to enforce the unfamiliar French procedures. Dartmouth was untrained in law and naturally relied upon the expert advice of the law officers of the crown. Solicitor General Wedderburn suggested the granting of the whole body of English criminal law, rather than merely the portion pertaining to capital punishment.[27] Dartmouth, accepting this suggestion, incorporated into the final form of the act more generous provision for common law than Carleton's Memorandum had recommended. Dartmouth hoped that this part of the act would pacify the English settlers, even though he realized that they would not like the system of government. His optimism appears in a letter to Governor Carleton in which he ventured to hope that "when the provisions of [the Quebec Act] have taken place, and His Majesty's gracious intentions with respect to the plan of the judicature that is to be established are made known, prejudices, which popular clamour has excited, will cease, and that His Majesty's subjects of every description will see, and be convinced of the equity and good policy of the bill."[28] Consultation and compromise also figure in the solution to the problem of civil law. At first it was proposed to convert the seigneurial holdings into free and common

---

[26] Early draft of Quebec Bill, Pub. Archs. Can., Dartmouth Papers, VII, 2351.

[27] From Wedderburn 2 March 1774, *ibid.*, VI, 2334.

[28] To Carleton, 10 December 1774, Pub. Archs. Can., Q. 12A, 137.

soccage. This might have pleased the English minority, but it was contrary to the customs of generations of *habitants*. Furthermore, it did not conform to Carleton's plan for a dutiful, feudal peasantry. Hillsborough also objected to this proposed change in the civil law.[29] When he learned of these objections, Dartmouth struck out the reference to English land-holding practice and thereby insured the continuation of seigneurial tenure in Quebec.[30]

Nearly one year later, Dartmouth defended his actions when Lord Camden made a motion to repeal the Quebec Act. Camden's motion arose from a petition from the British merchants in Montreal and Quebec. They complained that they had been deprived of many rights, including the writ of habeas corpus and trial by jury. In reply, Dartmouth noted that the petitioners claimed to speak for the inhabitants of the province, when in fact they were only a small minority. The petition itself was improper, since it had not come from the governor's office. The French Canadians, on the other hand, had presented Governor Carleton with a paper in which they expressed satisfaction with the new constitution. To accept Camden's motion to repeal the act would disappoint the majority, while the minority complaint was unreasonable. The provisions for English criminal law guaranteed habeas corpus writs and jury trials in criminal cases. On these grounds, Dartmouth concluded that "by no one rule of good policy, justice, or a regard to public faith, could it be expected that nearly 100,000 peaceable, loyal subjects should be rendered unhappy and miserable, purely to gratify the unreasonable request of two or three thousand persons. . . ."[31] Possibly the situation in Massachusetts in 1775 conditioned Dartmouth's opinion of the Quebec Act, but all his official communications from the colonies emphasized the smallness of the faction which was the source of opposition. Consequently, Dartmouth regarded petitions from the English merchants in Quebec as merely the "work of a faction." He assumed that these objectors to the Quebec Act would, by their own intemperate conduct, "mark out to every unprejudiced person the factious spirit with which they have been taken up."[32]

No single provision of the Quebec Act received more bitter denunciation than that dealing with the religious settlement. Yet, the final

---

[29] "Hillsborough's Objections in the Quebec Act," Pub. Archs. Can., Dartmouth Papers, VII, 2360. See note 22 above.

[30] To Hillsborough, 1 May 1774, *ibid.*, VI, 2343. Some of the seigneurial obligations remained in effect until as late as 1854, when a law was passed to free the *censitaire* from payment of *cens, lods et ventes* and other responsibilities to the *seigneur*. Marcel Trudel, *The Seigneurial Regime* (Canadian Historical Association booklet #6, Ottawa, 1956), 17.

[31] Debate in the House of Lords, 17 May 1775, *Parl. Hist.*, XVIII, 662.

[32] To Cramahé, 6 April & 4 May 1774, Pub. Archs. Can., Q. 12A, 134-5. To Carleton, 7 January 1775, *ibid.*, 142.

draft of this section reveals the least alteration, when compared to earlier versions. As early as December, 1772, Dartmouth had decided that it might be necessary to admit "some episcopal authority under proper restrictions" for the Catholic Church in Canada.[33] This step was not a radical innovation in form. Monseigneur Briand had exercised the powers of a bishop since 1766, although designated only a superintendent of clergy. His consecration had taken place in France by permission of the Rockingham administration, largely owing to Burke's influence. Dartmouth, at the Board of Trade at the time, undoubtedly knew of the arrangement. Briand's principal responsibility was to consecrate young French-Canadian priests, in order to avoid the necessity for importing clergymen from France. Even those who approved of this expedient often wondered whether it was contrary to existing statutes. Attorney General Masères, for example, wished the practice were sanctioned by an act of Parliament.[34] Dartmouth's attitude toward the question of a bishop for Quebec was perfectly consistent with the policy laid down by the Rockingham Whigs when they had been in power. Nine years later they opposed the Quebec Act as a whole.

Long before the Boston affair, Dartmouth had come to the conclusion that toleration of Roman Catholicism would be essential "to conciliate their [the *Canadiens'*] affections and to create that attachment to and dependence on the British government upon which the safety and prosperity of the colony depend."[35] When the Quebec Act was presented to Parliament, it contained a clause providing for the legal sanction of tithes. The so-called "establishment" of the Church of Rome was attacked on this ground, but there was never any intention of creating that close union of altar and throne customarily associated with established churches.[36] When the opposition in Parliament and outside of it condemned the North ministry for establishing "popery," they were really attacking religious toleration. The Age of Reason had promoted a high degree of toleration, but religious prejudice continued to appear in the debates of the time. Colonel Barré condemned the measure as "Popish from the beginning to the end."[37] Chatham took the most violent anti-Catholic position. His obsession with "No Popery" constitutes one of his less admirable qualities. Most of the opposition speakers in Parliament preferred to attack the legal and constitutional aspects of the bill, but

[33] To Cramahé, 9 December 1772, *ibid.*, 115.
[34] [Francis Masères], *Occasional Essays* (London, 1809), 368-70.
[35] To Cramahé, 9 December 1772, Pub. Archs. Can., Q. 12A, 115.
[36] Carleton's Instructions for 1775, *Documents relating to the Constitutional History of Canada* (Adam Shortt & A. G. Doughty, eds., Ottawa, 1918), II 603-5.
[37] Sir Henry Cavendish, *Debates of the House of Commons in the Year 1774 on the [Quebec Act]* (J. Wright, ed., London, 1839), 238.

Barré and Chatham knew that the religious provisions would excite more public emotion.

In New England the strongest denunciations were levelled at the religious provisions of the bill, as might well be expected. Ezra Stiles, president of Yale College, was amazed to learn that "a whole Protestant Parliament should expressly establish Popery over three Quarters of their Empire."[38] The Suffolk Resolves widened the range of attack somewhat, but did not omit the religious issue. They declared the Quebec Act to be "dangerous in an extreme degree to the Protestant religion and to the civil rights and liberties of all America, [because] the Roman Catholic religion and French laws" had been established in Canada.[39] Although strongest in Puritan New England, the same resentment arose in other colonies. The Continental Congress adopted a very bitter attack on the religious provisions when they accepted the draft of an address to the people of Great Britain. Its author, John Jay, professed great astonishment that the British would consent to the establishment in one of their colonies of "a religion that has deluged your island in blood, and dispersed impiety, bigotry, persecution, murder and rebellion through every part of the world."[40] The Congress spoke out of the other side of its mouth, however, when addressing the people of Canada. Then, they emphasized the legal and constitutional losses suffered by the inhabitants after the passage of the bill.[41] Dartmouth had only intended to solve a specific problem in one colony by providing for the financial support and administrative supervision of the Catholic clergy. In spite of these good intentions, the consequences of the Quebec Act were far-reaching and ominous.

The Quebec Act was not one of coercive acts, although the colonists considered it aimed at their future liberty. Whether it should be called humane and enlightened or punitive and vicious, depends largely on viewpoint. Carleton regarded the act in the larger context of continental problems. In 1776 he boasted to Lord George Germain that his policy had been perfectly consistent, for he had "had a war of this sort constantly in view. . . ."[42] Carleton, however, was only one of several persons responsible for the final draft of the bill. Each one was influenced by different motives and Dartmouth certainly based his support of the measure upon the sincere conviction that it was both necessary and humane. If Dartmouth had conspired

---

[38] Diary entry for 23 August 1774, *Letters on the American Revolution, 1774-1776* (M. W. Willard, ed., Boston, 1925), p. 19, n. 2.

[39] *Journals of the Continental Congress* (W. C. Ford, ed., Washington, 1904), I, 34.

[40] *Ibid.*, 88.

[41] *Ibid.*, 105-13; II, 68-70.

[42] Carleton to Germain, 28 September 1776, Shortt & Doughty, *Documents*, II, 675-6. Martin, *Empire and Commonwealth*, 114.

to destroy colonial liberty, one might expect to encounter overtones of congratulations in this confidential correspondence. Instead, he told Carleton on almost the very day of Lexington and Concord that "the confidence which I have in your firmness and discretion, encourages me to hope that every man in the colony that is not biassed by passion and prejudice will approve the steps which have been taken, which I can truly say have been founded in the most anxious good wishes for its welfare and prosperity."[43] Dartmouth regarded the Quebec Act as a measure of local application, drawn up before the coercive policy, and having no direct connection with events in New England. As he told Cramahé before introducing the bill to the House of Lords, "the measures now under consideration here for the final arrangement of the affairs of Quebec . . . are in a state of preparation for Parliament, and will certainly be brought forward this session unless the important consideration, now before both Houses, relative to the disorders in the Province of Massachusetts Bay, prevents it."[44] The Quebec Act became law in 1774, but not because it was part of the plan to punish Massachusetts. Far from hastening its passage, the coercive measures delayed it.

To the colonists the Quebec Act became one of five "intolerable acts." They denounced all its provisions (extended boundary, arbitrary government, foreign law code and established church), as conclusive evidence of the ministry's intentions to destroy all liberty. Joseph Reed was prepared to excuse Dartmouth from complicity in the plot, but obviously he believed that such a plot existed. He wrote to the Colonial Secretary: "The idea of bringing down the Canadians and savages upon the English Colonies is so inconsistent not only with mercy but justice and humanity of the Mother Country, that I cannot allow myself to think that your lordship would promote the Quebec Bill, or give it your suffrage with such intentions. Should it unhappily be applied in this way, it will wound the feelings of every man in this country so sensibly that I doubt whether any future accommodations or length of time would obliterate it."[45] There were rumors in the press that Carleton was going to send a contingent of "savages and Roman Catholics" to Boston to help Gage "butcher our suffering Protestant brethren."[46] Although this fear of a Canadian invasion existed in the minds of the colonists, there was little likelihood of its happening. Carleton learned on his return to Quebec that he could not fulfill his promise of loyal troops for the suppression of rebellion to the south. When he had suggested clauses in the act

---

[43] To Carleton, 15 April 1775, Pub. Archs. Can., Q. 12A, 149-50.

[44] To Cramahé, 6 April 1774, *ibid.*, 134.

[45] From Reed, 25 September 1775, *Reed's Corres.*, I, 79.

[46] Letter from New York, *London Evening Post*, 7-10 January 1775, Willard, ed., *Letters on the American Revolution*, 19.

designed to please the clergy and the seigneurs, he had erroneously assumed that they commanded the complete obedience of the peasantry. It was disillusioning for him to learn that the *habitant* could be as intransigent as a New England Yankee. Even when threatened by invasion from the rebel army, the *habitants* and the Indians refused to rally to Carleton's banner. Instead of sending thousands of obedient militiamen to the south, he required the assistance of regular troops to defend his own province. Far worse news arrived later: some *Canadiens* were actually aiding the enemy advance and were offering to supply canoes for crossing the St. Lawrence![47] It is ironic that the Quebec Act must be considered a failure from opposite viewpoints. It was a failure from Carleton's viewpoint, because it did not secure the loyalty of the French Canadians. Dartmouth, with different intentions, must also have considered it a failure, since it did not establish a permanent solution for the Canadian problems. At worst, however, the act antagonized the other colonists and helped to fan the flames of rebellion until they became inextinguishable.[48]

---

[47] From Carleton, 7 June & 26 June 1775, Pub. Archs. Can., Q. 11, 186 & 202. From Cramahé, 19 November 1775, *ibid.*, 331-2, enclosing Benedict Arnold to Montgomery, 8 November 1775.

[48] "Declaration on taking up arms," 6 July 1775, *Journals of the Continental Congress,* II, 145.

Chapter XIV

ENGLISH PLANS FOR CONCILIATION

L ORD DARTMOUTH expected the coercive policy to provide the basis for later conciliation. The course of history proved this to be a vain hope, but he continued to search for a plan of accommodation during his last year in the American Department. This last year must have been the most disillusioning, as he witnessed the failure of conciliation, the surprising unity of colonial opposition, and worst of all the beginning of actual war. The fundamental issue all during Dartmouth's three years as Colonial Secretary remained the same: how to reconcile centralized imperial control with colonial home rule. Dartmouth never solved this basic problem but, quite possibly, it was insoluble in the Eighteenth-Century political milieu. The origins of the conflict began long before Dartmouth accepted the seals of office, so it is not surprising that he failed to resolve it in only three years. "If men had been so blind as to allow affairs to reach a crisis," one student of the problem asks, "could they then overnight find a solution for it?"[1]

Of the several suggestions originating in England for the solution of the imperial problem, Dartmouth was concerned in varying degrees with three: Chatham's provisional bill, Franklin's plan for establishing a "durable union," and Lord North's conciliation proposal of 1775. None of these plans succeeded, but each one of them reveals an aspect of Dartmouth's career, illuminating both the sincerity with which he desired a peaceful accommodation and the handicaps with which he labored to stem the tide of history.

On the first of February, 1775, Lord Chatham asked the House of Lords to consider "a provisional act for settling the troubles in America and asserting the supreme legislative authority and superintending power of Great Britain over the colonies."[2] This proposal dealt with a number of grievances, but its general purpose was to repeal all of the so-called intolerable acts, including the Quebec Act, and to assure the colonists that their rights would be respected. For example, the admiralty courts would be restricted, colonial judges would be appointed for good behavior (*Quamdiu se bene gesserint*)

---

[1] Weldon A. Brown, *Empire or Independence: A Study in the Failure of Reconciliation, 1774-1783* (Baton Rouge, 1941), 8.

[2] *Parl. Hist.*, XVIII, 198-203.

rather than during the King's pleasure, and colonial charters would not be altered except by due process of law. A unique provision of Chatham's bill was the recognition of the Continental Congress as a legal institution. Chatham would even authorize Congress to collect taxes in America. Nevertheless his belief in the supremacy of Parliament was still strong. The provisional bill required the American Congress to acknowledge Parliament's right to regulate all imperial matters, especially trade and commerce. Chatham was prepared to yield more than the ministry in an effort to redress colonial grievances, even to the extent of recognizing the exclusive right of provincial assemblies to impose internal taxation, but he would never consent to the abandonment of "the legislative supremacy and great constitutional superintending power and control of the British legislature" over the Americans.[3]

What did Chatham hope to gain by this move? The proposal to recognize Congress and to repeal the coercive acts could never win acceptance in the Parliament of 1775, while the strong statement of parliamentary supremacy made it equally unacceptable to many Americans. Characteristically, Chatham had ignored the Rockingham group, making no attempt to secure parliamentary support for his bill in advance. Very likely he was appealing to an audience outside Westminster Palace, issuing a manifesto of peace and good will rather than a serious piece of legislation.[4]

When Chatham concluded his speech, Dartmouth rose to reply. He noted that the proposed measure was highly detailed and included such a variety of important matters that he could not state a definite opinion on such short notice. Dartmouth expressed his willingness to have the bill lie on the table, to be considered more fully at a later date.[5] Some of Dartmouth's colleagues on the government side of the House, however, were not prepared to acquiesce in this arrangement. Lord Sandwich, the First Lord of the Admiralty, denounced the bill in very strong terms and also moved that it be immediately rejected. During the debate which followed, Gower and Hillsborough attacked the proposed bill. Lord Privy Seal Grafton (who had fallen out with Chatham), joined the attack upon the measure. They complained about the manner in which the bill had been introduced, insisted that the colonists were already in rebellion, and contended that submission and suppression were the only possible remedies.

A number of lords supported Chatham's proposal and one of them especially commended Dartmouth's "candid proposal" that the bill be considered later. At this point, Dartmouth stood up again to say

---

[3] Chatham's speech in support of his provisional act, *ibid.*, 203.

[4] Turberville, *House of Lords,* 359. O. A. Sherrard, *Lord Chatham and America* (London, 1958), 357.

[5] *Parl. Hist.,* XVIII, 204.

that, after hearing so many noble lords speak against permitting the bill to lie upon the table, he had changed his mind. He could not accept the praise offered to him for his candor, for he would now vote to reject the bill immediately.[6] When the vote was taken, a large majority of sixty-one to thirty-two sustained Sandwich's motion.[7] Chatham's provisional act was rejected for all time. Franklin, who was naturally disappointed at this result, was inclined to think the worst of Dartmouth. The Agent complained that the Secretary had "no will or judgment of his own, being with dispositions for the best measures, easily prevailed with to join in the worst."[8]

Should Franklin's opinion be accepted and Dartmouth considered weak-willed, misguided and too easily swayed by others? Can anything be said in extenuation? If Dartmouth had voted in favor of Chatham's motion, what would have been gained? He would have taken sides in public against a fellow-minister, without affecting the results, for the majority of the House supported Sandwich. Chatham's disdain for possible support from Rockingham had foredoomed the measure. Another factor was the conviction of many lords that Franklin had been the real author of the bill and that, consequently, it must grant the rebels all they wanted.[9] Dartmouth did not speak in favor of the bill, but only in favor of tabling it for future consideration. However much he may have disapproved of Sandwich's peremptory rejection of the measure, the real choice for him was whether to reject the bill now or later. His final vote in this question, then, should be attributed to political necessity. The only course of action open to him, Franklin's opinion notwithstanding, was to join the majority in rejecting Chatham's provisional act. It is interesting to note, however, that he considered the draft measure worth preserving, for the complete text in seven large pages still rests among his personal papers. Did he read it in later years? And if so, did he experience regret at the outcome?

Dartmouth's concern for colonial reconciliation led him into secret negotiations with Benjamin Franklin. Although the men Franklin talked to were only intermediaries, he shrewdly suspected that Dartmouth received reports about their conversations. Evidence in the Earl's manuscripts confirms the Agent's suspicion. Information about the conversations comes largely from Franklin's own account, so Dartmouth's role in the affair is somewhat shadowy. Two private citizens, Dr. John Fothergill and David Barclay, approached Franklin in December, 1774, asking him to set down on paper the terms for

---

[6] "Account of the Negotiations in London," *Franklin's Writings* (Smyth, ed.), VI, 368-9.

[7] *Parl. Hist.,* XVIII, 217-18.

[8] *Franklin's Writings* (Smyth, ed.), VI, 369.

[9] Turberville, *House of Lords,* 359.

reconciliation. The Agent was somewhat reluctant to do this, because he knew that the First Continental Congress had been working on a petition for redress of grievances. He did not want to say anything inconsistent with their demands. When Fothergill and Barclay urged him, he composed a memorandum entitled "Hints for conversation upon the subject of terms that might probably produce a durable union between Great Britain and the colonies."[11] The seventeen points in this memorandum comprise all the specific grievances of the colonists, but the suggested remedies far exceed those of Chatham's proposal.

The question naturally arises, who initiated this negotiation? Although considerable mystery remains,[12] some logical inferences are possible. Dr. Fothergill and David Barclay were both members of the Society of Friends. As Quakers, they naturally favored a pacific settlement of all disputes. They would scarcely have undertaken such high-level conversations without some encouragement from government officials. Fothergill was Dartmouth's physician and in one of his letters to the Colonial Secretary he referred to "the noble lords who were pleased to intimate that our endeavours to promote a reconciliation would not be unacceptable."[13] David Barclay was a friend of Lord Hyde, the Chancellor of the Duchy of Lancaster, who was also working for a peaceful understanding with America. Dartmouth and Hyde both saw the results of the negotiations, for one copy of the Hints contains "corrections and interlineations" in their handwriting.[14] North was also informed about the conversations which Fothergill and Barclay were conducting. Whether the original suggestion for such a conversation came from Dartmouth, North, Hyde, or the Quaker intermediaries themselves would be impossible to say.

A further complication arises from the fact that another intermediary, Lord Howe, interviewed Franklin. Howe said nothing to Franklin about Fothergill and Barclay, but he assured the Agent that any proposals offered would reach Dartmouth, North and Hyde. Although Howe's mission had the appearance of independence, those who employed him had obviously seen the Hints. The ministers may have hoped to gain better terms, but Howe gave Franklin no inducements to alter his original proposal. When Howe suggested that special commissioners might go to America to hear the colonists' grievances first hand, Franklin raised no objection. He made a few

---

10 Dartmouth Manuscripts, 1129.

11 "Account of the Negotiations in London," *Franklin's Writings* (Smyth, ed.), VI, 328-330.

12 Brown, *Empire or Independence*, 37.

13 From Fothergill, 6 [February] 1775, Dartmouth Manuscripts, 1133.

14 According to B. F. Stevens, editor of the Hist. Mss. Comm., *14th Report, App. Part X,* 236.

alterations, in order to bring his proposals into closer conformity with the recently-arrived petition from the Continental Congress, but the memorandum which Howe took away with him was essentially the same as the Hints prepared for Fothergill and Barclay.[15]

The ministers could not accept Franklin's original proposals and the negotiations broke down with the failure to obtain better terms. The evidence which has survived reveals both the concessions which Dartmouth was prepared to make at this point and also the width of the gap which was growing between the two sides. Dartmouth and his conciliatory colleagues accepted five of Franklin's terms. They rejected only three entirely, but so qualified their acceptance of the remainder that Franklin decided they had rejected them in spirit if not in form.[16] It is interesting that Franklin's first point should be payment for the tea destroyed in Boston harbor. Dartmouth naturally agreed. The second suggestion, the repeal of the tea duty, was accepted only on the condition that: "The colonies having engaged to make the provisions hereafter to be agreed upon. . . ." Franklin's suggestion that the acts of trade and navigation be re-enacted in the several colonies was rejected out of hand. The next three points, however, met with unqualified acceptance: a naval officer appointed by the crown to reside in each colony and enforce the navigation acts; all acts restraining colonial manufacturing to be reconsidered; and all duties arising from the acts to regulate trade to be paid into the respective colonial treasuries for public use within the colony from which the revenue came. Dartmouth and his friends were prepared to make these concessions in mercantilist policy, but they rejected with a brief negative the proposal that customs officers be appointed by each colonial governor and not sent from England. Someone wrote on the manuscript beside this point that it was "not tenaciously supported," so they believed that they were rejecting only a minor point of difference.

The major difficulties arose from points of constitutional, rather than economic, divergence. Franklin proposed to end the dispute over taxation by a twofold remedy. In time of peace, Britain would agree to make no requisitions from the colonies, but allow them to provide their own governmental expenses. In Franklin's opinion, the monopoly of imperial commerce was sufficient compensation for the mother country. In time of war, however, the King might make requisitions based upon an agreed scale in proportion to the English land tax. Whenever Parliament levied an extra shilling at home, the

---

[15] "Account of the Negotiations in London," *Franklin's Writings* (Smyth, ed.), VI, 352-5.

[16] *Ibid.*, 372-3. Franklin says that *two* points were marked "inadmissible," but a copy preserved in Dartmouth's papers shows *one* point labeled "utterly inadmissible" and *two* others marked simply "no". Dartmouth Manuscripts, 1007.

colonial legislatures would raise a certain fraction of additional tax
for imperial defense. The ministers accepted this suggestion with
qualifications which Franklin considered tantamount to rejection.
They agreed that no requisitions would be made in time of peace,
if each colony established a "permanent fund for the support of the
[provincial government] after the precedents of the island of Ja-
maica." In time of war, however, "let requisitions be made as heretofore, in mutual confidence that America will not furnish less, nor
Great Britain expect more towards the general service than shall be
justly proportioned to the abilities and circumstances of each colony."
Massachusetts had resisted a permanent civil list for so long that
this could hardly be considered a conciliatory compromise; furthermore, it was precisely the lack of "mutual confidence" which had
precipitated the crisis in the first place.

Dartmouth and his colleagues regarded as "utterly inadmissible"
Franklin's proposal that no troops enter or quarter in any colony
except with the consent of its legislature. From the official point of
view, it would be just as unreasonable to require the consent of a
municipal council for the stationing of regular troops in any English
borough. They were willing to meet Franklin's suggestion to restore
Castle William to the Province of Massachusetts; although they preferred to phrase it thus: "Castle William to be put under the command of the governor, with a garrison paid by the province."

When the Agent coupled the Massachusetts Government Act and
the Quebec Act in requesting their repeal and "a free government"
for Canada, the ministerial reaction was typical. Dartmouth had
always regarded the two measures as unconnected. If he did not
write this comment, he agreed with it: "As to the Quebec Act, this
article rejected; the colonies with whom the present contest is, having
nothing to do with it." On the other hand, the ministers promised to
listen to any complaints the people of Massachusetts might make
about the "disadvantages and inconveniences" of the act altering their
charter.

The remaining Hints, dealing with grievances concerning the
judiciary, met with a mixed reception. Franklin asked that Parliament
formally disclaim the act of Henry VIII's reign which, by interpretation, made it possible to transport persons accused of treason to
England for trial. This act had been the basis of the problem which
Dartmouth had encountered in the *Gaspée* crisis, but he was also
aware of the difficulty of obtaining convictions from colonial juries.
The reply simply stated that the colonies must make provision for
the impartial trial of traitors, before the Tudor statute could be
restricted in application. Admiralty courts had long been a source
of grievance, so it is not surprising to encounter them in Franklin's
list. He suggested that they be "reduced to the same powers they

have in England and the acts relative to them [be] re-enacted in America." The response was a counter-proposal to establish exchequer courts in lieu of admiralty courts, if they would be "more agreeable to the people of America."[17] With respect to the appointment and payment of judges in the common law courts, Franklin made an alternative proposal. The judges' commissions might read "during good behavior" as they did in England, in which case the colonial assemblies would establish permanent salaries for them. Or, "If it is thought best that the King should continue to appoint *during pleasure* then the colony assemblies to grant salaries during their pleasure, as has always been the practice." Given such a choice, it was logical for the ministers to write: "Agreed to the first proposition." The comparable issue of the governor's salary appears last on Franklin's list, but the official attitude was that "governors' salaries will be included in the general estimate," rather than leave them to the mercies of the colonial legislatures' "voluntary grants."[18]

Although the ministers and the Agent were far apart on several points of controversy, Franklin's Hints might have provided a basis for reconciliation, had it not been for the constitutional issue. Judges' salaries, troops in Castle William, admiralty courts and mercantilism had all become secondary in importance. Dr. Fothergill understood the reason for the failure of his negotiations. He told Dartmouth that the coercive acts had created insuperable obstacles to agreement: "as a concession to pay a tax was the *sine qua non* on this side, so a rescinding of those acts, or rather repealing them, is the term of reconciliation on the other."[19] Fothergill concluded that further negotiation was useless, because "we had not permission to give any hopes that these acts would be repealed. . . ." In the same letter, however, he mentioned that Franklin had offered his personal fortune as a pledge that the tea would be paid for. Clutching at this straw, the conciliatory ministers urged another meeting, which was arranged for February 16th. The government's two unofficial representatives presented Franklin with a plan for conciliation which, significantly, began: "The Agent . . . should engage that the Tea

---

[17] Admiralty courts did not employ the jury system, while common law courts, like the Court of Exchequer, did. In England, the exchequer court usually took cognizance of customs cases, but this court had not extended its jurisdiction to America. The colonists would have preferred a provincial court, with a local jury, to decide their cases, but the offer of an exchequer court was a compromise. See Carl Ubbelohde, *Vice-Admiralty Courts and the American Revolution* (Chapel Hill, 1960), pp. 19, 75-76, & 146.

[18] Copies of Franklin's "Hints" with ministerial comments, including some in Dartmouth's handwriting, will be found in Dartmouth Manuscripts, 1007 & 1124.

[19] From Fothergill, 6 [February] 1775, Dartmouth Manuscripts, 1133.

destroyed shall be *paid* for."[20] This plan incorporated a number of ministerial modifications of the earlier Hints which Franklin had written, but he regarded further negotiations on these bases as impracticable. In his remarks on the plan for permanent union, he referred to the "numerous petitions" which individual colonies and the Continental Congress had sent to Britain. Any plan for reconciliation would have to redress the grievances complained of there.

A knowledge of the events of spring and early summer, 1775, makes this proposed plan seem almost ludicrous. The fate of several hundred chests of tea seems of minor importance. Franklin's Hints contained a simple, but unacceptable, alternative: America would pay permanent grants of revenue in return for Britain's surrender of the control of imperial commerce—or, America would submit to commercial regulation in return for Parliament's surrender of the right to tax. The choice between free trade and freedom from taxation was impossible for an Eighteenth-Century ministry to make. They continued to hope that Franklin would offer better terms, but he sailed for America in mid-March. Believing that further negotiations with North's government would be futile, he decided that he would not return to England until a change of administration had produced a more favorable attitude. While he was still on the high seas, the battles of Lexington and Concord put an end to whatever hopes he may have had for a peaceful settlement of differences.[21]

Although the departure of Franklin and the collapse of the negotiations must have been a disappointment, Dartmouth did not abandon all hope for accommodation. Before the secret negotiations with Franklin were two months old, Lord North presented his resolution on conciliation to the House of Commons (20 February 1775), surprising many of his own supporters and alarming the advocates of firmness. Franklin, who seldom underestimated his own influence, believed that his Hints had formed the basis for this resolution. There is evidence, however, that the proposal had a different source. For example, Barrington had made a similar suggestion to Dartmouth the previous December: "When three out of four taxes were repealed in the Duke of Grafton's ministry, I proposed in the House of Commons to repeal them *all,* where they had not been resisted, and to repeal *none* of them where they had. I mentioned somewhat similar last year to a meeting at Lord North's. If the tea duty were this season repealed in Canada, Nova Scotia, Georgia, East and West Florida, I cannot help thinking it would produce very good consequences; and would show the refractory colonies that obedience is

---

[20] "Plan for a *Permanent* Union Between Great Britain and the Colonies," [16 February 1775], Dartmouth Manuscripts, 1149.

[21] Van Doren, *Franklin,* 520-3. Brown, *Empire or Independence,* 37.

a sure way to be relieved."[22] This suggestion would have appealed to North, for it combined firmness with conciliation. Dartmouth, too, must have appreciated the conciliatory element in this suggestion, together with the maintenance of parliamentary supremacy.

Lord North consulted his stepbrother at every point in drafting his resolution. The cabinet, consisting of Lord Chancellor Apsley, Lord President Gower, Sandwich of the Admiralty, the two principal Secretaries of State (Suffolk and Rochford), and the two stepbrothers (North and Dartmouth), discussed the proposal as early as January 21st. Thus, all the government leaders knew the wording of the resolution a full month before its presentation to Parliament. Franklin believed that the original proposal had been longer than the one actually read to the House of Commons. He was correct, but he erred in assuming that it had once contained more of his own ideas and had then been altered in the direction of firmness. Quite the contrary. In January, the ministers: "Agreed that an address be proposed to the Houses of Parliament to declare that if the colonies shall make sufficient and permanent provision for the support of the civil government and administration of justice and for the defence and protection of the said colonies, and in time of war to contribute extraordinary supplies, in a reasonable proportion to what is raised by Great Britain, we will in that case desist from the exercise of the power of taxation, except for commercial purposes only. . . ." Up to this point Franklin might have recognized his own ideas, but he should have noticed that the ministry promised only to desist from the "*exercise* of the power of taxation"—just as Dartmouth had proposed to Reed and Cushing—not the abandonment of the right of taxation. The cabinet minute continued, ". . . that whenever a proposition of this kind shall be made by any of the colonies, we will enter into the consideration of proper laws for that purpose. . . ." When read to the Commons, the resolution ended at this point, but originally the ministers had planned to conclude: "and in the meantime to entreat his Majesty to take the most effectual methods to enforce due obedience to the laws and authority of the supreme legislature of Great Britain."[23] Although Franklin would not have approved of this conclusion, much less have claimed authorship of it, there was nothing in the draft resolution to offend either Dartmouth or Sandwich. The fact remains, however, that the version presented to Parliament appears more, rather than less, conciliatory than the original.

Governor Tryon, on leave in England, had warned Dartmouth against employing "half measures." He criticized Dartmouth for

---

[22] From Barrington, 24 December 1774, *Barrington-Bernard Corres.*, xiii.
[23] Cabinet Minute, 21 January 1775, Dartmouth Manuscripts, 1093. Cf. *Parl. Hist.*, XVIII, 320.

"holding out the olive branch in one hand and the rod of chastisement in the other."[24] This warning went unheeded. The King's address to the Lords and Commons had said, in part, that some of the colonists had gone to such lengths in resisting the authority of the supreme legislature that a rebellion actually existed in Massachusetts.[25] Rockingham attempted to postpone a discussion of the address by moving that a petition from some merchants be heard first. Dartmouth helped to foil this parliamentary strategem, however, by recommending the address on the grounds that it promised the colonies "would be tenderly and gently treated, if they return to their obedience."[26] The bitter and confused debate which followed lasted until two o'clock in the morning, but the house rejected Rockingham's proposal by a majority of 104 to 29. They then concurred in the Commons' address without a division.[27]

In replying to the joint address of both houses, the King assured them that he would enforce all due obedience, but that whenever "any of my colonies shall make a proper and dutiful application, I shall be ready to concur with you in affording them every just and reasonable indulgence."[28] A few days later, Lord North introduced his resolution for conciliation in the modified form noted above. Considering the origins and background of this proposal, North's debt to Franklin's Hints was very small. It is true that the ministry offered to suspend taxation when colonies supported their own governments and imperial defense, but no responsible English official would recommend free trade at this time. Still, the proposal seemed too lenient to some administration supporters. North felt compelled to justify the measure to the more militant members by pointing out that it would tend to divide the colonies. By making it possible for some of them to become reconciled, it would at the same time make it easier to subdue the remainder.[29] Edward Gibbon reported: "We went into the House in confusion, every moment expecting that the Bedfords would fly into rebellion against those measures. Lord North rose six times to appease the storm. . . ."[30] North's Machiavellian logic satisfied the Bedford faction, but it also provided the opposition with an argument against the resolution, as though North's primary and exclusive purpose was to apply the principle of *divide et impera*. Burke condemned the measure on the grounds that no specific sum

---

[24] From Tryon, 19 January 1775, Dartmouth Manuscripts, 1112.
[25] *Lords' Journals*, XXXIV, 305-6.
[26] *Parl. Hist.*, XVIII, 292.
[27] Turberville, *House of Lords*, 360.
[28] *Parl. Hist.*, XVIII, 298.
[29] *Ann. Reg.*, 1775, 95-7.
[30] Gibbon to J. B. Holroyd, 25 February 1775, *Miscellaneous Works* (Lord Sheffield, ed., London, 1796), I, 490.

had been named and that, therefore, the colonies would be forced to bargain and haggle over the amount to be paid for defense.[31] Other Whigs, both in and out of Parliament, denounced the plan as insincere and insufficient to redress grievances. Franklin compared it to the method of a highwayman, who expected his victims to pay until he decided they had paid enough.[32]

In spite of the ferocity of the attack, the plan was not without its defenders and chief among them was Dartmouth. Burke's arguments may have given him some uneasiness about the details of the proposal, for he consulted with Hutchinson, in order to clarify the meaning of "contributing their proportion."[33] There can be no doubt, however, about his support of North's resolution. He pinned all his hopes for conciliation upon this measure and was greatly disappointed by its failure. His official dispatches to all the colonial governors reflect his deep personal concern with the much-desired success of the proposal. To his relative, Governor Legge of Nova Scotia, for example, he reported that the government's majorities on recent motions respecting America "have been more than three to one, and I trust that the firmness which has appeared in the nation to preserve the colonies in a state of due dependence, tempered with that indulgence, in point of taxation, which is so properly held out in the last resolution of the Commons, will convince the Americans of the error of their conduct and have the effect to restore the public tranquillity."[34] On the same day he wrote to General Gage in Boston that Britain would temper firmness with indulgence, with respect to "any reasonable proposition that shall be offered by the colonies" regarding taxation.[35] "Reasonable" in this context required the demonstration of "a resolute attachment to the principles of the constitution," a phrase subject to only one interpretation in Dartmouth's mind. He saw nothing incompatible in a policy of combined coercion and conciliation. Yet, the rod of chastisement was never far from the olive branch, especially since the recent increases in the army and navy estimates, and the introduction of bills restraining New England commerce and closing the Newfoundland fisheries to rebellious Yankees. These measures were more than "firm" and appeared to be based on intentions the opposite of conciliatory.

After Parliament approved North's resolution on February 27th, Dartmouth forwarded copies of it to each colonial governor, together with a letter in which he strongly recommended its acceptance. He

---

[31] *Parl. Hist.,* XVIII, 335-7.

[32] Franklin to Joseph Galloway, 25 February 1775, *Franklin's Writings* (Smyth, ed.), VI, 314.

[33] Hutchinson's *Diary,* I, 387 (22 February 1775).

[34] To Legge, 22 February 1775, Pub. Archs. Can., Nova Scotia Papers, A. 93, 146-7.

[35] To Gage, 22 February 1775, *Gage Corres.* (Carter, ed.), II, 185.

assured the colonists that the King had "no object nearer to his heart than the peace and prosperity of his subjects in every part of his dominions. At the same time, his Majesty considers himself as bound by every tie to exert those means the constitution has placed in his hands for preserving that constitution entire and to resist with firmness every attempt to violate the rights of Parliament; [and to resist every attempt] to encourage in the colonies ideas of independence inconsistent with their connection with his kingdom."[36]

Dartmouth believed that North's resolution constituted a just and moderate plan for reconciliation. The principle of parliamentary supremacy must be acknowledged first, and then the details of reconciliation could be discussed. Dartmouth always maintained that complete independence was the only alternative, in which case the colonies could not expect the benefits of membership in the British empire. He failed to understand the colonial viewpoint, that without guarantees that Parliament would respect their rights, they could not submit to the principle of legislative supremacy. Even without the bloodshed at Lexington, this divergence of constitutional opinion would have made permanent peace difficult, if not impossible.

The suspicion that North's proposal was aimed only at the division of the colonies gained widespread support. Franklin reflected this fear when he said: "All the colonies but those of New England . . . may still make peace for themselves by acknowledging the supreme unlimited power of Parliament, but those [New England colonies] are absolutely to be *conquered*. After which possibly they may obtain a Quebec constitution."[37] North may have used the argument that his resolution would divide the colonies primarily to appease the Bedfords, but many highly placed persons confidently expected that New York would accept the terms, thus isolating New England.[38] North assured the King in the middle of February that the plan would not give up any right, but would "greatly facilitate the passing" of the bill for restraining New England's trade. The King replied that he approved of the resolution, because it would put an end to congresses.[39] If, however, the King and North plotted the division and conquest of the colonies, they might have used greater wisdom in constructing their strategy. Only a profound misunderstanding of colonial grievances and the rapid development of colonial unity can account for the hopes placed upon the resolution of 27 February 1775. It failed to offer sufficient concessions to tempt any one of the

---

[36] Circular Letter to the Governors in America, 3 March 1775, Dartmouth Manuscripts, 1177. Printed in *N. Y. Col. Docs.*, VIII, 546.

[37] Franklin to Charles Thompson, 13 March 1775, *Franklin's Autobiography* (Bigelow, ed.), II, 256. Franklin's italics.

[38] Brown, *Empire or Independence*, 65.

[39] North to King, 19 February 1775, and King's reply, same date, *Corres. of George III* (Fortescue, ed.), III, 176-7.

Thirteen Colonies. Consequently, it must be considered a failure whether its purpose was true reconciliation or something more ominous.

Events at Lexington and Concord naturally colored the reception of North's plan in the colonies. Both individuals and provincial assemblies reacted with marked lack of sympathy. In Philadelphia it was said that "Lord North's motion would be slavery."[40] John Penn noted that "Lord North's conciliatory resolution has been ill-received here [Philadelphia]. Since the late action all the provinces have applied themselves to military exercise. . . ."[41] Even New York, the most loyal of the older colonies, disappointed the King's expectations. The city council plainly stated that there was no longer any hope for conciliation on the terms recommended in Dartmouth's letter.[42] None of the Thirteen Colonies would consider the proposal independently. Each one referred it to the Continental Congress for joint action. "If it were the wish," Governor Tryon wrote "it is not the power of any one province to accommodate with Great Britain. . . ."[43]

If the colonies refused to treat separately, there was even less hope of securing the approval of the Congress. After considering the resolution, Congress reported on the last day of July that: "the proposition is altogether unsatisfactory, because it imports only a suspension of the mode, not a renunciation of the pretended right to tax us. . . ."[44] They rejected the offer as inadequate, since North had failed to consider the redressing of the other grievances contained in various petitions. During the debate on this report, a viewpoint exactly parallel to Franklin's appeared: the colonies would contribute to the defense of the empire only if they were allowed to trade freely with all parts of the world. They were prepared to give Britain either a fixed grant of supply, or else a monopoly of colonial commerce, but not both.[45] North's resolution could not provide a remedy for this problem, because it retained the right of taxation without abandoning mercantilism.

The story of colonial policy in 1775 is largely an account of a losing battle in which only the extremists appeared to succeed. Mod-

---

[40] Anon. to Brig. Gen. Robertson, 25 May 1775, enclosed in Robertson's letter of 13 June 1775, Dartmouth Manuscripts, 1316.

[41] John Penn to William Baker, 5 June 1775, Dartmouth Manuscripts, 1292 (Intercepted).

[42] Wilbur C. Abbott, *New York in the American Revolution* (N. Y., 1929), 134.

[43] From Tryon, 4 July 1775, *N. Y. Col. Docs.,* VIII, 589. For South Carolina's reaction to North's resolution, see the letter from Alexander Innes, 16 May 1775, Dartmouth Manuscripts, 1270, printed in B. D. Bargar, "Charles Town Loyalism in 1775: The Secret Reports of Alexander Innes," *South Carolina Historical Magazine,* LXIII (July, 1962), 127.

[44] *Journals of the Continental Congress,* II, 231.

[45] Brown, *Empire or Independence,* 70.

erates like Dartmouth, who hoped for a peaceful solution to Britain's colonial problems, were doomed to disappointment. The growth of American radicalism and British conservatism forced the two sides farther from reconciliation with each passing day. Because the Bedford group was so aggressive, North had to adopt strong measures in order to retain their support for his government.[46] The bill for restraining New England commerce is one example of this policy. When it arrived in the House of Lords, Dartmouth moved that it be committed on March 16th and, a few days later, that it be read a third time.[47] He must have felt this an uncongenial task, for he limited his own part in the debate to answering one question. Some of the lords wondered why the restrictions were to apply only to New England. The Earl of Buckinghamshire, for example, felt so strongly about this issue that he proposed an amendment, including the southern colonies, on the grounds that they had been "equally culpable with those of New England." Lord Effingham then asked why New York should not be included as well, since he had heard that they had also refused to allow ships to unload cargo in that port. Dartmouth, however, opposed the extension of the restrictions by tactfully answering Effingham: "It is not in my power directly to contradict or affirm the intelligence of the noble lord. All I can say on the subject is that the last account I received was from a gentleman of veracity on the spot, who writing on the Saturday, and informing me of the arrival of a vessel, assures me that the goods would be landed on the Monday following."[48] This soft answer apparently turned away Effingham's wrath. Buckinghamshire's amendment was defeated (52 to 23) and the bill passed in its original form (73 to 21).

Dartmouth attempted unsuccessfully to apply a difficult policy during his last year in the American Department. He wanted to punish the wrongdoers in Boston, while at the same time protecting other colonists from extreme measures. Accepting the doctrine of parliamentary supremacy as the basis of the imperial constitution, he supported coercive measures in the House of Lords. Here he used what little influence he had to "cover" the colonies. When he supported the bill to restrain New England commerce, he also prevented its wider application. At this time he was still counting upon North's motion to effect a reconciliation with some, if not all, of the colonies. He continued to hope, even after receiving news of Lexington and Concord, that the middle colonies would not support the rebellion.[49] Holding fast to this futile hope, he tried to keep the door open for

---

[46] Fitzmaurice, *Shelburne*, I, 478.

[47] *Parl. Hist.*, XVIII, 430 & 455.

[48] *Ibid.*, 457.

[49] To Gage, 1 July 1775, *Gage Corres.* (Carter, ed.), II, 200.

negotiations with individual colonies. In leaning upon North's resolution, Dartmouth had chosen a very weak reed. It proved to be unacceptable to any of the Thirteen Colonies. Both contemporaries and recent scholars have condemned it as utterly inadequate.[50] From Dartmouth's point of view, it had the advantage of official sponsorship, parliamentary approval, and an appeal to colonial legislatures, instead of secret agents and extra-legal congresses. He might better have explored some of the other proposals for reconciliation which Americans in the colonies were framing.

---

[50] Brown, *Empire or Independence,* 45.

Chapter XV

AMERICAN PLANS FOR CONCILIATION

SEVERAL suggestions for a peaceful accommodation originated in America. In his capacity as Secretary of State for the Colonies, Dartmouth received three of them: the petition from the First Continental Congress, the New York Assembly's petition, and the Olive Branch extended by the Second Continental Congress. Although none of these attempts to preserve the first empire succeeded, each concerned Dartmouth during his last year in the American Department. He had the strongest desires for a peaceful settlement of colonial problems, but he was unable to accept any one of these American proposals as a basis for reconciliation. A strong faction in the government and in Parliament preferred to force colonial submission, rather than bargain with "rebels". The King favored strong measures of coercion and disapproved of extra-legal congresses. No one in high office appreciated the growth of unity in America, and Dartmouth's reliance upon North's resolution prevented him from giving the congressional petitions the serious consideration which they deserved.

The First Continental Congress, which met in Philadelphia in autumn of 1774, contained a broad spectrum of colonial opinion. One conservative member, Joseph Galloway of Pennsylvania, proposed a Plan of Union which would have provided for a separate legislature for America, with a President General appointed by the King. Since the Congress rejected this proposal, it never came to Dartmouth's official attention. A few radicals, like Sam Adams, may have had dreams of complete independence, but the majority of members were moderate. Their opinions produced a declaration of rights and resolves, admitting that Great Britain should regulate imperial commerce, but insisting upon the redress of a long list of specific grievances. They thought that it was "unconstitutional" for the King to appoint councilors during his pleasure. They also condemned the Declaratory Act and all other acts passed after 1763, which affected "life, liberty and property" in America.[1] In order to secure the repeal of all these offensive acts, Congress authorized a

[1] Declaration of Rights and Resolves, 14 October 1774, *Journals of the Continental Congress*, I, 63-74. L. H. Gipson, *The Coming of the Revolution, 1763-1775* (*New American Nation Series*, Commager and Morris, eds.), 230.

non-importation and non-exportation Association. This method had worked very well in the time of the Stamp Act, so there was some reason to believe that it would persuade the imperial government to redress colonial grievances. But the necessary allies of 1766, the British merchants, did not give unanimous support to the colonists in 1775.[2]

Since all the delegates had received instructions to work for reconciliation, they also agreed to petition the King.[3] The Secretary of State's office is the normal channel of communication between Crown and subjects, so this petition eventually arrived in Dartmouth's department. It was very dutiful in tone, but it reflected moderate American opinion that colonial policy should be returned to the position of the years before 1763. British officialdom never appreciated this degree of moderation. The Continental Congress, in the opinion of the American Department, was not a legally constituted assembly. Dartmouth had condemned its work in advance, as "propositions that lead to inevitable destruction."[4] Thus, it is not surprising that the petition met a cool reception when it reached London. The principal objection, however, was the method rather than the content of the petition. Dartmouth complained to Gage that: "I can not but lament that the King's subjects in America should have adopted so dangerous and unconstitutional a measure seeing that any representation they might have to make of inconveniences they suppose themselves to lie under would have come with greater weight and propriety from each colony in its separate capacity. . . ."[5]

Benjamin Franklin persuaded some of the agents from other colonies to join him in presenting the petition to Dartmouth on December 21st. Pownall had informed his chief the previous day that the petition had arrived in the country. He understood it to be written in "a very high tone and with very offensive expressions."[6] Dartmouth, however, told the agents that the King would accept the petition and that it appeared to be "decent and respectful."[7] Three days later, Christmas Eve, he informed the agents that "His Majesty received your petition very graciously and, for its importance, would lay it before his Houses of Parliament when they met."[8] Dartmouth's cordial reception of the agents and their petition is rather surprising in view of his official dispatches concerning the Congress.

---

[2] B. D. Bargar, "Matthew Boulton and the Birmingham Petition of 1775," *William and Mary Quarterly*, XIII (January, 1956), 26-39.

[3] *Journals of the Continental Congress*, I, 115-121.

[4] To Dunmore, 3 August 1774, P.R.O., CO 5/1352, 134 (L. C. Trans.)

[5] To Gage, 8 September 1774, *Gage Corres.* (Carter, ed.), II, 172-3.

[6] From Pownall, 20 December 1774, Dartmouth Manuscripts, 1088.

[7] Arthur Lee to R. H. Lee, 22 December 1774, *Amer. Archs.* (Force, ed.), I, 1058.

[8] Same to Same, 24 December 1774, *ibid.*

While Dartmouth might display "firmness" on paper, he could never be rude in person. If the agents expected an equally cordial reception in Parliament, they were misled.

Dartmouth was disappointed with the work of the Congress. He wrote the Lieutenant-Governor of New York that "it can not but be the wish of every candid and unprejudiced person that the proceedings of the general congress had been of such a colour and complexion as to have united accommodation without provoking the vengeance of the mother country." At the same time, he believed that union "upon some general constitutional plan is certainly very just and I have no doubt of its being yet attainable through some channel of mutual consideration and discussion."[9] The petition of the Continental Congress, however, did not satisfy Dartmouth's own definition of a "general constitutional plan," because it failed to acknowledge the principle of parliamentary supremacy. His reception of the petition, then, reflects only his code of gentlemanly courtesy, not his political principles.

North may have been inclined to negotiate with the colonists on the basis of their petition,[10] but the King's attitude was decisive in this instance. As early as November, 1774, George III had confided in his first minister: "I am not sorry that the line of conduct seems now chalked out . . .; the New England governments are in a state of rebellion, blows must decide whether they are to be subject to this country or independent. . . ."[11] As a confidential advisor to the Crown and stepbrother to the first minister, Dartmouth must have known of this sentiment. If he had been less polite, the agents might have been less disappointed by the ultimate fate of their petition. When Parliament re-assembled after the Christmas recess, the petition was sent to them without any special recommendation from the King. Rather, it was buried (as #149) in a large bundle of papers "relating to the disturbance in America."[12] One explanation for this cavalier treatment may have been the fact that Congress had also voted to aid Massachusetts and George III would naturally regard the offer of assistance to rebels as inconsistent with professions of loyalty and obedience. Thus, suspicions of insincerity and duplicity handicapped both the petition from Congress and North's resolution.[13] It is also possible that the government chose to ignore the petition, because they hoped to get better terms later. This reasoning, however, was no more accurate in this instance than it had been in the

---

[9] To Colden, 7 January 1775, N. Y. Col. Docs., VIII, 529.

[10] Fitzmaurice, Shelburne, I, 476.

[11] King to North, 18 November 1774, Corres. of George III (Fortescue, ed.), III, 153.

[12] Franklin to Cushing, 28 January 1775, Franklin's Writings (Smyth, ed.), VI, 302. Stevens' Facsimiles, #850. Parl. Hist., XVIII, 74 et seq.

[13] Brown, Empire or Independence, 19.

negotiations with Franklin. Thomas Jefferson believed that the petition contained only the minimum number of grievances requiring attention in order for reconciliation to take place. He noted that Congress had refrained from mentioning "the monopoly and regulation of trade, and all the acts of Parliament prior to 1764. . . ."[14] Jefferson also said that a settlement at the date of writing would require additional concessions from Britain. Lexington had rendered the moderate terms of the first petition unacceptable to the Americans themselves. If the ministry expected to obtain more favorable terms by delay, they were mistaken.

Although the government never made an official reply to the petition, conciliation remained in the realm of possibility. In fact, North's resolution was still in the future when the petition was given its indecent burial in the House of Commons. Since one complaint about the petition had been its method of framing, it would seem reasonable to expect that a petition drawn up in the proper manner would be acceptable. The fate of the petitions from the colony of New York demonstrates that such was not the case.

New York was generally considered to be the most loyal of the Thirteen Colonies. Because of this loyalty and also because of her strategic position, it might be assumed that her grievances would be heard with more sympathy than those of some other colonies. The New York Assembly had declined sending representatives to the First Continental Congress. They decided instead to make their grievances the subject of separate petitions. No doubt they took their cue from Dartmouth's letter to the Lieutenant-Governor in which he said that any complaints would "come from each colony with greater weight in its separate capacity," than from a general congress, "of the propriety and legality of which there may be much doubt."[15] Colden responded that he would make immediate inquiries of the members of the colonial legislature, to ascertain "whether I may expect that they will propose conciliatory measures, and pursue the method which your Lordship so justly points out as the most proper."[16]

In the autumn of 1774 there seemed to be every reason to expect that a dutiful petition from New York would receive favorable response from the imperial government. The basis for this short-lived affection, however, was that the New Yorkers had not officially challenged the doctrine of parliamentary supremacy. Dartmouth informed Colden before Christmas that the ministry took a very favorable view of his province, because "the wishes which they have in general

---

14 Jefferson to ?, 25 August 1775, Dartmouth Manuscripts, 1461 (Intercepted). J. P. Boyd, ed., *Papers of Thomas Jefferson* (Princeton, 1950), I, 240-43, identifies the addressee as John Randolph.

15 To Colden, 7 September 1774, *N. Y. Col. Docs.*, VIII, 487.

16 From Colden, 2 November 1774, *ibid.*, 510.

expressed that all violence might be avoided, and the sovereign
authority of the supreme legislature might be supported, are graciously considered by the King as evidences of their respect and affection
for his Majesty, and of the just sense they entertain of the rights of
the British Empire."[17]

Acting upon Dartmouth's hint that complaints from individual
assemblies would be more readily heard, the moderate elements in
the New York government passed resolutions condemning violent
and precipitate measures. They then proceeded to draw up a petition
to the King, a memorial to the House of Lords and a representation
and remonstrance for the House of Commons. So long as the moderate authors of these documents remained in power, New York
abstained from official participation in congresses. Colden praised
his legislature for their refusal to appoint delegates to the Second
Continental Congress, but noted that the "disaffected party are however exerting their utmost influence to obtain the appointment of
delegates by the people. . . . Your Lordship may however be assured that a great part of the people are against appointing delegates
to meet the May congress. . . ."[18] Officials of the Crown tended
to exaggerate the numbers and importance of the friends of the government, while disparaging their opponents as merely "the disaffected
party," but Colden's description of the state of affairs may have been
accurate at the date of writing. The arrival of the news of the opening
battles of the Revolution, however, caused a change in public opinion. The radical elements in the colony made good use of this exchange of shots and the shedding of American blood by the King's
troops. Debtors in other colonies refused to pay their New York
creditors, unless that province joined the Association to present a
united front to the mother country. Against this pressure the moderates were defenseless. The revolutionaries took control by June,
1775. A provincial congress, with the aid of local committees, carried on the functions of government, just as in twelve other colonies.
Tories suffered various degrees of discomfort and danger. The mob
deprived even soldiers of the garrison of their baggage while they
were transferring to a ship in the harbor.[19]

While the New Yorkers were rushing toward revolution, their
petitions were making their slow way to England. The petition to the
King eventually came to Dartmouth's office.[20] It recited the usual
grievances regarding taxation and various acts of Parliament, with
the request for redress. But the most significant part of the petition
was the desire that the King confirm "such a system of govern-

---

[17] To Colden, 10 December 1774, *ibid.,* 514.

[18] From Colden, 5 April 1775, *ibid.,* 566.

[19] From Colden, 3 May & 7 June 1775, *ibid.,* 571, 579-83.

[20] N. Y. Gen. Assem. to King, 25 March 1775, Dartmouth Manuscripts,
1191.

ment . . . as will ascertain and limit the authority claimed by the British legislature." The colonies and the mother country had drifted far apart indeed, when the moderate elements of "loyal" New York suggested the limitation of the illimitable. How could Dartmouth continue to hope for a peaceful accommodation with Massachusetts, when not even New York shared his view of the constitution?

The New York petitions to the two houses of Parliament were no more successful. Burke presented the representation and remonstrance to the lower house on May 15th, but they decided not to permit the reading of a paper which denied the right of Parliament to tax the colonies in all cases whatsoever.[21] Although the memorial to the House of Lords was probably the most dutifully phrased, a similar fate awaited it there. Burke had encountered some difficulty in finding a friendly peer to present the memorial, but when the Duke of Manchester offered it to the Lords on May 18th, they rejected it unread.[22]

This refusal to consider a document containing uncongenial sentiments may seem somewhat petulant to the modern reader. It was certainly unrealistic, for the two Houses of Parliament chose to stand on their dignity at a time when the supremacy which they claimed was rapidly vanishing in revolutionary war. Of course, news of the opening shots had not yet arrived in England, so Dartmouth did not realize that the last, or perhaps the penultimate, opportunity for reconciliation had just disappeared. When he wrote to the Governor of New York, to thank him in the King's name for the petition from the "faithful subjects in New York," he regretted that the petitions to the two Houses of Parliament had contained "claims which made it impossible for Parliament consistent with its justice and dignity to receive them. . . ." Had it not been for these denials of parliamentary supremacy, Dartmouth insisted, the New York petitions might have provided the "foundation of that conciliation we have so long and so ardently wished for."[23] Dartmouth's regret at this time was tempered by two considerations. First, he did not yet know of the fighting in Massachusetts and, secondly, he still counted upon North's plan for reconciliation. In the same letter to Tryon, he expressed the hope "that the resolution of the House of Commons of the 27th Feb[ruar]y will remove all obstacles to the restoration of public tranquillity. . . ."

Within a few days Dartmouth realized that this was a vain hope. The blood shed in Massachusetts had already rendered the New

---

[21] *Parl. Hist.*, XVIII, 643 *et seq.* Burke to the Committee of Correspondence, 7 June 1775, Dartmouth Manuscripts, 1295 (Intercepted).

[22] *Lords' Journals*, XXXIV, 461. From Burke, 9 May 1775, Dartmouth Manuscripts, 1264.

[23] To Tryon, 23 May 1775, *N. Y. Col. Docs.*, VIII, 574-5.

York petitions inadequate as instruments of reconciliation. Parliamentary rejection of them, unheard, played directly into the hands of the opposition forces in the erstwhile loyal colony and ensured New York's active participation in the struggle. The provincial Association informed the Lieutenant-Governor that: "To their inexpressible grief they have found that the most dutiful applications for redress have not only been rejected, but have been answered by reiterated violations of their rights."[24] Public opinion was incensed, as numerous letters intercepted by the Post Office demonstrate. After the rejection of their petitions, the people of New York believed they had no alternative but to join forces with the other colonies and to "defend their liberty by a vigorous opposition."[25] J. H. Cruger deplored the treatment accorded the petitions, on the grounds that it "irritated and greatly vexed many of the moderate well-disposed people and will hasten on the scene of confusion, ruin and anarchy."[26]

Was there any possibility for the success of conciliation in 1775? When the gestures from England were deemed inadequate and insincere, and when even the most moderate petitions from the colonies were rejected, there would seem to be no alternative but war. If conciliatory measures failed prior to the outbreak of fighting in April, how could they succeed in repairing an already shattered peace? If one accepts the concept of inevitability in history, then the battles of Lexington and Concord may constitute a point of no return. In this case, subsequent efforts at conciliation, like the Olive Branch, appear futile and unworthy of serious consideration. As a matter of fact, contemporaries did not regard the Olive Branch as futile at all. It is true that a state of war already existed, but no one could prophesy the future course of the war in 1775. James Warren, one of the leading Massachusetts radicals, for example, wrote in July of that fateful year: "I fear nothing now so much as the small pox in our army . . . and proposals of a conciliatory nature from England. The first would be dreadful, but the last more so. . . . I did not expect another petition."[27] If Dr. Warren regarded conciliation proposals as worse than smallpox, there was some hope for the Olive Branch.

The Second Continental Congress faced the same official discouragement and disapproval as the first. George III had expressed the hope that North's resolution would put an end to congresses, and Dartmouth had directed the colonial governors to obstruct the meet-

[24] Address of the N. Y. Association to Colden, 11 May 1775, *ibid.,* 584.

[25] Isaac Seagrove to John Blackburn, 2 July 1775, Dartmouth Manuscripts, 1348 (Intercepted).

[26] J. H. Cruger to Henry Cruger, Jr., 5 July 1775, *ibid.,* 1356 (Intercepted).

[27] Warren to John Adams, 20 July 1775, *Warren-Adams Letters,* I, 84.

ing. His circular letter of January 4th pointed out that the first Congress had engaged in unwarrantable proceedings; consequently, each governor should take steps to prevent the selection of delegates. This meeting would be "an unjustifiable proceeding, which cannot but be highly displeasing to the King. . . ."[28] The ministry, like the Bourbons, had apparently learned nothing and forgotten nothing. They might have realized the hopelessness of trying to prevent the Congress from meeting. Governor Wentworth's reply to Dartmouth's instructions aptly illustrates the difficulty of the situation. He frankly stated that there was "not sufficient force in the government" of New Hampshire to prevent the two delegates from representing that colony in Philadelphia.[29] The governors of larger colonies experienced the same frustration.

Before the meeting was called to order in May, fighting had already broken out in Massachusetts. The prospects of a peaceful settlement seemed even more remote than at the time of the first Congress. Yet, there remained a strong sentiment in favor of making another attempt at reconciliation. The result was the last petition to the King, usually called the Olive Branch.[30] In spite of the opposition of Adams and the radicals in Congress, the moderates carried the vote to prepare a petition. The actual drafting of the document was entrusted to Jefferson, but when Dickinson objected to some offensive phrases in it, Jefferson allowed him to revise it. The result was an eminently moderate petition, strongly opposed by the radicals, which passed only after a bitter debate.[31]

The Olive Branch invited the King to draw up a suitable plan for reconciliation. The colonists desired a sacred charter of rights, comparable to Magna Carta. Specifically, they offered to submit to a strict regulation of trade, if Britain would surrender the power to tax them; alternately, they offered to pay a share of the costs of empire in return for the right to trade freely with all parts of the world. Actually, they were still hoping for a return to the conditions that existed before the Peace of Paris, when they had enjoyed the benefits of mercantilism without suffering unduly from its restrictions. This proposal might have provided a basis for discussion and negotiation, if the ministry had given it more serious consideration.

The members of Congress signed the Olive Branch on July 8th and commissioned Richard Penn to deliver it to London. Before the completion of his journey, however, an event occurred in Britain which greatly altered the complexion of his mission. The House of

---

[28] To the Governors in America, 4 January 1775, *N. Y. Col. Docs.,* VIII, 527-8.

[29] From Wentworth, 28 March 1775, Mass. Hist. Soc., *Proceedings,* XIV, 343.

[30] For text, see *Journals of Cont. Cong.,* II, 158-62.

[31] Brown, *Empire or Independence,* 28-30.

Commons had earlier carried a resolution declaring some of the colonies in a state of rebellion, but the wheels of government had turned so slowly that no official proclamation had yet been issued. Pressure began to build during the summer for an immediate declaration of rebellion. Dartmouth, away on his annual holiday, received a letter on the subject from each of his undersecretaries. Pownall expressed the opinion that the proclamation should be issued soon, because a number of foreign officers were interested in American affairs. He mentioned specifically some French officers who were visiting General Israel Putnam's camp.[32] Knox, who also thought the situation perilous, ominously referred to "an intercourse of a nature which ought to be prevented," but said that he could see no remedy, "without a proclamation declaring the rebellion."[33]

It was regular procedure for one undersecretary to correspond with Dartmouth when he was away from his office, but it was unusual for both of them to address him letters on the same subject and on the same day. Although strong pressure was developing in favor of a proclamation, Dartmouth resisted their urgings. He continued to hope for conciliation, possibly on the grounds to be provided by the second petition from Congress. His reply to Knox reveals that he was no longer an inexperienced minister. He could at least control his own staff, even if the course of events was beyond all human control. Referring to a newspaper report from America, he told Knox: "I rather wish than expect a settlement of our differences upon the ground of the terms stated in the article from Philadelphia. However, I see no reason why we may not set our feet upon that or any ground that can be given, and though both sides will have a great way to go before they will be within the sound of each other's voice, it is not impossible that they may come near enough to shake hands at last. If they mean to admit duties for regulation of trade, and will add to that a revenue for the support of civil government, and such military force as they shall themselves desire to have among them, I think we may soon be agreed. God send that day as soon as may be."[34]

Although Dartmouth was willing to listen to moderate proposals, even from an extra-legal Congress, the day of the moderate was over. Extremists had already begun to lead each side away from that road where they might shake hands. His letter to Knox succeeded only in ending the agitation within the American Department for a proclamation. At least, in mid-August Pownall agreed that the proclamation should be delayed until after Penn had delivered the Olive Branch.[35]

32 From Pownall, 5 August 1775, Dartmouth Manuscripts, 1427. Cf. ibid., 1471.
33 From Knox, 5 August 1775, ibid., 1424.
34 To Knox, 6 August 1775, Hist. Mss. Comm., Knox Mss., 120-1.
35 From Pownall, 15 August 1775, Dartmouth Manuscripts, 1441.

A new and more dangerous insistence upon immediate action, however, appeared outside the Colonial Office. Both North and Thurlow favored issuing the proclamation. In Dartmouth's absence, Pownall could only urge Suffolk to postpone action on this business. It is doubtful whether Suffolk, of all people, sympathized with Dartmouth's policy, but for some reason, probably bureaucratic red-tape, the proclamation was delayed.

This inter-office rivalry had little effect upon the ultimate results. Richard Penn and Arthur Lee sent a copy of their petition to the American Department on August 21st. Two days later, the Privy Council approved the proclamation for suppressing rebellion and sedition in America.[36] It was not until the first of September that Dartmouth came up to London from Sandwell in order to receive the official copy of the petition in person.[37] The proclamation had been delayed until after the delivery of the unofficial copy, it is true, but the extremists triumphed over moderation and conciliation. The timing of the proclamation converted the agents who delivered the Olive Branch from loyal subjects petitioning for redress into rebels with an ultimatum.

What was Dartmouth's state of mind on the occasion when he received Penn and Lee? His conflict of emotions must have been very great. On the one hand, there was his own inclination to deal leniently with the colonies. Some of the correspondence which came to his hand supported this inclination. David Barclay, for example, informed Dartmouth that the Olive Branch was the product of the group in Congress who sincerely desired conciliation. To reject this petition would inevitably alienate a large number of moderates in every colony, for they "think from the reception of the New York memorial there is no disposition, on this side, for reconciliation. . . . Nothing can exceed their firmness and unanimity. . . ."[38] On the other hand, Dartmouth knew perfectly well the official opinion of the Congress, and that it was generally accepted that only a small but noisy minority dominated its proceedings. An old friend, Sir James Augustus Oughton, bluntly told him that "treating with rebels, while they have arms in their hands, would demonstrate a weakness in government which no victory could compensate for."[39] In all probability, Oughton was more truly representative of British opinion than Barclay. The actual beginning of hostilities had convinced many people that independence was the real goal of the Americans and

---

[36] *Acts of the Privy Council (Colonial Series)*, V, 417.

[37] To Richard Penn and Arthur Lee, 24 August 1775, Dartmouth Manuscripts, 1458. The copy of the petition which Penn and Lee sent to Dartmouth will be found in *ibid.*, 1451.

[38] From David Barclay, 23 August 1775, *ibid.*, 1454.

[39] From Oughton, 24 August 1775, *ibid.*, 1459.

that petitions were only meant to gain time for the rebels to build up their strength.

Whatever Dartmouth's thoughts may have been, he accepted the petition in silence and delivered it to the King. He never gave the colonists any official reply, resorting to a rather lame excuse in order to avoid a commitment: "as his Majesty did not receive it on the Throne, no answer would be given."[40] Dartmouth may have been trying to soften the blow instead of delivering an outright rejection, but the colonists regarded this answer as more insulting than the deliberate burial of their first petition in a paper grave. The opposition in the House of Lords, refusing to allow the matter to rest on so inconclusive a note, insisted upon a more definite answer. The Olive Branch was read to the peers and a motion was made on November 7th that it afforded grounds for conciliation. A point of order delayed its consideration until the tenth. The Duke of Richmond then advocated accepting the petition and arranging for conciliation on the basis suggested in it: that is, the repeal of the offensive acts and the restoration of peace. Richard Penn, who was called to give testimony, assured the House that independence was not the colonists' goal, and that complete freedom of trade was not required for the restoration of peace.

In the debate which followed, Dartmouth successfully opposed Richmond's motion.[41] On this occasion, Dartmouth very clearly stated his opinion of the Olive Branch and the unfeasibility of accepting it. In the first place, he contended, it would be impossible to recognize a petition from Congress, "without at the same instant relinquishing the sovereignty of the British Parliament."[42] This attitude, of course, corresponded to his earlier insistence that peace proposals should come from individual colonies. It revealed, however, an unfortunate inability to recognize the realities of the situation as they existed after the rejection of the New York petition. Dartmouth also claimed that the basis of the dispute had changed: "It was no longer a question about taxation, about the quantum to be raised, or the mode of raising it; it was not the conquest, but the allegiance of the colonies, which administration were desirous of obtaining." When Dartmouth spoke of allegiance, he assumed that allegiance to the Crown alone was insufficient and even dangerously Tory in its

---

[40] *Journals of Cont. Cong.*, III, 343 n.

[41] *Parl. Hist.*, XVIII, 895 *et seq.* Dartmouth's halfbrother reported that, "Lord Dartmouth shone prodigiously. I never heard him speak nearly so well, indeed I scarcely ever heard a better speech." Bishop of Worcester to Guilford, [n.d.], Ms. North, d.26:24-25. Dartmouth's own account of the debate was no less enthusiastic but more modest: "I don't remember ever to have heard a debate in which the majority had a more clear and decided superiority of argument as well as numbers." To Guilford, 11 November 1775, *ibid.*, d.16:67-68.

[42] *Parl. Hist.*, XVIII, 919-20.

implications. Since the Glorious Revolution and the Hanoverian Succession, the King-in-Parliament had been the source of sovereignty. The development of dominion status years after Dartmouth's death proved that he was wrong, but he had no way of knowing that in 1775.

Finally, Dartmouth attempted to justify his actions in receiving the petition without comment. He insisted that it was an accepted custom for the King not to "give an answer to any petition, unless presented to him on the throne. It would have been highly indecent, therefore, in the secretary, to have given an answer unauthorized." He confessed by implication, however, that this refusal to answer was more than just a technicality of protocol. He conceded: "If the silence was construed into a disapprobation of the Petition, it was . . . a very justifiable construction. The Petition, in terms, was unexceptionable, but there was every reason to believe that the softness of the language was purposely adopted to conceal the most traitorous designs." Here, then, is the real reason for the rejection of the Olive Branch: not because it contained objectionable phrases, like the petition from New York; not because it originated in an extra-legal gathering, like the petition of the First Continental Congress; but because there was so little faith and understanding left between Britain and her colonies, that the words of the petition were not believed!

The rejection of the Olive Branch destroyed the last hope of the moderates. The propaganda of the radicals carried more conviction than before, for no middle ground existed between complete submission and absolute independence. What is the evidence in support of Dartmouth's charge of "most traitorous designs"? There is some, although it is far from conclusive. Many of the radicals in the Congress voted for the petition entirely for their own purposes.[43] Assuming that the government would reject it, the radicals hoped to undermine the moderates' position. By voting for conciliation, they were really aiming at uniting the opposition under their leadership. Whether this duplicity of a few was sufficient to contaminate the work of the whole group is a question which might as well be directed at North's resolution as the Olive Branch. Whatever the answer might be, an unhappy coincidence apparently decided the issue. General Burgoyne had intercepted some of John Adams' letters. The general sent them to England, where they arrived about the same time as Richard Penn.[44] The Adams letters convinced the ministry that the colonists in general were aiming at independence, and that all petitions were mere dissimulation. It is ironic that the rejection of the Olive Branch did more than anything else to encour-

---

[43] Brown, *Empire or Independence,* 64-5.
[44] *Ibid.,* 30-2.

age the independence movement. The colonists became convinced that petitioning was futile. No important or influential American bothered to frame peace proposals after 1775. It now became Britain's responsibility to initiate a plan of conciliation, but until 1778 all her attempts were half-hearted and accompanied by coercion. When British officials were willing to grant every concession the colonies required, short of independence, the offer came too late.[45]

How can Dartmouth's role in the sad story of the failure of colonial conciliation be evaluated? Due allowance must be made for the fact that his reputation as a conciliator had been exaggerated. Those who remembered that he had helped to repeal the Stamp Act in 1766 were inclined to overlook his support of the Declaratory Act. The contrast which he presented to his predecessor may have helped to inflate his reputation as Hillsborough's policy of firmness was accompanied by bluster and rudeness. Dartmouth's policy differed only slightly, but his manner was polite, tactful, and perhaps misleadingly friendly. Nevertheless, Dartmouth intended, when he took office in 1772, to restore harmony and tranquillity in colonial policy. Not only did he fail to carry out this plan, but in three short years all hopes for conciliation had disappeared. Many writers have blamed Dartmouth's weakness of personality for this failure. Agreeing that he was pious, good, well-intentioned, and amiable, his critics dismiss him as hopelessly weak. Yet, how much control would a man of stronger personality have had? The King's insistence upon the sanctity of "the constitution," the Bedfordites' vehement resentment of any sign of leniency, and the hardening of public opinion against the colonies after the first bloodshed, were all barriers to conciliation which would have obstructed the path of even the most determined Secretary of State. It is also important to note that the events of the day occurred so rapidly and so far from the center of imperial administration that Dartmouth rarely learned about them until six weeks or two months later. Any decision on policy required an additional month or more to take effect in the colonies. Furthermore, the long-delayed news which reached his office was always biased: letters from his unofficial correspondents, like Joseph Reed, usually emphasized the strength and unity of colonial opposition, while dispatches from governors and army officers exaggerated the opposition's lack of unity and stressed the fact that the "best people" did not join the mob around the Liberty Tree. Faced with this contradictory information, Dartmouth quite naturally relied more heavily upon official reports, with the result that his information was not only out of date but far from accurate.

---

[45] R. G. Adams, *Political Ideas of the American Revolution* (Durham, N. C., 1922), 38. (Third Edition, N. Y., 1958, page 63).

Whatever his correspondents told him about affairs in America, there was one further obstacle to conciliation: the doctrine of parliamentary supremacy. Not even Burke or Chatham would have surrendered the right of Parliament to legislate for the colonies,[46] yet the pressure of events in America was producing the opinion that this doctrine was incompatible with liberty. As early as 1768, Franklin had acknowledged that it was easier to make a case for one of the two extremes, while the middle ground had become less tenable: either Parliament had the right to make all laws or it had no right to make any laws for the colonies.[47] By 1775 this conclusion had become inescapable to most Americans. If Dartmouth had accepted the American interpretation of the imperial relationship, he would have had to resign from the ministry. Conversely, his firm and consistent avowal of parliamentary supremacy made it impossible for him to accept the most moderate proposals from the colonies. The failure of conciliation was a great tragedy and no one man should bear the entire responsibility for it. The pressure of historical events and the incompatibility of constitutional theories far outweighed the influence of any individual.[48]

---

[46] *Ibid.,* 27-8. (Third Edition, 52-4). Sir Lewis Namier believed that it was "extremely doubtful whether Burke and his friends, if in power, would have succeeded in saving the First British Empire." *England in the Age of the American Revolution* (Second Edition), 39. Furthermore, Brigadier General Robertson reported to Dartmouth that the "best intelligence" from Philadelphia stated that the colonists "fear Lord Chatham: he is for having the supremacy acknowledged. . . ." See the letter dated 25 May 1775, enclosed in Robertson's note of 13 June 1775, Dartmouth Manuscripts, 1316.

[47] Franklin to William Franklin, 13 March 1768, *Franklin's Writings* (Smyth, ed.), V, 115.

[48] Without reviving the Whig historians' concept of "tyranny," recent scholars have placed more emphasis upon the King's responsibility for insisting upon "firmness" as a general policy, while leaving the details up to the ministry. Labaree, *Tea Party,* 178-79. Piers Mackesy, *The War for America, 1775-1783* (Cambridge, Mass., 1964), 38.

Chapter XVI

THE MISERIES OF CIVIL WAR

HORACE WALPOLE, who could find something insulting to say about even his best friends, once turned his acidic attention to the description of the chief ministers of North's administration. Of them all, he said, "Lord Dartmouth only stayed long enough to prostitute his character and authenticate his hypocrisy."[1] It is unfair to call Dartmouth a hypocrite, although the situation in which he found himself in the year 1775 was filled with irony and apparent contradiction. His chief objective had been the preservation of the empire, but the continued insistence that unity depended upon colonial submission to Parliament was the very doctrine which destroyed the first empire. Dartmouth supported measures, designed to secure recognition of parliamentary supremacy, which were both coercive and conciliatory. This ambivalent policy not only failed to maintain parliamentary supremacy; it also deprived the empire of thirteen of its colonies. Certainly, he had been warned of the possible consequences of coupling firmness with friendliness. Joseph Reed, for one, admonished him in June, 1774, that a "civil war will ensue before Americans will submit to taxation by Parliament."[2] Three months later, while the coercive policy remained in effect, Reed again prophesied that "we are on the verge of a civil war not to be equalled in history for its importance and fatal consequences."[3] At the same time, of course, Dartmouth's official correspondents were emphasizing the divisions among the opposition elements and the growth of support among the better sort of colonists.

Dartmouth and the conciliatory members of the government had been apparently willing to stake everything upon North's resolution of February, 1775. Although condemned at the time and later as inadequate and insincere, this proposal actually failed because of the commencement of hostilities in Massachusetts. Governor William Franklin, for example, in replying to Dartmouth's earnest recommendation of the plan, noted that the skirmishes at Lexington and Concord would prevent it from having a proper hearing. He personally approved of North's proposal and reproached Gage for precipitating an open conflict. The governor of New Jersey thought that some warning should have been sent that military action was

---

[1] Walpole, *Memoirs of George III*, IV, 56.
[2] From Reed, 10 June 1774, *Reed's Corres.*, I, 68-70.
[3] From Reed, 25 September 1774, *ibid.*, 80.

likely.[4] Dartmouth ruefully agreed with Franklin's estimate of "the fatal effects of General Gage's attempt at Concord." Furthermore, Dartmouth was convinced that except for that "unfortunate event" North's proposal would have been accepted. He said, the "happy moment of advantage is lost and, instead of reconciliation, all North America, except Quebec, Nova Scotia, Georgia, and the Floridas, is in arms against Great Britain and committed in rebellion that menaces to overthrow the constitution."[5]

When General Gage ordered the fatal march to Concord, he was convinced that the ministry had commanded him to take decisive action. A dispatch, which Dartmouth had signed on January 27th, finally arrived in Boston after a prolonged delay. As Gage interpreted it, this dispatch became his marching orders and led directly to the war for independence.[6] Did Dartmouth really intend to start a war? Was Walpole correct in calling the conciliator a hypocrite? The answer to this complex problem requires a consideration of several factors: Gage's relationship with the ministry, the King's role in the formulation of colonial policy, and finally, the wording of the famous dispatch itself.

Gage was both Commander-in-Chief of the royal troops in America and also Governor of Massachusetts Bay colony. He had arrived in Boston in May, 1774, with a complete set of instructions to enforce the coercive policy.[7] That policy, it is recalled, was developed during the Parliamentary session of 1774, without waiting to see how the Port Act was received. As the later bills became law, Dartmouth transmitted them to the Governor, but Gage's relationship with the ministry was unhappy, to say the least. He soon discovered that his unenviable task was impossible. He could not enforce the intolerable acts in Massachusetts, because the Provincial Congress had assumed control of most of the colony. Consequently, he sent very unwelcome reports to the American Department. He told the ministers that the resistance had become nearly universal and that he must have more troops in order to execute his orders. Until a large force arrived, he recommended the temporary suspension of the coercive acts.[8] The result of this information was not a change in policy, but a loss of confidence in Gage. Dartmouth had received and shown to the cabinet many conflicting reports from America. The ministry preferred to believe the governors who emphasized the division of colonial opinion, but here was the Governor of Massachusetts talking nonsense about united resistance. The official dis-

---

[4] From William Franklin, 6 May 1775, *N. J. Archs.*, X, 590.

[5] To William Franklin, 5 July 1775, *ibid.*, 645-7.

[6] J. R. Alden, "Why the March to Concord?" *A.H.R.*, XLIX (April, 1944), 446-454. Same author, *General Gage in America*, Chapter XIV.

[7] To Gage, 9 April 1774, *Gage Corres.* (Carter, ed.), II, 158-62.

[8] Alden, *Gage in America*, 234.

patches had maintained all along that the "patriots" were a small faction of noisy malcontents, while the better sort of colonists would support the government in case of lawlessness or destruction of property.

Both Gage and Dartmouth complained that the other failed to communicate full and accurate information. The General told his friend and colleague, Secretary at War Barrington, that he was waiting "with impatience for further orders as offensive measures are becoming necessary. . . ."[9] Yet, only a short time before this complaint, he had written to Dartmouth in a very optimistic tone, reporting that the "disposition of the people [was] cooling down," and that arresting the most obnoxious leaders of the resistance would meet with "less opposition than expected a few months since."[10] Gage's letters to Barrington were much more complete than those he addressed to Dartmouth. The Secretary at War occasionally relayed this information to the American Department, but many of Gage's observations on colonial affairs were endorsed "private" and Barrington did not show them to anyone else.[11] When Dartmouth realized that the Governor was sending more pertinent reports to his friends than to the American Department, he reproved him: "your letters hitherto have not been so full and explicit as I wished them to be."[12] On the other hand, Dartmouth had sent Gage several statements of general policy but not specific orders the General expected. In addition to instructions to enforce the coercive acts, Gage had received Dartmouth's circular letter to all the governors in America. This dispatch assured the colonial executives of the King's determination to uphold the doctrine of parliamentary supremacy. Dartmouth also enclosed the resolutions of both houses, supporting the coercive policy, as evidence of the state of political opinion at home.[13] Gage may have felt aggrieved and impatient for orders, but Dartmouth had stated the ministry's policy in several letters and was waiting for Gage to execute it. He might even have allowed himself to hope for success, upon reading Gage's report that tempers were "cooling" and opposition lessening.

Whatever the reason for the mutual misunderstanding about an exchange of information and orders, Gage had lost the confidence of the ministry. Many of the King's advisors thought that he was altogether too soft and cautious in subduing the rebellious colony. Lord Suffolk, for example, was convinced that Gage should be removed

---

[9] Gage to Barrington, 10 February 1775, enclosed in letter from Barrington, 28 March 1775, Dartmouth Manuscripts, 1193.

[10] From Gage, 18 January 1775, *ibid.*, 1108. Received 20 February 1775.

[11] Both sets of letters will be found in Carter's edition of the *Gage Corres.*

[12] To Gage, 1 July 1775, *Gage Corres.* (Carter, ed.), II, 201.

[13] To the Governors in America, 10 December 1774, *N. Y. Col. Docs.*, VIII, 515.

from not only the command of the army but also the post of governor of Massachusetts.[14] Gage's enemies at court may have persuaded the King that his Commander-in-Chief was incompetent, but there is no doubt that he was disappointed at Gage's failure to crush the rebellion.[15] The King insisted that Dartmouth take a strong line in his dispatches to the Governor. On one occasion, he instructed his Secretary of State for the Colonies to add a paragraph to "the dispatch to General Gage, . . . assuring him that, though the conflict is unpleasant, Great Britain cannot retract. . . ."[16] The King believed that such a statement would give Gage "resolution, and without it I should fear he would think there was some wavering which [at] the present moment I . . . cannot allow to be the case with the most gentle minds." Thus, in one brief note, the King rejected Gage's suggestion to suspend the coercive acts and at the same time guided the hand of the gentle-minded Dartmouth in the drafting of an official dispatch. Nevertheless, the King remained unsatisfied with his general. Early in 1775, George III decided to replace Gage. He did not, however, adopt Suffolk's drastic plan for complete dismissal; rather, he would have permitted Gage to remain as Governor of Massachusetts. If the King had been able to persuade Lord Amherst to accept the assignment, Gage would have ceased to command the troops in America. Much to his own chagrin, the King had to inform Dartmouth that Amherst had refused.[17]

The King's interest in colonial policy extended to many details beyond the question of appointments and personalities. Even before the failure of the plan to replace Gage, he was commenting upon the news from America. In mid-December, 1774, he told Dartmouth that, "nothing can be more provoking than the conduct of the inhabitants of Massachusetts Bay; some measures must undoubtedly be adopted after Christmas to curb them, and by degrees bring them to due obedience to the mother country, but reason not passion must point out the proper measures."[18] The principal result of this determination was the dispatch which the cabinet authorized Dartmouth to send to Gage and which he signed on January 27th. The dispatch represented the dissatisfaction which many members of the government, including the King, felt with respect to General Gage: his reports were infrequent and contained unwelcome news; his inac-

---

[14] From Suffolk, 22 November 1774, Dartmouth Manuscripts, 1078. Alden, *Gage in America*, 235.

[15] *Ibid.*, 234, citing *Corres. of George III*, III, 154.

[16] From the King, 10 October 1774, Hist. Mss. Comm., *11th Report, App., Part V*, 439. Photostat of this letter supplied by William Salt Library, Stafford.

[17] From the King, 31 January 1775, Hist. Mss. Comm., *13th Report, App., Part IV*, 501.

[18] From the King, 15 December 1774, Hist. Mss. Comm., *11th Report, App., Part V*, 439. Photostat supplied by Salt Library.

tivity in his province appeared to some ministers as incompetence. Dartmouth followed the will of the cabinet in drafting the dispatch and signed it as the last available measure for securing the recognition of parliamentary supremacy.

The American Department continuously suffered from certain constitutional defects and personality conflicts which prevented it from becoming a strong, permanent branch of the government. Until colonial policy could be concentrated in the modern Colonial Office, decisions which affected America were often taken in other offices or in cabinet meetings where Dartmouth was only one of five or seven ministers. His relationship with North would have prevented him from resigning, even when his proposals were defeated in the cabinet. Dartmouth confronted many difficulties in this period. Governor Hutchinson recorded in his diary that the Secretary of State "intimated that measures were now determined with respect to America: he wished they could have been accompanied with other measures which he had proposed, particularly the appointment of commissioners to go to America. . . ." Dartmouth had apparently adopted as his own a proposal contained in Lord Howe's negotiations with Franklin at this same period. The futility of all conciliatory proposals, however, became obvious. Hutchinson quoted Dartmouth as saying that he "hoped something would yet be done, though he added, 'when I proposed it, it was scouted at'."[19]

Ministers who favored "firmness" won this particular argument within the cabinet, but Dartmouth made one further effort for conciliation. The dispatch did not go immediately to America, but was deliberately delayed until the negotiations with Franklin came to their unsuccessful end. North, who was privy to these negotiations, assuredly supported his stepbrother. Even after these hopes for a peaceful accommodation were dashed, further delay occurred. Adverse winds prevented the ships from sailing at once with the dispatch and its official copy. Communication across the ocean was painfully slow, even at best, but the net result of this combination of delays, both deliberate and accidental, was that Gage did not receive Dartmouth's dispatch until mid-April. The duplicate copy arrived first, on April 14th, but Gage added two more days' delay to the story when he chose to await the arrival of the official dispatch.[20] If one regards Dartmouth's letter of January 27th as the cause of the war for independence, it would be fair to say that the resulting march to Concord and the Battle of Lexington were several weeks late.

Dartmouth, of course, did not instruct Gage to begin a war. His dispatch[21] contained some very strongly worded passages, balanced

[19]Hutchinson's *Diary*, I, 362-3. Entry for 25 January 1775.
[20] Alden, *Gage in America*, 240-1.
[21] To Gage, 27 January 1775, *Gage Corres.* (Carter, ed.), II, 179-83.

by three separate "saving clauses". For example, Dartmouth said that it would be impossible to send the 20,000 men Gage had requested. He noted that the general had enough at least to capture the ringleaders. Dartmouth conceded that such a step might well provide "a signal for hostilities, yet it will surely be better that the conflict should be brought on, upon such ground, than in a riper state of rebellion." The strength of certain phrases, such as the preceding, indicate that Dartmouth was prepared to accept the possibility of armed resistance in one colony. He may have felt other New Englanders would support Massachusetts, but he had not yet learned to appreciate either the degree or the extent of American sympathy for resistance. Since he was still counting upon the strength of loyal elements in New York and more southern regions, he had no way of knowing that the "conflict" would result in revolutionary war. He was determined to secure Massachusetts' acknowledgment of the supremacy of parliament, even if he had to employ drastic measures. Owing to the distance in time and space separating him from the rapidly changing scene in New England, Dartmouth fully appreciated the danger of giving Gage unalterable instructions. The more belligerent phrases were tempered by sentences like the following: "It must be understood, however, after all I have said, that this is a matter which must be left to your own discretion to be executed or not as you shall, upon weighing all circumstances, and the advantages and disadvantages on one side and the other, think most advisable. . . ." Realizing that he lacked full information about affairs in Massachusetts, Dartmouth also told Gage: "I sincerely wish that the information which we have received of the state of the province would enable me to instruct you upon every case, in which you may wish to receive such instruction; but in a situation where everything depends so much upon the events of the day, and upon local circumstances, your conduct must be governed very much by your own judgment and discretion. . . ." To impress Gage with the importance of using his own judgment, Dartmouth inserted even a third "saving clause," when he authorized Gage to declare martial law in the colony. The law officers of the Crown had assured Dartmouth that such a declaration would be legal, but he reminded the governor that "the expedience and propriety of adopting such a measure must depend upon your own discretion under many circumstances that can only be judged of upon the spot."[22]

Since Dartmouth did not order Gage to march to Concord and since he reiterated the discretionary nature of his instructions, how can this dispatch be considered the cause of the war for indepen-

[22] Alden, *Gage in America*, 240-3. While noting the existence of "a saving clause," Alden minimizes both the number and the force of the three distinct injunctions which Dartmouth inserted into his dispatch to Gage.

dence? The answer lies in the fact that Gage interpreted Dartmouth's letter as a call for action. He used his discretion about what type of action to take. The dispatch specifically instructed him to arrest the leaders of the provincial congress. Gage himself had recommended this step, suggesting that it would meet "less resistance" than previously expected. For reasons which must have seemed sound to Gage at the time, he did not attempt to arrest the only leader left in Boston, Dr. Warren. John Adams was safely out of his reach, but all the other "actors and abettors" of the provincial congress were assembled at Concord. Still, Gage waited until after the congress had adjourned, before he ordered the ill-fated march into the countryside on the 19th. He made no effort to apprehend Samuel Adams or John Hancock, who were near the route of march, nor did his troops hold Paul Revere after capturing him.[23] Gage used his own judgment: he ignored one specific instruction in favor of an entirely different kind of action.

Actually, Gage had decided to capture the arms and ammunition which he knew the provincial congress had sequestered at Concord. In adopting this course of action, he was executing, knowingly or otherwise, a much earlier instruction. Dartmouth had instructed all the American governors to "take the most effectual measures for arresting, detaining and securing any gunpowder or any sort of arms or ammunition which may be attempted to be imported into the province under your government. . . ."[24] The ban on the exportation of gunpowder had originated in a series of reports, which Suffolk relayed to Dartmouth, saying that large quantities purchased in the Netherlands were destined for America.[25] In spite of counter measures, the goods managed to reach the colonies. In January, ten chests of arms arrived in New York assigned to "some persons in Connecticut." When the customs officer attempted to confiscate this cargo, the Sons of Liberty assaulted him.[26] Gage's attempt to capture a store of arms at Salem in February had been equally unsuccessful, so the march to Concord would appear to be a logical sequel to that futile action. The date of the second attempt to carry out the instructions to seize arms coincided with a fortnight's adjournment of the provincial congress. This fact, together with the intentional omission of baggage and artillery, indicates that Gage was trying to avoid conflict, rather than to precipitate it under specific orders from home.[27]

---

[23] *Ibid.*, 242.

[24] To the Governors in America, 19 October 1774, *Gage Corres.* (Carter, ed.), II, 176.

[25] From Suffolk, 31 August 1774, P.R.O., CO 5/138, Part II.

[26] From Paul Wentworth, 18 February 1775, Dartmouth Manuscripts, 1151. Extract of a letter to Mr. Williams, 6 January 1775, *ibid.*, 1092.

[27] Allen French, *General Gage's Informers* (Ann Arbor, 1932), Chap. I.

Whatever action Dartmouth had expected Gage to take, he was shocked by the reports of bloodshed which eventually reached his office. George III, on the other hand, was quite content with the results. When Dartmouth relayed the news of Lexington and Concord to his royal master, the King refused to consider it "bad news." He even insisted that Gage had no reason to be displeased with the results of his sally into Massachusetts countryside, saying: "The object of sending a detachment was to spike cannons and destroy military stores, this has been effected, but with the loss of an equal number of men on both sides; the dye [sic] is cast. I therefore hope that you will not see this in a stronger light than it deserves."[28] Knowing the later results of this "loss of an equal number of men," one may think the King rather callous. His attitude toward the empire, however, had a certain quality of simplicity about it. As he confidently told Dartmouth: "Distant possessions standing upon an equality with the superior State is more ruinous than being deprived of such connections."[29]

Dartmouth was quite right in viewing the situation in a very strong light. One by one his hopes for a peaceful settlement had evaporated. In March, 1775, he had been prepared to write off most of New England. He told Governor Hutchinson then that he was "very apprehensive that the New England people will resist the King's troops. . . ."[30] Even if fighting should erupt there, Dartmouth was still counting upon the "loyalty" of New York and the effectiveness of North's Resolution. He had hoped to preserve the empire by a policy of conciliation. The battles of Lexington and Concord spelled the end of conciliation in New England, but the failure of that policy did not necessitate Dartmouth's resignation. His main object remained. It was now necessary for the empire to be preserved by military means. Even before the first shots had been fired, Dartmouth informed Gage that he approved the latter's plan "to convince the people under your government of the dreadful delusion they have suffered themselves to be drawn into, and to show them that if they come to be involved in the miseries of civil war, it will be the consequence of their own intemperance and folly, and of their ignorance of the real disposition of this country towards them." In the course of this communication, Dartmouth demonstrated his belief that armed force was a last resort, to be used only after the failure of "reason and argument." But he was not afraid to use force to preserve the empire. He described it as "that compulsive force, with which every govern-

---

[28] From the King, 29 May 1775, Hist. Mss. Comm., *11th Report, App., Part V*, 440. Photostat supplied by Salt Library.

[29] From the King, 10 June 1775, Hist. Mss. Comm., *13th Report, App., Part IV*, 502.

[30] Hutchinson's *Diary*, 419, Entry for 29 March 1775.

ment must be armed for the support of its own authority, and for the protection of those who submit themselves to its laws."[31] Dartmouth's belief that the use of force was justified in suppressing rebellion and to protect loyalism explains his remaining in office after the failure of conciliation. He executed all the necessary orders for the conduct of the war, although it may appear incongruous that "the good Lord Dartmouth" with his reputation for piety and conciliation had become a war-minister.

The "bad news" from Massachusetts did not come first from Gage. One Captain Darby, whose account was highly sympathetic to the "patriot" cause, carried it posthaste across the ocean. Dartmouth sent for him three times, but he refused to attend the Secretary in his office and set sail again before he could be apprehended.[32] Dartmouth was still impatiently waiting for confirmation of the events of April 19th, when he wrote to Governor Wentworth on June 7th. Thus far, he said, he had heard only a "very vague and uncertain account" of the skirmish. He believed that the rumor was intended only to convey misrepresentation and create alarm, but "it has had no other effects than to increase that just indignation which his Majesty's faithful subjects in this kingdom feel for the insult and violence offered to the constitution. . . .[33] When later news confirmed the rumor, he told Gage, "let the event be what it may, the rash and rebellious conduct of the provincials upon this occasion, evinces the necessity, and will manifest to all the world the justice of the measures which the King has adopted for supporting the constitution, and in which His Majesty will firmly persevere."[34]

The situation rapidly deteriorated in New England and throughout North America. When Gage reported the battle of Bunker's Hill in a private letter, he confessed that the "number of killed and wounded is greater than [the King's troops] could afford to lose."[35] Boston was besieged by a rebel army supposed to number 20,000, while Gage's army suffered greatly from sickness.[36] More disappointing than the worst reports from New England, however, were the dispatches which Dartmouth received from other colonies. The single spark struck on April 19th fell into highly inflammable material and soon the colonies to the south were ablaze. The various governors and other officials, who had previously underestimated the strength and determination of the discontented elements, were surprised at the rapid spreading of the revolt. Their dispatches made it clear that

---

[31] To Gage, 7 April 1775, *Gage Corres.* (Carter, ed.), II, 189-90.
[32] Warren to John Adams, 20 July 1775, *Warren-Adams Letters*, I, 84.
[33] To Wentworth, 7 June 1775, Mass. Hist. Soc., *Proceedings*, XIV, 343.
[34] To Gage, 1 July 1775, *Gage Corres.* (Carter, ed.), II, 199-202.
[35] From Gage, 25 June 1775, Dartmouth Manuscripts, 1335.
[36] From A. Pepperrell, 13 August 1775, *ibid.,* 1438.

Dartmouth would have to deal with more than a local rebellion. He appreciated the widespread nature of the resistance for the first time early in July, when he observed to Wentworth that "not only the four New England governments are in arms, but that almost every other colony has 'catched' the flame, and a spirit of rebellion has gone forth that menaces the subversion of the Constitution."[37]

The widespread nature of the rebellion did not at first diminish Dartmouth's determination. He still believed that "strong measures" would suffice to punish the wicked and protect the loyal. Although the prosecution of a civil war could not have been a pleasant experience for him, he found it necessary to perform new duties. During the early months of the tragic conflict, he issued all the necessary orders to Gage, Howe, Carleton and Guy Johnson, concerning their respective commands.[38] Gage had complained ever since the adoption of the coercive policy that he needed more troops. The cabinet had done very little about this problem until the fighting actually began. They then decided to send additional troops to Boston from Great Britain, Ireland and Canada.[39] Secretary at War Barrington had earlier warned the ministry that there were not enough troops in the British Isles to conquer and control the colonies. He had opposed using the army on several grounds: the expense would be prohibitive, the bloodshed would be terrible, and there were more effective ways to reduce the colonists to obedience, such as a coastal blockade. Barrington believed that it would be more efficient to allow the Americans to suffer their own anarchy and to contend with the Indians unassisted. In the long run he was more concerned about stripping England of her defenses than about the conquest of the colonies.[40] The ministry did not follow the Secretary at War's recommendations, but proceeded to deal with the problem of augmenting the forces. The French-Canadians seemed to present the nearest and best solution. Governor Carleton undoubtedly had based his suggestions for the Quebec Act on the desire to secure the loyalty of the seigneurs. He believed that they had eighteen thousand men at their beck and call.[41] In the present emergency, it was natural for the ministry to rely upon Carleton's optimistic judgment. On June 21st, Dartmouth recorded in a cabinet minute the decision to raise a force of "2000 Canadians to be employed as light infantry under Gage." By the first of July this number was increased to 3,000, while Dart-

---

37 To Wentworth, 3 July 1775, Mass. Hist. Soc., *Proceedings,* XIV, 343-4.

38 Dartmouth Manuscripts, 1410 *et seq.*

39 Cabinet Minute, 15 June 1775, *ibid.,* 1319.

40 From Barrington, 24 December 1774, Shute Barrington, *Political Life of William Wildman, Second Viscount Barrington* (London, 1815), 152-3. Barrington to the King, January 1776, *ibid.,* 162-3. *Barrington-Bernard Corres.,* page x *et seq.*

41 Chester Martin, *Empire and Commonwealth,* 113-4.

mouth informed the Governor of Quebec that the "King relies upon the loyalty and fidelity of his Canadian subjects for their assistance to suppress rebellion. . . ."[42] At the same time, Dartmouth admitted to Gage that it would be impossible to send reinforcements from Britain until the following year. But he assured the General that Carleton's Canadians would be of great assistance in the meantime, especially in recapturing Ticonderoga and Crown Point.[43]

The news from America continued to be dark and discouraging. Undersecretary Pownall had scarcely ordered the clothing for 3,000 Quebec troops, when the ministry decided to double the number.[44] A larger force was necessary for suppressing the rebellion, but they might just as well have tried to raise ten times as many Canadians, for Carleton had greatly overestimated their gratitude and loyalty. Instead of leading a vast army of *habitants* southward, the Governor was forced to confess to the Secretary of State that "the blind perverseness of this people" had caused "an unprecedented defection." He complained bitterly of the "base desertion of the Canadian peasantry."[45]

Among the many orders which Dartmouth issued during the opening months of the revolution, the most surprising one authorized the employment of American Indians as auxiliaries to the King's troops. It is difficult to conceive of this kindly, pious man actually signing an order to initiate the horrors of Indian warfare. The justification for this action, however, was the fact that the rebels had already attempted to secure the red men's support for their side of the conflict. Early in August Dartmouth acknowledged Gage's report concerning the presence of Indians in Washington's camp: "The steps which you say the rebels have taken for calling in the assistance of the Indians, leave no room to hesitate upon the propriety of your pursuing the same measure."[46] At the same time Dartmouth prepared to send presents for the natives to Colonel Guy Johnson, in order to facilitate the superintendent's efforts to "induce them to engage in His Majesty's service. . . ."[47]

The use of Indians was a significant decision, for the campaign took on more of the appearance of actual war, instead of merely an expedition to restore Colonial allegiance to the Crown. It would have been impossible to keep the natives neutral. Since the frontiers-

---

[42] Cabinet Minute, 21 June 1775, Dartmouth Manuscripts, 1326. To Carleton, 1 July 1775, Pub. Archs. Can., Q. 12A, 155-6.

[43] To Gage, 1 July 1775, *Gage Corres.* (Carter, ed.), II, 201-2.

[44] Pownall to Harley, 12 July 1775, P.R.O., CO 5/154, 231 (L. C. Trans.), Pownall to Harley, 19 July 1775, *ibid.*, 241. To Carleton, 24 July 1775, Pub. Archs. Can., Q. 12A, 165.

[45] From Carleton, 20 November 1775, Pub. Archs. Can., Q. 11, 319.

[46] To Gage, 2 August 1775, Dartmouth Manuscripts, 1412.

[47] To Johnson, 24 July 1775, *ibid.*, enclosure.

men had given them so little cause to love or trust them, they naturally preferred the King's side. Furthermore, the full horrors of Indian warfare did not appear until later, when the conflict had spread to the western frontier. Indians were useful in the East as scouts and messengers, but they were outnumbered by white soldiers who usually kept them under control. Even when they were permitted to fight, their opponents were also armed. It was quite a different story in the Ohio country, however, where non-combatants were the victims and Henry Hamilton acquired his not altogether deserved title, "The Hair-Buyer General."[48]

In spite of the application with which he executed strong measures, Dartmouth's temperament was not that of a war-minister. As the area of conflict widened and the differences between the two sides became more acrimonious, Dartmouth realized that the war would last a long time. He had adopted short-term policies, designed to suppress rebellion as quickly as possible and restore imperial harmony. The appointment of Lord George Germain as his successor in November, 1775, spared him the necessity of directing the long war which ensued. Germain immediately reversed a number of Dartmouth's orders, an action which partially obscures his policies and makes it difficult to evaluate them. For example, Germain's attitude toward Indian warfare was entirely different from Dartmouth's. The Earl's reluctant authorization for Gage to recruit some natives had resulted from the report that the Americans were doing so. Germain, on the other hand, insisted that Indian warfare should become a part of British strategy. He ordered Carleton to recruit more of the red men, not merely as scouts but rather as warriors. He actually envisioned a campaign of deliberate savagery, which would terrorize the rebels into submission.[49]

Among the last orders which Dartmouth signed as Secretary of State, there was a series of communications with the generals in America. He directed Gage to make the necessary arrangements to return to Britain for consultation. He sent Howe a commission as Commander-in-Chief during Gage's absence, but at the same time he acknowledged Carleton's seniority. Howe's appointment was only temporary. As soon as the hypothetical French-Canadian army joined Howe's troops, the command would devolve upon Carleton.[50] Germain's handling of this arrangement is widely known. Largely out of personal spite, he restricted Carleton to his own province, then commissioned Burgoyne to lead the Canadian forces southward

[48] J. D. Barnhart, *Henry Hamilton and George Rogers Clark in the American Revolution: with the Unpublished Journal of Lieut. Gov. Henry Hamilton* (Crawfordsville, Indiana, 1951), Chap. VII.
[49] Alan Valentine, *Lord George Germain* (Oxford, 1962), 185.
[50] To Gage, 2 August 1775, Dartmouth Manuscripts, 1410, enclosing copies of commissions and letters to Howe and Carleton.

to New York.[51] This change of one of Dartmouth's policies led indirectly, but nonetheless disastrously, to the battle of Saratoga.

Dartmouth's last official act in connection with the direction of military affairs was granting permission for Howe to evacuate Boston. He authorized the new Commander-in-Chief to remove his besieged troops to New York or some other port to the southward. The dispatch which Dartmouth signed suggested that this move might have a strategic advantage in the possibility of a surprise attack upon the southern regions which "if it has not the effect to subdue, will at least strike terror to the rebellious colonies. . . ."[52] Whether Dartmouth's strategy would have produced either submission or terror is doubtful, but the fact remains that Germain countermanded this order as soon as he became aware of it.[53]

How can Dartmouth's activity in issuing orders for the conduct of the war be reconciled with his reputation as a friend of the colonies? How could the advocate of conciliation give firm, strongly-worded instructions to various officials for the transportation of troops, supplies and presents to the Indians?[54] Should he be commended for performing an uncongenial duty, or branded as a hypocrite? Several factors must be considered in explanation of his conduct. Throughout the course of his brief secretaryship, including the critical years 1774 and 1775, he had consistently carried out the express will of Parliament. He regarded parliamentary supremacy as one of his "unalterable principles." While he may have felt some personal regret at the more extreme portions of some acts, he enforced them to the best of his ability once they had become law. Furthermore, the lack of speedy and complete reports from colonial officials was a great handicap. Dartmouth did not appreciate the full extent of the opposition until the summer of 1775. The protection of the loyal and moderate elements in America was an obligation which came second only to the enforcement of parliamentary supremacy. Finally, Dartmouth continued to hope for the ultimate success of conciliation. The strong measures which he pursued in the meantime were not intended to be the opening campaign in a long and bitter war, but rather to protect property and maintain Britain's authority wherever possible.

---

[51] Valentine, *Germain,* chap. XII.

[52] To Howe, 5 September 1775, Pub. Archs. Can., Nova Scotia Papers, A. 94, 165 *et seq.*

[53] Hutchinson, *Diary,* II, 22 & 24. Howe had already written that the lack of transportation made it impossible to execute Dartmouth's order. From Howe, 26 November 1775, Mass. Hist. Soc., *Proceedings,* XIV, 354-8.

[54] See *Gage Corres.* (Carter, ed.), II *passim.*

Chapter XVII

RESIGNATION FROM THE
AMERICAN DEPARTMENT

DARTMOUTH had reluctantly joined North's administration in 1772 primarily to support his stepbrother. In spite of the failure of conciliation, he could not resign from the American Department, until and unless he could obtain a different post of honor within the government. His "unalterable principles" had not been violated; there was no reason for him to register a protest against the policies of the government. To have resigned in 1775 would only have strengthened the faction who still desired North's downfall. Perhaps Dartmouth remembered the advice he had given another minister a decade earlier. When Rockingham had considered resigning in the midst of the Stamp Act crisis, Dartmouth had urged him to remain in office "while there is the least shadow of hope of doing good. . . ."[1] If Dartmouth followed his own advice, the reports which reached him during the course of 1775 clearly revealed that even the "shadow of hope" was rapidly disappearing. His original policy of watchful waiting had failed when the colonists refused to allow old grievances to die. Instead, they found new and more serious ones. The coercive policy failed in Massachusetts, where it led to bloodshed rather than peaceful submission. Conciliation on the basis of unconditional submission to Parliament was impossible, although Dartmouth did not fully appreciate this in 1775. When the opening of hostilities in April killed whatever chances North's resolution might have had, Dartmouth continued to see a "shadow of hope" in the possibility that the other colonies would not support Massachusetts. As late as mid-July, he told Carleton: "There is still room to hope that the colonies to the southward may not proceed to the same lengths with those of New England."[2] Even this hope evaporated in 1775 as the southern colonies rapidly joined the revolutionary movement.

Undoubtedly, the reports which the various royal governors sent to the Colonial Secretary caused his thoughts to turn toward retirement. For years these same officials had underestimated the strength and unity of the opposition faction. Now, suddenly, they were driven from their very capitals by the revolutionaries. Governor Dunmore

---

[1] To Rockingham [12 February 1766], Rockingham Manuscripts, R. 1, f.344.
[2] To Carleton, 12 July 1775, Pub. Archs. Can., Q. 12A, 163.

of Virginia, for example, had filled his official correspondence with minor complaints and details of his own troubles: the loss of his furniture at sea, a dispute with the Governor of Pennsylvania about jurisdiction over the Pittsburgh area, the limitations on his patronage, and other trivia.[3] Dartmouth had often read dispatches containing such trifling matters, until the very eve of the revolution when the governors were forced to face the realities of their situations. Dunmore suddenly discovered that some of the members of his Council sympathized with the opposition, that he had no power to prevent the election of delegates to Congress, and that even the justices of the peace had accepted the authority of the Continental Congress.[4]

The governors had failed to give Dartmouth prompt and accurate information. When at last they awoke to the dangers of revolution, their diagnosis was superficial and misleading. The people of Virginia had prevented the courts from opening until the governor summoned the Burgesses. Dunmore concluded that the reason for this "opprobrious" action was "to engage their English creditors, who are numerous, to join in the clamor of the country, and . . . to avoid paying the debts in which many of the principal people here are much involved." Although he admitted that his authority was insufficient to suppress the rebellion, Dunmore nevertheless prophesied that it would collapse of its own accord. He felt non-importation and non-exportation agreements would assuredly ruin Virginia, because the inhabitants could not live without the products of the mother country. If a few vessels blockaded the coast, in order to cut off Virginia's commerce with other colonies, Dunmore believed that the trouble would soon blow over.[5]

Dartmouth encountered as much difficulty in obtaining information from Virginia as from Massachusetts. In April he sent Dunmore a sharp rebuke for failing to describe fully Virginia's reactions to the proceedings of the Second Continental Congress.[6] The situation was beyond Dunmore's control even before the news of Lexington and Concord reached the Old Dominion, but hostilities ended the possibility of conciliation once and for all. Dartmouth's "shadow of hope" rested upon the belief that "men of spirit and property" would come forward in support of the government, but Dunmore was forced to seek safety on board a Man of War.[7]

---

[3] Dartmouth's correspondence with Dunmore will be found in P.R.O., CO 5/1351-1353 passim (L. C. Trans.). See also, B. D. Bargar, "Lord Dartmouth's Patronage, 1772-1775," William and Mary Quarterly, XV (April, 1958), 191 et seq.

[4] From Dunmore, 24 December 1774, P.R.O., CO 5/1353, 46 (L. C. Trans.).

[5] Ibid., 45-48.

[6] To Dunmore, 5 April 1775, ibid., 143-4.

[7] From J. Blackburn, 14 July 1775, ibid., 154, 237.

Royal governors of other colonies experienced similar awakenings. Their dispatches to the Colonial Office cannot have contributed to Dartmouth's peace of mind. Governor Martin of North Carolina had been very confident in April that "firmness and perseverance on Britain's part will extinguish the democratic zeal in these colonies."[8] Not long afterwards, Dartmouth received word that Governor Martin had fled to the safety of a fort on the Cape Fear.[9] Lord William Campbell, newly arrived in South Carolina, had to acknowledge that the opposition was more than a noisy crowd of malcontents. A few weeks after the reading of his commission he sought refuge aboard H.M.S. *Tamar* in Charles Town harbor.[10] In this confusion of information, one thing was clear to Dartmouth: whatever hope he may have entertained vanished when even the Carolinas joined the revolutionary movement. By the end of the summer, all the King's representatives had been forced to abandon their governments. This fact was especially difficult to comprehend after receiving so many optimistic and encouraging reports earlier in the year. Many of the unofficial correspondents substantiated the tale told by the officials. Nathaniel Walker had confidently informed Dartmouth in January that the "disturbances are entirely due to a few people from different provinces aiding the Bostonians."[11] In March, Captain Webb estimated that three-fourths of the people were loyal and would rally around the royal standard.[12] In spite of so many reports of loyalty, colony after colony joined Massachusetts. By autumn, Dartmouth could read the truth in an intercepted letter which said that the colonies were entirely beyond Britain's control and that "no civil officer can exert any power unless directed by Congress."[13]

---

[8] From Martin, 20 April 1775, Dartmouth Manuscripts, 1227.

[9] From Martin, 15 July 1775, *ibid.*, 1373. From Earl of Loudon, 17 July 1775, P.R.O, CO 5/154, 247 (L. C. Trans.).

[10] From Campbell, 19 July, 19 August, & 19 September 1775, Dartmouth Manuscripts, 1375, 1446, & 1521. See also the letters from the Governor's secretary, Alexander Innes, printed in *South Carolina Historical Magazine,* LXIII (July, 1962), 127. Governor Penn's reports from Philadelphia told a different story (P.R.O., CO 5/1286), but Dartmouth relied more heavily upon the information supplied by royal governors. Even the proprietary governor of Maryland, however, shared the opinion that resistance was the work of a minority: "In popular assemblies particular men generally govern the rest, and the proceedings take their colour from the temper and views of a few leaders. The moderate and diffident are carried with the stream; and their silence and acquiescence by swelling the apparent majority indicate an approbation of violences they really condemn." From Gov. Eden, 29 January 1773, P.R.O., CO 5/1285, 87 (L. C. Microfilm).

[11] From Walker, 12 January 1775, Dartmouth Manuscripts, 1101.

[12] From Captain Webb, 1 March 1775, *ibid.*, 1172.

[13] Rev. George Panton to Rev. Dr. Chandler, 2 September 1775, *ibid.*, 1477 (Intercepted letter received from Mr. Todd, 11 October).

The news from Quebec, whose loyalty the Act of 1774 had supposedly insured, was equally disheartening. Carleton not only failed
to recruit an army of French-Canadians, he was having great difficulty defending his province from an invasion by the rebels. The
defenses of the capital were in poor repair, while the *habitants* were
either apathetic or openly supporting the invasion. Since no reinforcements could reach Quebec in the wintertime, it looked as though
Canada would fall to the Yankees.[14] This discouraging news from
every quarter must have conditioned Dartmouth for retirement. The
half-hearted manner in which he conducted the business of his office
in August, September and October, reflected his desire to escape from
the terrible responsibilities which had accumulated in the previous
six months. When the last "shadow of hope of doing good" disappeared with the rejection of the Olive Branch, it only remained for
Dartmouth to find a suitable opportunity to escape.

The King's ministers usually enjoyed a month's holiday during
August or September, and Dartmouth was no exception. He always
found pleasure and relaxation at Sandwell Park, although he was
not completely isolated from the business of his department. Pownall
or Knox could always communicate with him about matters of
major importance. In fact, crises often occurred during the customary holiday, as in the instance of the *Gaspée* affair. If Dartmouth
appeared unconcerned with office business, the time element must be
remembered. It required six or more weeks for a dispatch to cross
from the colonies to England. If the news it contained was of great
importance, one of the undersecretaries could send it to Dartmouth's
country house in a matter of hours. If a major crisis erupted, the
Colonial Secretary could do little about it by himself. The cabinet
would have to meet, before a policy decision and a response could
begin their slow journey back across the ocean. In the Vandalia
problem, for example, Rochford and Dartmouth had had to wait
for other confidential advisers of the King to return from their
respective holidays. Ordinarily, there was no reason for Dartmouth
to remain at his Whitehall office during the summer months. News
from the colonies would reach him in the country in reasonable time.

The summer of 1775 was not an ordinary summer, however, in
either England or America. Dartmouth's holiday in Staffordshire
was unusually prolonged, not because he lacked a sense of crisis,
but because he found the direction of warfare uncongenial. As his
hopes for the restoration of peace vanished, his basic dilemma remained. How could he escape the onerous duties of his office with-

---

[14] Various letters from Quebec in September, 1775, calendared in Hist. Mss.
Comm., *14th Report, Pt. X,* pp. 383-87, described the deteriorating situation in
Canada for Lord Dartmouth's edification. These letters are now in the Public
Archives of Canada, Dartmouth Manuscripts, III, pt. 2.

out injuring North's political leadership? Just when he decided to seek an escape is impossible to say. The important orders for Generals Gage, Howe and Carleton indicate that he was still actively concerned with American military affairs as late as August 2nd. It was not his intention to pave the way for his successor, for Germain began his administration by reversing the orders which Dartmouth had previously sent to Howe.[15] Apparently, the comforts of family life at home, combined with the darkening prospect reflected in dispatches from America, caused Dartmouth to yearn for an honorable release. All that was lacking was the opportunity.

Whatever Dartmouth thought about during the summer of 1775, his actions are clear. He returned to London only rarely after the beginning of the customary holiday period. He remained absent from his office long after other officials had returned to town and occasionally, important papers were sent to Sandwell for his signature. But more often Pownall sent letters directly to American officials over his own signature. After the other two Secretaries of State had returned from their holiday, Pownall drafted the dispatches and submitted them to Lord Suffolk for signing.[16]

The opportunity which Dartmouth sought arrived when the Duke of Grafton resigned his post as Lord Privy Seal. There has been a great deal of misunderstanding about this exchange of positions. William Knox, for example, believed that the King wished to have Lord George Germain in charge of the American Department and the result was a cabinet shuffle.[17] Recent accounts tend to give more credit to Grafton, who supposedly resigned because blood had been shed in America, than to Dartmouth, who continued to support the government.[18] One might conclude that Dartmouth had abandoned his conciliatory policies, while Grafton had resigned on a matter of principle. It would be indeed surprising if the notorious Grafton proved to have higher principles than the "good Lord Dartmouth." Such was not the case. Grafton had accepted the Privy Seal in the North government, but he had refused a seat in the cabinet and the responsibility for ministerial policy which that post would imply. In the fall session of Parliament he had spoken out strongly against its policies. Grafton saw nothing inconsistent in accepting the King's stipend and attacking his Majesty's government at the same time. He apparently hoped that North's administration would disintegrate in the near future. In that case, he was immodestly and unrealistically assuming that the King would call upon him to form a new govern-

---

[15] Valentine, *Germain,* 139-41.

[16] Suffolk to Legge, 16 October 1775, Pub. Archs. Can., Nova Scotia Papers, A. 94, 201. Cf. *Canadian Archives Report* (1894), pp. 335 *et seq.*

[17] William Knox, "Memoranda of November 1775," Hist. Mss. Comm., *Knox Mss.,* 256.

[18] Feiling, *Second Tory Party,* 127.

ment. Although he voted against administration-sponsored measures, like the amendment to the Militia Act, he was not prepared to give up the salary attached to his sinecure office.[19] George III, however, took a different view of the matter. He let it be known that he would send for the Privy Seal, if Grafton did not resign of his own accord.[20] It is obvious that Grafton resigned on November 6th, in order to avoid dismissal.

This was the opportunity for which Dartmouth had been waiting. He requested Grafton's former office for himself, in order to escape the responsibility for directing a war against the colonists. Perhaps the King wished eventually to place Germain in charge of American affairs, but the initiative came from Dartmouth at this point in time. In fact, he was so determined upon this course of action, that he risked the displeasure of the King and the embarrassment of Lord North, in order to have his own way. Quite uncharacteristically, Dartmouth refused to acknowledge any of the obstacles in his path. The first of these obstacles was Lord Weymouth's insistence that he had a prior claim to the Privy Seal. The King suggested what he considered the best solution: Dartmouth should become Groom of the Stole, in order to honor Weymouth's claim. This sinecure position in the royal household would permit Dartmouth to retain his seat in the cabinet, where North still needed his support. The King specifically noted that: "Many that have held the office of Groom of the Stole have attended cabinet meetings;. . . . I would propose he [Dartmouth] should attend them. . . ."[21] The King obviously expected Dartmouth to be accommodating and yield to Weymouth: "The good sense of Lord Dartmouth will I trust engage him to heal all differences," he said.

Contrary to all expectations, Dartmouth remained adamant in his desire for the Privy Seal. His refusal to accept any other office caused the exasperated monarch to write rather tartly to Lord North: "If Lord Dartmouth would one moment permit his own amiable temper to examine the state of affairs cooly, he would certainly deem the office of Groom of the Stole equally honourable with that of Privy Seal, they have ever been esteemed so and when called to the effective cabinet, is certainly so."[22] North realized the seriousness of the situation and frankly told the King that, unless Dartmouth and Weymouth could both be pacified, "the ministry will be dissolved."[23] Dartmouth's importance as a personal supporter of his stepbrother

---

[19] George Selwyn to Lord Carlisle, 28 October [1775], Hist. Mss. Comm., *15th Report, App., Part VI,* 300.
[20] King to North, 3 November 1775, *Corres. of George III* (Fortescue, ed.), III, 276.
[21] Same to Same, 6 November 1775, *ibid.,* 277.
[22] Same to Same, 7 November 1775, *ibid.,* 278-9.
[23] North to King, 7 November 1775, *ibid.,* 279.

in the multi-factional ministry had not diminished during the three years of his secretaryship. Rather, it had increased as Weymouth and his friends, the Bedfordites, had become more menacing. But there was an additional complication. North, anticipating Dartmouth's compliance, had already approached Germain. Offering the American Department to a successor, before Dartmouth had resigned, proved to be highly embarrassing for North. He confessed that he was "greatly perplexed how to extricate himself from present difficulty."[24]

If North expected Dartmouth to solve this problem for him by accepting the office of Groom of the Stole, he was mistaken. Dartmouth remained firm in his decision to refuse that office, regardless of the King's exasperation. Somewhat later, on November 7th, North found what he believed to be the perfect solution. He proposed to pension off Lord Rochford, a move which would open the Southern Department for either Dartmouth or Weymouth and leave the Privy Seal for the other.[25] This "solution" created a new problem for Dartmouth, who asked for time to think it over. The next day, John Robinson, North's principal political aide, urged Dartmouth to accept the seals of one of the older secretaries, "and so relieve Lord North of much anxiety."[26] There was no intention of removing Dartmouth to a position of obscurity. The original proposal to invest him with the groomship had included a seat in the cabinet. Now, according to this new expedient, Dartmouth would become Secretary of State in one of the two older departments, traditionally more important than the American Department. The only outstanding question was whether he would occupy Rochford's place or whether Suffolk would advance to the Southern Department, leaving a vacancy in the Northern Secretaryship for Dartmouth. In either case, this would mean a decided promotion, with additional responsibilities.

This solution also failed, because neither Lord would abandon his claim for the Privy Seal. Dartmouth, in fact, was so determined, that he decided to remain in the Colonial Office rather than accept any other post, even the older secretaryship. North reported these wholly unexpected developments to the King on November 8th: "Lord Dartmouth expresses a great dislike to the office of secretary of state, as he did to the other arrangement. Indeed, Lord Dartmouth wishes either to have the Privy Seal or to stay where he is [and] he will never be persuaded to accept any other office."[27] Dartmouth's de-

---

24 From North, 7 November 1775, Dartmouth Manuscripts, 1587.

25 From North, 7 November 1775, *ibid.*, 1588. North to King, 7 November 1775, *Corres. of George III*, III, 279-80.

26 From John Robinson, 8 November 1775, Dartmouth Manuscripts, 1590.

27 North to King, 8 November 1775, *Corres. of George III*, III, 282.

termination is all the more remarkable, considering that he already knew of Germain's agreement to succeed him in the American Department. In retaining the Colonial Office, he was causing North acute embarrassment, but his reply to Robinson made his own feelings on the subject quite clear: "If I take the seals that are offered me, I shall render myself ten times more miserable than I am."[28] Dartmouth could be very amiable and complaisant, but in this instance he remarked that Weymouth might be equally accommodating and withdraw his claim to the Privy Seal. While appreciating his stepbrother's anxiety, Dartmouth also faced a dilemma which he described as "my dread of a situation in which I foresee no satisfaction to myself on the one hand, and my love for Lord North on the other." The possibility of simply resigning had also occurred to Dartmouth, for he confided to Robinson: "I would with all my heart go quite out of employment, but that would look unkind to him [North]." Under these circumstances, he regarded his request for the Privy Seal as both reasonable and modest. If anyone were to give way, it should be Weymouth.

Robinson replied that North had no desire to press upon Dartmouth an office which would make him miserable, but would attempt instead to urge Weymouth to accept the secretary's seals. If all went well, Robinson assured Dartmouth on November 9th, he could have the Privy Seal that same day.[29] Although this message was intended to encourage, it seems to have increased Dartmouth's agitation. He replied: "The suspense in which I have been since I received your note is a state of no small agony. Relieve me if you can."[30] But first it was necessary to persuade the King to accept the final arrangements. North described his stepbrother's problem in the best possible light, reporting that Dartmouth thought "it not creditable to quit the seals of the American Department at this time, and that he is rather sorry he ever made the proposal, but having applied for the Privy Seal, he will certainly abide by his first request."[31] North said nothing about Dartmouth's misery in office. He wished to impress the King with the necessity of concurring in the proposed changes, because "it might personally hurt Lord North's credit extremely, if Lord Dartmouth were to resign, even though he supports administration, as he would do in that case, with utmost zeal and cordiality." The King, at that moment, was very annoyed with his Colonial Secretary's determination: "Lord Dartmouth I cannot say has been in the

---

[28] To John Robinson, 8 November 1775, Hist. Mss. Comm., *10th Report, Appendix VI (Abergavenny Mss.)*, 12.

[29] From John Robinson, 9 November 1775, Dartmouth Manuscripts, 1593.

[30] To John Robinson, 9 November 1775, *Abergavenny Mss.*, 12.

[31] North to King, 9 November 1775, *Corres. of George III*, III, 283-4.

least accommodating . . . this is carrying obstinacy greatly too far . . . he cannot continue so obdurate."[32]

In the end, however, the royal wrath subsided and Weymouth came around to a more accommodating position. North informed his stepbrother of this happy turn of events and Robinson gave him the requested relief with word that the Privy Seal was at last ready for delivery.[33] On November 10th, then, the exchange of seals, which Dartmouth had initiated, took place. The ministerial crisis was solved with apparent satisfaction to all parties. The King retained Lord North; North retained Dartmouth's support; Dartmouth obtained an honorable, though less taxing post in the cabinet. Simultaneously, the Bedfords were pleased by the appointment of one of their number to the important position of Secretary of State for the Southern Department. Even Lord Suffolk, the other Secretary, was content, because he was counting upon the new American Secretary, Lord George Germain, to assist him in undermining Lord North.[34]

---

[32] King to North, 9 November 1775, *ibid.*, 282-3.

[33] From North, 9 November 1775, Dartmouth Manuscripts, 1595. From Robinson, *ibid.*, 1596.

[34] William Knox, "Memoranda of November 1775," Hist. Mss. Comm., *Knox Mss.*, 256.

Chapter XVIII

THIS UNHAPPY EMPIRE

ARTMOUTH remained a member of the government after the delivery of the Privy Seal on November 10th, but the change in the colonial secretaryship caused great alarm and suspicion among the friends of America. Lord George Germain's aggressive opinions were well known. His appointment suggested that the ministry had abandoned all hope of conciliation and were now determined upon a policy of complete coercion and unconditional submission.[1] There was considerable speculation about the reason for Dartmouth's transfer from an active to an honorary office. All the evidence points to his own initiative and request, as the motivating factor in this exchange of ministries, but members of the opposition suspected some dark design behind the new arrangement. It became necessary for Dartmouth to justify his position and to explain the apparent inconsistencies in his conduct.

Only five days after Dartmouth received the Privy Seal, his predecessor, the Duke of Grafton, challenged him in the House of Lords. The Duke made a formal motion designed to learn how many troops had been engaged in America before the outbreak of hostilities. The Earl opposed this move with the reasonable argument that "when it could be no longer doubted that we were in an actual state of war," it would have been highly improper to disclose precise information regarding the troops.[2] This was the first time Dartmouth had revealed in public that he appreciated the situation in North America in all its seriousness. It was no longer a matter of a rebellion staged by a small group in three or four colonies. An "actual state of war" required a different approach, involving stronger measures and a high degree of cabinet unity in the face of the enemy. The change in his opinion must have occurred sometime previous to its public revelation. Possibly, it coincided with his decision to leave the American Department. While the recognition of an actual state of war would naturally prompt his retirement from active duty, it would at the same time inhibit him from resigning completely. It was now a matter of loyalty not only to Lord North but also to the King's government. Dartmouth could not leave the administration in this time of crisis,

---

[1] Guttridge, *Whiggism*, 84-5. J. Steven Watson, *The Reign of George III, 1760-1815* (*Oxford History of England*, Vol. XII), 203.

[2] Dartmouth's speech, 15 November 1775, *Parl. Hist.*, XVIII, 945-6.

he could only sigh with relief that he had been able to escape to a position of less responsibility.

In March, 1776, he was forced to defend himself and the government. When Grafton made a motion for conciliation, he accused the ministry of deserting the policy announced in the King's speech to Parliament, in North's resolution and in Dartmouth's own declaration that the administration intended only to restore allegiance. The Duke interpreted Germain's attitude and policies as an indication that "the new doctrine of unconditional submission" had replaced the older concept of conciliating differences. As final proof, Grafton cited Dartmouth's resignation, alleging that Dartmouth "was not thought so proper a person to carry the designs of government into execution. . . ." Dartmouth had often assured the House that "no intention was entertained by administration of 'subduing America.' "[3] The new Colonial Secretary, Grafton maintained, was deliberately contradicting his predecessor.

Grafton's motion was highly impractical. He would have repealed the coercive acts and issued a proclamation inviting the colonies to petition for the redress of grievances. Past experience with the fate of petitions would have precluded any colony from responding to this belated suggestion.[4] The significance of this debate, however, lies in Dartmouth's reply. His speeches in Parliament were rare, but this one reveals much about Dartmouth's attitude toward both his term of office and his resignation. While Secretary of State for the Colonies, Dartmouth replied, he had been willing "to suppose that the disorders in the country were local, and had chiefly pervaded the hearts of an inconsiderable number of men, who were only formidable, because they possessed the power of factious delusion and imposition." This view of colonial opposition was quite reasonable, especially for the early months of Dartmouth's tenure and considering the general tenor of his official correspondence. It reveals, however, that he underestimated the development of unity and determination, as described in numerous unofficial communications. Dartmouth further conceded, "I all along expected that the body of the people, when they came to view the consequences attentively, would soon perceive the danger in which they were precipitating themselves, and return to their duty. Urged by those expectations, I was anxious to treat them with tenderness and even to give way to their prejudices, so far as it could be done with safety." An American might have interrupted Dartmouth at this point to insist that his concessions had always been minor ones, while nothing was accomplished in the way of accommodating major differences. Dartmouth, however, continued by posing a rhetorical question: What have been the conse-

---

[3] Grafton's speech, 14 March 1776, *ibid.*, 1247-1249.

[4] Turberville, *House of Lords,* 363.

quences of these tender feelings? "They have treated those marks of favor as so many indications of national imbecility . . . backwardness and want of ability to assert our rights."[5]

After this condensation of his colonial policy, Dartmouth gave Grafton a specific answer to his accusations of inconsistency. He denied that there had been any fundamental change in policy since he had last assured the House that conciliation was the true goal of the administration. He had retained a post in the cabinet because of this conviction. He continued to believe that the colonies should recognize the supremacy of Parliament, re-affirming the principle of the Declaratory Act. The Bostonians, however, had resorted to violence, so force was necessary to persuade the colonies to accept this principle. In line with this reasoning, Dartmouth strongly opposed Grafton's motion. It had become too late for tenderness and peaceful reconciliation. Only firm measures would hold the colonies in allegiance. Nevertheless, Dartmouth continued to believe that coercion might serve the cause of conciliation. Troops must be sent to North America in order to "awe the colonies into submission," but this should not "preclude an accommodation." It was not intended to conquer America, as Grafton had maintained, but what Dartmouth termed the "true subordination and constitutional relation" between mother country and daughter colonies must be restored. Dartmouth insisted that there was a difference between requiring unconditional submission and "a resolution on our part not to cease hostilities till America submits so far as to acknowledge the supreme authority of [Parliament]."[6]

The unprejudiced mind may find it difficult to reconcile the militant policy of Germain with the pacific protestations of Dartmouth. But his opposition to Grafton's motion was consistent with his position during the final month as Colonial Secretary. In October, 1775, he had declared, "it was never supposed, if America united, that to reduce them would be the work of one summer; the measures of the last session were directed to the protection of Massachusetts Bay entirely; as such, they had been wisely planned, and must have been successful, if a variety of events, impossible to be foreseen or provided against, had not united to defeat them; such, in particular, was the change of sentiments in the people of New York, and the unexpected unanimity and unforeseen measures adopted by the continental congress."[7] The judgment of history favors Grafton's side in

---

[5] Debate on Grafton's motion, 14 March 1776, *Parl. Hist.*, XVIII, 1254. Jack P. Greene, "Bridge to Revolution: The Wilkes Fund Controversy in South Carolina, 1769-1775," *Journal of Southern History*, XXIX (February 1963), 26, points out Dartmouth's willingness to omit one controversial item from Governor Lord William Campbell's instructions.

[6] Debate on Grafton's motion, 14 March 1776, *Parl. Hist.*, XVIII, 1254.

[7] Debate on the address of thanks, 26 October 1775, *ibid.*, 718-19.

this particular argument, but he was mistaken in his charge that Dartmouth had been removed contrary to his own wishes. Furthermore, Dartmouth was correct in maintaining that he could still work for conciliation, in spite of Germain's appointment. Unfortunately, all his new efforts to arbitrate colonial differences also proved unsuccessful.

Dartmouth's role in the North government until its fall in 1782 consisted largely of passive support. As Lord Privy Seal, he participated in very few cabinet meetings. Probably the most important policy decision which he influenced concerned the terms of the peace commission given the brothers Howe in 1776. Governor Franklin of New Jersey and other officials had previously suggested that special agents be sent to discuss grievances with the Continental Congress.[8] Lord Howe, in his secret negotiations with Benjamin Franklin in 1775, had included a similar suggestion in his program for reconciliation. None of these plans, however, was implemented before 1776, when it was already too late. The new Colonial Secretary, who apparently enjoyed the waging of war far more than Dartmouth, disapproved of the idea of sending peace commissioners. Hoping to nullify their efforts at the start, Germain insisted that the colonies must acknowledge the supremacy of Parliament as a primary basis for negotiations.[9] North agreed that the colonies must ultimately recognize Parliament's supremacy, but he objected to Germain's proposal, making it a necessary preliminary to discussion. Dartmouth felt even stronger about this restriction to be placed upon the brothers Howe. He threatened to resign and to "speak out" against Germain's plan.[10] This was no idle threat on Dartmouth's part. North also considered resigning over this issue.[11] A major cabinet crisis developed when Germain countered with a similar threat. He preferred to reduce the colonies with the forces which he had collected before treating with them. Moreover, he feared that once peace had been restored, neither Parliament nor the ministry would have the will to renew the conflict for the sake of a formal declaration of legislative supremacy.

Before anyone resigned, however, the crisis was settled by a compromise. After consulting Lord Mansfield about the legal technicalities involved, North decided that the commissioners should not demand colonial submission as a prerequisite to negotiations (which satisfied Dartmouth), but instead they should wait for each colony to ask for pardon (which satisfied Germain). In no case would the King's peace be restored without an acknowledgment of

---

8 From William Franklin, 28 June 1774, *New Jersey Archives,* X, 464-5.

9 G. H. Guttridge, "Lord George Germain in Office, 1775-82," *A.H.R.,* XXXIII (October, 1927), 27. Valentine, *Germain,* 306 *et seq.*

10 "Memoranda of November 1775," *Knox Mss.,* 259.

11 *Ibid.* See also, Brown, *Empire or Independence,* 84-5.

parliamentary supremacy, although it was possible that further instructions might be issued to the commissioners on this point.[12] Lord Howe and his brother took with them a copy of the information which Dartmouth had requested all the governors to supply in 1773,[13] but they had little success in their commission. Neither the Olive Branch nor the rod of chastisement which they carried restored peace to the empire. Dartmouth's determination in opposing Germain at this time, however, indicates that he still fondly believed that there was hope for a peaceful accommodation in 1776. As time proved him mistaken, he retired further from active politics. Private life on his Staffordshire estate appealed to him more than cabinet discussions about the war in America. There were rumors to the effect that some higher post than Lord Privy Seal had been offered to him. In October, 1776, for example, it had been possible that Dartmouth would become Lord Lieutenant of Ireland. His retiring temperament led him to reject this and all similar offers of advancement, saying that he feared they were "certain to be productive of disgrace and misery to himself and to the public."[14]

During the years when he held the Privy Seal, Dartmouth continued to receive information and reports about American affairs. He had no responsibility for policy decisions, except as one member of a cabinet dominated by Lord George Germain. His opinions of the matters which came to his attention went unrecorded. Still, the fact that he bothered to retain so many private and official papers in his personal collection indicates a continuing interest in colonial problems. In most cases, he was powerless to act; he could only follow with frustration and regret the course of events in the American Revolution. A few Loyalists addressed their petitions to him. Whenever possible, Dartmouth used his influence with his stepbrother to secure a measure of relief for them.[15] The British Treasury was not rich enough to give the Loyalists everything they asked and pay for a war as well. North and Dartmouth, however, did their best.

The new Lord Privy Seal had to assist a number of former dependents. Germain "accepted the resignations" of Undersecretary Pownall and of Ambrose Serle, who had also worked in the American Department.[16] Pownall had already obtained a seat in the House

---

[12] *Knox Mss.*, 259-60. Brown, *Empire or Independence*, 85-6. Hist. Mss. Comm., *6th Report*, 399-404 contains a calendar of Sir Henry Strachey's papers, including instructions to the Howe Commission, of which Strachey was secretary.

[13] Strachey Papers, W. L. Clements Library.

[14] To John Robinson, 8 October 1775, *Abergavenny Mss.*, 15.

[15] From Thomas Danforth, 25 August 1778, Dartmouth Manuscripts, 1875. From the same, August 1778, *ibid.*, 1876. From Samuel Hopkins, 24 July 1780, *ibid.*, 1909. From North, 14 June 1781, *ibid.*, 1915.

[16] From Germain, 23 January 1776, *ibid.*, 1654.

of Commons, but through Dartmouth's influence he was appointed one of the Commissioners of the Excise in 1776. In gratitude, he thanked Dartmouth for this "cup of comfort."[17] Serle secured the post of Clerk of the Reports and accompanied the army to America. From New York and Philadelphia, he sent long and often misleading letters to Dartmouth. Quite unwittingly, he encouraged his patron to hope for an early and successful end to the conflict.

In July, 1776, Serle wrote an enthusiastic letter from a ship in New York harbor. The troops with whom he had crossed the Atlantic were in excellent health and anxious to attack the enemy. Burgoyne was expected in the near future and the enemy was in a state of panic.[18] Serle's next report from New York was even more encouraging. The rebels had destroyed their own mortars. Their army was suffering from small pox and everyone was distressed by the lack of imported goods, especially clothing.[19] A disturbing note crept into Serle's letter, when he mentioned the failure of Sir Peter Parker's expedition to Charles Town, South Carolina. Dartmouth realized the extent of this disaster when William Knox, who was still undersecretary in the American Department, sent him a full report.[20]

During his last year as Secretary of State, Dartmouth had received a number of secret dispatches from Alexander Innes, the private secretary of the Governor of South Carolina. Like so many royal officials, Innes had emphasized the division of opinion in Charles Town. He had asserted that the loyal element was large, but intimidated. He declared if the ministry sent a strong force to the colony, the "friends of government" would stand firm against the "mob." Dartmouth showed at least one of these reports to the King, who apparently liked the idea. In time, the expedition to Charles Town was mounted, with disastrous results. Those landing in Carolina on Long Island foundered in the tide-swept inlet separating it from Sullivan's Island. The ships assigned to bombard Fort Sullivan inflicted slight damage, but suffered 201 casualties. Admiral Parker and the exiled governor, Lord William Campbell, were slightly wounded, and one of the ships, the *Actaeon,* ran aground and was burned by her crew to prevent the capture of her twenty-eight guns.[21]

Serle refused to be discouraged by this defeat. He told Dartmouth that the Hessians had arrived in New York, which was completely in British possession. The members of the Continental Congress were quarreling with each other and issuing paper money of little value. The Pennsylvania Assembly was quarreling with the Provincial Con-

---

[17] From John Pownall, 16 January 1776, *ibid.,* 1653.
[18] From Ambrose Serle, 25 July 1776, *ibid.,* 1694.
[19] From same, 12 August 1776, *ibid.,* 1697.
[20] From Knox, 22 August 1776, *ibid.,* 1701.
[21] "Précis" enclosed in Knox's letter, *ibid.*

vention, while General Carleton was enjoying great success on Lake Champlain. All was going well in November, 1776, and one more campaign would teach the Americans a lesson in obedience.[22] The next few months appeared to justify Serle's optimism. Early in the following year, he reported that rebels were coming into New York "by hundreds" and that he was kept very busy, making out pardons for them.[23] The consensus at New York was that the rebellion was nearly crushed. Serle was already looking forward to Howe's expedition to Philadelphia.

In the meantime, Dartmouth was familiar with the broad outline of the arrangements for the coming campaign. He probably attended cabinet meetings in January and February, 1777, when Germain secured his colleagues' consent for his program. On January 10th, the cabinet agreed to add 4,000 troops to Howe's army, while near the end of February, they accepted Germain's nomination of General Burgoyne to lead the invasion from Canada.[24] Dartmouth had no knowledge of the devious method which Germain would employ to implement this general plan.[25] No one foresaw the disaster which would result from the confusion and mutual misunderstanding of the Secretary's correspondence with his generals in America.

Dartmouth continued to receive encouraging reports from his friends in the colonies. Serle introduced Joseph Galloway—the Loyalist—to his patron, by trans-Atlantic post.[26] Galloway assured Dartmouth that many Americans were already sick of the rebellion and, in the middle colonies especially, resistance was waning.[27] In their subsequent correspondence, Galloway discussed his proposals for accommodating the differences between Britain and her wayward colonies. A certain natural sympathy developed between the Pennsylvanian and the evangelical Earl. Dartmouth gracefully used his influence to obtain an appointment for Galloway as superintendent of civil affairs in Philadelphia. In return, Galloway supplied Dartmouth with various reports and accounts of local developments.[28]

While Serle and Galloway contributed to Dartmouth's hope for an early and successful conclusion to the war, another correspondent sent the Earl news from the North. Colonel Philip Skene kept Dartmouth informed of the progress of Burgoyne's army. In spite of the difficulties encountered en route, Skene assured him that the army

---

[22] From Serle, 5 & 25 September 1776, 7 November 1776, *ibid.*, 1703, 1708 & 1709.

[23] From same, 1 January 1777, *ibid.*, 1727.

[24] Cabinet Minutes, 10 January & 25 February 1777, *ibid.*, 1729 & 1738.

[25] Valentine, *Germain*, chap. XVI.

[26] From Serle, 25 March 1777, Dartmouth Manuscripts, 1743.

[27] From Galloway, 3 December 1777, *ibid.*, 1807.

[28] From same, 23 January 1778, *ibid.*, 1829, with nine enclosures.

From a copy of an original attributed to Sir Joshua Reynolds

Lord Dartmouth

tion had only a few more years of life. When the end eventually came in 1782,[40] Dartmouth willingly surrendered the Privy Seal. The King, who had long since forgiven him for his obstinacy in 1775, sent him a touching little note, expressing general regret that North and his colleagues must resign. George III concluded his affectionate farewell by saying that he wished Dartmouth to know how very near he would "always be to my heart, and that I have ever esteemed him since I have thoroughly known him in another light than any of his companions in the Ministry."[41] Although Dartmouth's views on religion were the source of ridicule on the part of some of his contemporaries, George III respected his evangelicalism. The retiring Lord Privy Seal could appreciate the pious invocation in this same letter: "What days has it pleased the Almighty to place me in when Lord Dartmouth can be a man to be removed but at his own request, but I cannot complain, I adore the will of Providence and will ever resign obediently to His will. My heart is too full to add more."

When the Fox-North ministry was formed in 1783, Dartmouth accepted the honorable post of Lord Steward, but this experience added nothing to his political biography beyond additional proof of his loyalty to his stepbrother. It was North's sad fate to end his days in total blindness.

But "good Lord" Dartmouth had a more comfortable old age, surrounded by a large and devoted family. Not even death in 1801 ended the Earl's association with America. In 1826, the authorities of Dartmouth College became agitated over the disappearance of a portrait of their benefactor. When this painting by John Singleton Copley could not be found, they applied to the then Earl of Dartmouth for another portrait. The second Earl's grandson replied that he would send the college a copy of the only canvas he possessed. The original, probably painted by Sir Joshua Reynolds, was copied by a Mr. Reynolds, and dispatched to America in 1829. By coincidence, it happened to arrive in the port of New York just before the celebration of Independence Day. At the request of the City Fathers, Dartmouth's portrait was displayed in the Hall of Justice, beside those of Washington, Franklin and other important citizens.[42] His reputation as a friend of America survived the years of war; half a century after his administration, the good citizens of New York were paying their respects to him on the Fourth of July. Did any one present appreciate the irony of the situation?

---

[40] I. R. Christie, *The End of North's Ministry, 1780-1782* (London, 1958), 370-2.

[41] From the King, 27 March 1872, Hist. Mss. Comm., *11th Report, App. Part V*, 442.

[42] William Wood to 4th Earl of Dartmouth, 4 & 6 July 1826, Dartmouth Manuscripts, 1969.

Chapter XIX

CONCLUSIONS

THE LIFE and political career of the second Earl of Dartmouth reveal a number of interesting facets of Eighteenth-Century history: the importance of family connection, the nature of the various offices which he held, his own view of the imperial constitution. All these factors impinge upon a broader sphere of historical interpretation, involving the origins of the American Revolution. Although Dartmouth cannot claim a position in the front rank of British statesmen, he was important. He occupied a high office at an extremely critical period of history. His family connections, rather than considerations of policy, had propelled him into the American Department. What he did and thought there are of significance in the larger story of the revolt of thirteen of the colonies.

Most modern historians of the period content themselves with listing his name in the index, either as "Dartmouth, second Earl of," or "Legge, William, etc.", followed by three or four page references. Turning to these pages one finds the traditional adjectives repeated in several variations: "good," "amiable," "well-intentioned," "pious," "ineffectual," and so on. There is more to the story, however, than this string of adjectives would imply. During his life, the "good Lord Dartmouth" was almost universally admired. His wide circle of friends expressed great affection and esteem in their letters to each other. His piety and philanthropy earned him the confidence of the American colonists. His religious convictions were more in accord with those of the King than Lord Bute realized, when rejecting Dartmouth as a Gentleman of the Bedchamber. He stood at the opposite end of the spectrum from those noble members of the Hell-Fire Club who practiced obscenity. In fact, if virtue alone were an acceptable substitute for political wisdom, the American Revolution might never have begun. But Dartmouth's most admirable qualities were non-political in nature. He developed from a completely inexperienced administrator in 1765 into a minister who was at least competent within his own office, but he never demonstrated outstanding efficiency or constructive drive.

While personality factors are undoubtedly significant, it is too easy a solution to dismiss Dartmouth's administration as "weak" and "amiable" but "ineffectual." Each of the offices which he held suffered from certain constitutional handicaps, which might well have frustrated a more determined man with a constructive policy.

[192]

The Board of Trade was concerned with economic problems in general, not just colonial affairs. It had already lost the important power of appointing colonial officials before Dartmouth became its president, and it never acquired the responsibility for the direction of colonial policy which Dartmouth desired in 1766. In this office, Dartmouth could only review the information available and draft reports for other ministers to accept or reject. The Board was neither a policy-formulating nor an executive body. By the time Dartmouth acquired secretarial seals in 1772, the imperial connection had been considerably weakened. The enactment of Townshend's duties and the subsequent repeal of all but one of them had convinced some colonists that their program for resistance would always succeed. The vacillations of British politics and policies had played into the "Patriots'" hands. Hillsborough's "firmness" had not persuaded them that the government might someday draw a line, beyond which they could not safely go.

Meanwhile, the belated establishment of the office of Secretary of State for the Colonies aroused political jealousy and constitutional doubts. Dartmouth should have been able to promote a conciliatory policy. North's dependence upon him, however, precluded any dramatic departures from past policy, for they might have disturbed the equilibrium of the Cabinet. The older Secretaries of State were not only jealous of the third secretaryship, as the quarrel over troop transfers demonstrates, but were also working for the eventual overthrow of Lord North. In this precarious situation, Dartmouth found that he must reckon with opposition on two fronts: the colonial radicals who denounced all imperial taxation and the parliamentary firebrands, who demanded even more stringent measures against the colonies. It is doubtful whether a stronger personality could have accomplished more than Dartmouth in these trying circumstances.

The role of the two undersecretaries of the American Department, John Pownall and William Knox, raises an interesting question. To what extent was the policy of the North Administration formulated by the second-in-command, or civil servant, in the absence of a strong personality in the ministerial office? Dartmouth could have nominated his own assistants, but he preferred to retain the services of Hillsborough's. This decision gave more continuity to the routine business of the newly-created department, but it lends color to the suspicion that Pownall and Knox prevailed upon Dartmouth to adopt their policy as his own. In the early months of Dartmouth's secretaryship, Pownall frequently advised his superior upon both minor appointments and major policy decisions. Dartmouth did not always accept his undersecretary's advice as his colleagues in the Cabinet were more likely to influence his policy than the subordinates in the American Department. Both Pownall and Knox complained of their lack of influence in colonial business. This development often gave the advocates of "firmness" a greater voice in the formulation of colonial policy, but to fix the responsibility upon the undersecretaries is unrealistic. One or the other undersecretary drafted the dispatches which Dartmouth signed, but he would never have signed a communication which violated his own principles. It is possible, however, that he might have expressed that policy in softer words. Comparison of various drafts in the Dartmouth collection reveals that he often edited his documents, searching for just the right words. Finally, if one regarded it as ominous that Pownall and Knox remained in office, one has only to contrast the dispatches signed by Hillsborough with those sent over Dartmouth's signature. The first Colonial Secretary used language which was much more offensive to Americans. If Dartmouth's dispatches, particularly the later ones, contain phrases which reflect "firmness" it must be accepted that the policy which they implemented was his own, not his undersecretaries'.

Did Dartmouth abandon his original hope for conciliation when he adopted the coercive policy? Was it inconsistent for him to supervise the initial military movements at the opening of the war for independence? Throughout the period of the North Administration, Dartmouth remained faithful to the principle of the Declaratory Act, an Act which he had helped to pass as a member of the Rockingham government in 1766. His attitude today may seem somewhat doctrinaire in the political environment of the 1770's, but at least he was devoid of hypocrisy. To regard him as hypocritical is to misunderstand both his reputation for conciliation and his view of the constitution. Dartmouth never regarded the Stamp Act as unconstitutional, although those who identified him with its repeal often overlooked this point. To say that the man who helped repeal the Stamp Tax later implemented the Coercive Acts, may have appeared to prove that he prostituted his character, as Walpole said. To state the proposition more correctly, it should be said that the man who regarded the Stamp Act as inopportune took his stand upon the Declaratory Act and supported the coercive policy of 1774. But this question of Dartmouth's attitude toward the constitution of the First Brtish Empire raises far broader issues involving the origins of the American Revolution.

There were ample reasons for the policy which Dartmouth pursued, however disastrously. Needless to say, the establishment of tyranny was not one of them. From his point of view, the best defense against tyranny (*i.e.,* the unlimited exercise of the royal prerogative, as in the case of Louis XIV's absolutism), was the doctrine of parliamentary supremacy. The Glorious Revolution of 1688, the basis of all Whiggism, had determined that no English King could be an absolute monarch, but that the King-in-Parliament was omnicompetent. There was no constitutional bar to changing a colonial charter by an Act of Parliament (*i.e.,* a bill which had secured the consent of both houses and the king). On the contrary to have recognized the equal competence of colonial legislatures would have established a revenue for the Crown beyond the control of the Parliament at Westminster. This would have led to a revival of the independence of the royal prerogative, to Toryism, and to the dissolution of the Empire! English and American constitutional concepts had grown so far apart that the opinions of Whigs on one side of the Atlantic were held by Tories on the other.

Dartmouth expressed his view of the constitution many times, in private letters, such as those sent to Joseph Reed, and in formal dispatches to the governors and generals in America. His ideas were not original, but they are significant, because they reflect the view shared by most British officials in the same period. It is easy to say that he was incorrect, or that American principles were superior to English concepts. The fact remains that the Secretary of State for the Colonies consistently entertained one particular view of the constitution. Dartmouth's opinion in this respect was very similar to Edmund Burke's, although the latter was a strong opponent of the North government. In his famous speech on the question of American taxation, Burke stated that he continued to support the principle of the Declaratory Act of 1766.[1] Like Dartmouth, Burke believed that the "Parliament of Great Britain sits at the head of her extensive empire . . . ;" that Parliament, not the Crown, should superintend "all the several inferior legislatures." Even while opposing the coercive policy, Burke admitted that it was "necessary to coerce the negligent, to restrain the violent, and to aid the weak and deficient, by the overruling plenitude of [Parliament's] power." To request contributions from the colonies, Burke argued, would be an admission of limitations on parliamentary supremacy, while these "powers must be boundless." Dartmouth would have agreed with all these sentiments, as well as with Burke's conclusion that this boundless power should be used only in emergencies. The principal difference between them in 1774 was whether the contemporary situation represented one of those emergencies. If Burke and his friends had been in power in the 1770's, they probably would have had no greater success in preserving the First British Empire. "Their ideas were no

---

[1] The speech on American taxation has been printed in many collections, for example, Burke's *Works* (Boston, 1871, Fourth Edition), II, 75-6. A convenient one-volume edition is: Ross J. S. Hoffman and Paul Levack, eds., *Burke's Politics* (New York, 1949). The phrases quoted above appear on pages 59 & 60 of the latter work. One indication of Dartmouth's continuing interest in his former political associate is the preservation among his papers of a newspaper clipping containing Burke's speech to his Bristol electors in 1774; Dartmouth Manuscripts, 981.

less hierarchical and authoritarian than those of George III and Lord North. . . ."[2]

In the years following Dartmouth's death, British statesmen and colonial officials found alternative solutions to conflicts between Britain and her colonies. But these alternatives depended upon fully developed responsible government and a concept of empire which did not exist in the Eighteenth-Century. George III's cabinet was not a model Victorian ministry: it lacked party solidarity and cohesion, it was supported by a coalition of parliamentary factions, while the King himself was more a "prime minister" than Lord North. Great Britain had to develop a system of cabinet responsibility first in the Nineteenth-Century, before it was possible for Nova Scotia and the other provinces of British North America to adopt similar solutions. None of the Thirteen Colonies was able to apply this solution, since it had not yet evolved.

Given these circumstances, it is possible to understand, if not agree with, Lord Dartmouth's position. A colony which failed to acknowledge the supremacy of the imperial Parliament was automatically independent. There was no middle-ground, in his opinion, in spite of the colonists' protests that they did not desire independence. Parliament provided certain benefits for North America: ships to suppress piracy and invasion, troops to control the Indians, bounties to enable planters of marginal crops, like indigo, to make a profit, and so forth. If the colonists were to enjoy these advantages, then they must acknowledge the controls and restrictions which were an essential and normal consequence. None of the colonial empires had yet experimented with completely free trade; mercantilism was the generally accepted policy.

While attempting to implement this policy for the empire as a whole, Dartmouth found himself in the political structure of Georgian England. Unlike some great lords, Dartmouth was not the patron of seats in the Commons. He had certain political obligations, connected with his social position in Staffordshire, but purely local politics was not his major interest. In each case where a question about his own political career arose, the importance of the family connection provided the most satisfactory explanation of his conduct. It was neither politics nor policy which drew Dartmouth into the Rockingham administration. The only policy which the Old Whigs had possessed in 1765 was to share the important offices of state and prevent the return of Lord Bute to power. Dartmouth was too inexperienced to have had a more specific policy, but not too young to have incurred some obligation to the Duke of Newcastle. According to the usages of the Eighteenth-Century, he regarded Newcastle as a

---

[2] Namier, *England in the Age of the American Revolution,* 44-45 (Second edition, page 39).

kind of "cousin." Family connection became the dominant factor in 1772, when he entered North's administration. Dartmouth's relationship with Rockingham became progressively cooler after 1770, while admiration for his stepbrother's ability grew. Unable to overcome his preference for the private life in 1771, he had declined North's first invitation and incurred the reprimand of his stepfather, Lord Guilford. After this family quarrel, it was virtually impossible for him to refuse a second invitation. Granted, he had acquired some reputation for colonial conciliation which may have made him more useful to his stepbrother's plan, but it was personal support which North needed. Hillsborough's resignation had threatened North's position as leader of a coalition government. Dartmouth's accession replaced that support, but to say that he was appointed *because* he favored conciliatory policy is to overlook the significance of the family connection.

The origins of the American Revolution will not be found in the tyranny of George III, nor in the materialistic motives of the colonists. Constitutional divergence provides the best key. The colonists and the mother country had developed to a point where constitutional theory and terminology no longer had the same meaning on both sides of the Atlantic. Liberty in England required the protection of Parliament, while in the colonies it required protection from Parliament. Whiggism in America included the recognition of increasing sovereignty of the colonial legislature, while British officials could only regard this doctrine as inimical to the principles of the Revolution of 1688, and therefore more akin to Toryism. Benjamin Franklin may have thought that the Crown was the common link between America and Britain, but Lord Dartmouth regarded Parliament as the essential bond. One may criticize him for failing to be ahead of his times, for failing to invent the modern concept of dominion status, for failing to foresee that the modern cabinet system would provide a solution to the problem; but one cannot doubt his sincerity and his consistency in advocating constitutional principles which he held. His view of the constitution was as incomprehensible to the colonists, as theirs was to him. The result of this divergence in constitutional theory was the War for Independence.[3]

---

[3] R. W. Van Alstyle, "Parliamentary Supremacy versus Independence: Notes and Documents," *Huntington Library Quarterly,* XXVI (May, 1963), 201-233, provides an analysis of British constitutional theories in the 1770's.

FINIS

BIBLIOGRAPHY

Part I: Source material for Lord Dartmouth's Life and career.

The recent *Guide to Manuscripts relating to America in Great Britain and Ireland* (B. R. Crick, M. Alman, *et al.*, editors, published for the British Association for American Studies by the Oxford University Press, 1961), provides a very extensive survey of the material. In many ways it supersedes the *Guides* compiled by Charles M. Andrews early in the present century. Where Andrews (his collaborator on one of the *Guides* was Frances G. Davenport) principally concerned himself with the Public Record Office and the British Museum, Crick and Alman have cast a wider net and included many other repositories and private collections. The student will still find Andrews' introductions valuable for information about the nature of the P.R.O. and B.M. collections, but Crick and Alman are unrivalled for completeness. In their otherwise commendable effort to include everything, Crick and Alman are occasionally misleading. This is particularly true in the case of their description of the Dartmouth Manuscripts (pp. 411-418), although anyone familiar with the collection of papers now in the William Salt Library, Stafford, would have no difficulty in recognizing the duplications and omissions.

When the editors describe the collection as "Letters unless otherwise stated," they are obscuring the fact that many of the items are public papers. Following the Eighteenth-Century custom, Lord Dartmouth carried a large number of reports and other official papers with him from his office to his home. The result is that one may find duplicate items in the private collection of Lord Dartmouth and among the public papers in the P. R. O. In some cases I have cited footnote references for both, but it seems an unnecessary duplication to do so in every instance. A scholar familiar with P. R. O. material, however, will recognize many of my quotations and citations from Dartmouth Manuscripts which are not letters.

Crick and Alman, in an effort to be as complete as possible, cite all the volumes of the Historical Manuscripts Commission's reports on Lord Dartmouth's manuscripts, including the *Second Report*. This report, published in 1871, is very cursory in nature and contains some inaccuracies, which Crick and Alman dutifully reproduce. For example, the "letters from Judith Reed at Philadelphia" (H.M.C. p. 12; Crick and Alman, p. 413) obviously refers to Joseph Reed's letters. All the items listed in the *Second Report* are calendared in greater detail in subsequent reports, so the student who turns to this 1871 report will only duplicate his effort.

In what is intended as a helpful and timely footnote, Crick and Alman tell the reader that "two supplementary N.R.A. Reports, both 5197," contain recently discovered Dartmouth papers (p. 412, note 2). An examination of a mircofilm, kindly supplied by the Registrar of the National Registry of Archives in London, reveals that these two reports ("both 5197," whatever that may mean) are something less than sensational. First of all, they contain a large number of papers relating to earls of Dartmouth other than the second Earl. Those few items which concerned the second Earl are largely estate records and private papers. While these manuscripts might provide interesting reading for the social or economic historian, they cannot throw any more light upon the political career of the "Good" Lord Dartmouth than the papers I have already consulted.

When I examined the Dartmouth Manuscripts, the collection was located in the residence of the seventh Earl of Dartmouth, Patshull House, near Wolverhampton. In fact, some early works cite these manuscripts as "Patshull Papers," although this is doubly misleading, for they have little to do with the estate and are no longer located there. They are now in the William Salt Library, Stafford, where they remain the property of the present Earl, but in the care of the Librarian. Reference to these papers presents a number of problems, owing to the various dates when they were discovered, catalogued and subdivided. In 1887 the Historical Manuscripts Commission issued a calendar or report on the manuscripts in the possession of the then Earl of Dartmouth. Only a few of the items in this *Eleventh Report, Appendix, Part V,* however, concern the second Earl. Later (1895), a *Fourteenth Report, Appendix, Part X,* appeared with the subtitle, "The Manuscripts of the Earl of Dartmouth, Volume II, American Papers." The bulk of the items in this calendar directly concern the second Earl, many of them being important public documents of the reign of George III. A third and final volume was issued by the Historical Manuscripts Commission in 1896, the *Fifteenth Report, Appendix, Part I.* Some of the items in this calendar relate to the second Earl, although most of them concern his ancestors, his mother and his sons.

Two difficulties arise from this tri-partite catalogue. The first problem stems from the fact that the manuscripts themselves follow the order prescribed by the three different calendars. Thus the papers of the second Earl are in three distinct series. In fact, related documents for the year 1775, to take one example, will be found in widely separated boxes of papers. The William Salt Library, which understandably uses its own system of cataloguing, has in some ways compounded the difficulty. The papers listed in the *11th Report* of the Historical Manuscripts Commission are designated D.1778/I, with a special subdivision for those belonging to the second Earl, D.1778/I/ii. The papers calendared in the *14th Report* are designated D.1778/II by the Salt Library. In citing these manuscripts in the preceding pages, I have not used this system of reference, primarily because it did not yet exist at the time I consulted the manuscripts at Patshull House. Perhaps, I should apologize in advance for any confusion which the footnotes may cause scholars, but I feel confident that the date, together with other pertinent information supplied in the footnotes, will enable the researcher to identify the reference in both the appropriate calendar published by the Historical Manuscripts Commission and the original document. Should all methods of self-help fail, the very obliging staff of the William Salt Library will doubtless turn up the desired manuscript.

The second difficulty is the absence from the manuscripts collection of several items listed in the various *Reports*. A few items are irretrievably lost, but a number of missing manuscripts will be found in other collections. Thus, the correspondence between Lord Dartmouth and Eleazer Wheelock, concerning the Indian School, now rests in the Dartmouth College Library. This loss of these documents from the collection is only relatively regrettable, for there are typewritten copies in the appropriate boxes of the Dartmouth collection. A more serious problem concerns the Canadian papers. B. F. Stevens noted in his introduction to the *14th Report* that he invited Douglas Brymner, the Archivist of Canada, to assist him in calendaring the papers relating to British North America. Dr. Brymner subsequently obtained permission to extract from the bulk of the collection all those items concerning North American colonies which remained part of the British Empire. The result of this further subdivision of the collection can be seen in the Public Archives of Canada, Ottawa, where there are fourteen large volumes of Dartmouth manuscripts. Most of the Canadian items are listed in a separate section of the *14th Report* (pages 545-606), but Dr. Brymner's diligence in obtaining material for his government's archives was not limited to that section. Dartmouth's correspondence with Governor Legge of Nova Scotia, Governor Carleton of Quebec, and with other officials and private residents of present-day Canada, will be found in Ottawa, although many of these items appear in the correct chronological order in the calendar. The student should be cautioned, then, that having located a document in one of the three volumes of the Historical Manuscripts Commission's *Reports* on the Dartmouth Manuscripts, he may find the actual document in Stafford, in Ottawa, in Hanover, New Hampshire, or—alas—not at all! Unfortunately, it is essential in many cases to refer to the original document, since there are occasional inadequacies and errors in the calendars themselves. (For one highly misleading error, see Chapter VI, note 41.)

In addition to the calendars of papers belonging to Lord Dartmouth (11th., 14th., & 15th. *Reports*), the Historical Manuscripts Commission has published reports of other collections in which letters from, to, or about the second Earl of Dartmouth appear. For example, the *6th Report* includes a series of letters written by Governor Tryon from New York to Lord Dartmouth (pp. 399 *et seq.*), while the *13th Report* reproduces the contents of several letters from King George III (499-502). In order to read the complete series of royal letters, one must correlate this group with those calendared in the *11th Report,* pp. 437 *et seq.* The King sent various personal and political messages to Lord Dartmouth during the decade beginning in 1773, but the chronological sequence was disturbed in the following century. Those letters which were unavailable in 1887 (*11th Report*) appeared a few years later in time for the *13th Report.* Photostats, supplied by the Salt Library, substantiate the accuracy of the calendars in all the more important instances.

If all the second Earl of Dartmouth's private papers were in one place, carefully arranged in chronological order, it would be of great assistance to the student of his career. But it would not be sufficient to tell us all we need to know about his life and times. The extensive collection of Dartmouth Manuscripts (there are 2,000 items in the "American Papers" alone) must be supplemented by reference to several other collections, public and private, which are scattered even more widely. The Public Record Office in London is, of course, a vast storehouse of official papers. It would be difficult to know where to begin amidst this *embarras de richesses,* if it were not for Charles M. Andrews' *Guide to the Materials for American History, to 1783, in the Public Record Office of Great Britain* (Washington, 1912 & 1914, 2 vols.). Among the many manuscripts in the P.R.O., the following were the most informative of Dartmouth's official career:

Colonial Office 5/27: Orders in Council, 1771-1772;
CO 5/28:   Orders in Council, 1773;
CO 5/145: Correspondence with the Treasury, 1772-1774;
CO 5/146: Correspondence with the Treasury, 1775;
CO 5/138: Correspondence with other Secretaries of State, 1775 (Part I) [*sic*] & 1772-4 (Part II);
CO 5/154: Promiscuous and Private Letters, 1772-1775;
CO 5/159 & 160: Correspondence with Law Officers, 1772-1775;
CO 5/161: Correspondence with Ordnance, 1772-1775;
CO 5/228: Plantations General Entry Book, 1771-1774;
CO 5/241: Plantations General; Dartmouth's correspondence with American governors and other officials begins on folio 428 and continues through the following:
CO 5/242: Plantations General Dispatches;
CO 5/246: Private Letters, 1771-1777; letters to and from Dartmouth, ff.44-72;
CO 5/247 & 248: In Letters;
CO 5/232 & 253: Précis of Letters.

The student who can manage only a brief visit to Great Britain is fortunate in having available several collections of transcripts on this side of the Atlantic. The Library of Congress holds transcriptions of many of the above-mentioned documents and I found it very convenient to refer to the correspondence between Dartmouth and the governor of Virginia, Lord Dunmore, in this form. The Public Archives of Canada has also transcribed extensively from P. R. O. collections. Using the Nova Scotia Papers (Vols. A.88 through A.95) and the Quebec Series (Vols. Q.10 through Q.12A) in Ottawa proved to be especially valuable both as an introduction to the materials to be found in the Public Record Office and also as a great saving of time, when I eventually visited the London repository.

More recently, the Library of Congress has adopted the generous policy of providing microfilm of P. R. O. manuscripts under the terms of Inter-library Loan. This service has made it possible for me to inspect the correspondence between the Colonial Secretary and the governors of the non-royal colonies in CO 5/1284-1286. In my opinion, this exchange between Dartmouth on the one hand and the governors of Connecticut, Rhode Island, Pennsylvania and Maryland on the other had little influence upon colonial policy. Dartmouth reposed little confidence in Governor Wanton of Connecticut after that gentleman made public a letter which Dartmouth had written him in confidence during the *Gaspée* crisis. Deputy Governor Penn neglected to inform the Colonial Secretary in advance of the growing opposition to the tea cargo destined for Philadelphia. Although his letters in 1774 and 1775 contain more information, even Penn expressed "great surprise" that his own assembly "unanimously" approved the proceedings of the First Continental Congress and appointed deputies to meet the Second [Penn to Dartmouth, 31 December 1774, P.R.O., CO 5/1286, f.7]. In these circumstances, it was only natural for Dartmouth to rely principally upon the numerous officials who had been appointed by the Crown, rather than the few remaining elective or proprietary governors.

Official papers, however, can be disappointing, if one is searching for a clue to a man's personality or for some insight into his motivation. Most of them were written by some clerk's hand, even though the P.R.O. might label them "promiscuous" and "private". Dispatches which bear Dartmouth's signature usually reflect only the results of a discussion held in private. When the decision on policy came from the Cabinet and the phraseology from a clerk, Dartmouth's personal role disappears into the background. Unfortunately, no diary kept by Dartmouth or other source of confidential information has come to light, so we must depend upon other collections of private papers in order to fathom his mind. It would be useful to know exactly what he *thought* were the reasons why he joined Rockingham's government, or why he accepted the secretarial seals from North, or why he rejected the Olive Branch, or any number of other critical decisions in his career. In the absence of a confidential journal, we shall never know for certain, but we can speculate about these and other answers, on the basis of records which appear in other collections.

The Newcastle Papers in the British Museum provide abundant material for the life and political career of the old Duke. The manuscripts relating to Lord Dartmouth are mercifully few in number but rich in information. I have drawn upon this source for the period of the Grand Tour and presidency of the Board of Trade. Newcastle was genuinely fond of the young Earl, but by the 1760's the Duke had played politics for so many years that making ministries and forecasting parliamentary votes had become a habit for him. It is difficult to know whether he persuaded Dartmouth to join Rockingham's government as a favor to the youthful nobleman or as a desperate measure to construct the last ministry in his long political career. Apparently he supported Dartmouth's desire for a full secretaryship in 1766 out of personal attachment, since the administration was about to collapse anyway. The Wentworth-Woodhouse Papers in the Sheffield Public Library are perhaps best known for the light they shed upon Edmund Burke's political career. Since Lord Dartmouth and the Marquess of Rockingham exchanged several letters in the period 1765-1770, this collection was also enlightening, especially the portion classified as R. 1.

More rewarding from the point of view of personal information are the North Manuscripts or Ms. North, as listed in the Bodleian Library, Oxford. These are not the papers of Frederick (Lord) North, but rather of his father, the first Earl of Guilford, Dartmouth's stepfather. There are numerous references to Dartmouth, as well as several letters from him, among the correspondence of various members of the North family. The following were the most informative:

Ms. North, c.75: Lady Kay's Accounts, 1739, revealing some of the extent of Dartmouth's family inheritance;

Ms. North, c.76: Accounts of rentals kept for Lord Lewisham Minor [*i.e.,* Dartmouth];

Ms. North, d.10-22: Guilford's correspondence, 1765-1790;

Ms. North, d.23-26: Guilford's correspondence with various members of the North family, 1714-1790.

Although this collection contains very little information about Lord North's administrative policy, it provides many insights into the warm, close relationships between Dartmouth and his various brothers and sisters (step-, half-, and blood relatives).

The William L. Clements Library in Ann Arbor, Michigan, is justly famous for its extensive collections of manuscripts. Several of these collections relate to Lord Dartmouth's political life:

The Gage Papers are especially useful for the correspondence between the American Secretary's office and General Gage as Governor of Massachusetts;

The Knox Papers contain the manuscripts of Dartmouth's undersecretary of state, William Knox;

The Strachey Papers include the interesting "census of 1773," which Dartmouth initiated by asking each colonial governor a score of questions about his province; those who answered supplied statistics which the Howe Commission thought would be useful in their mission of conciliation;

The Wedderburn Papers consist of legal reports and opinions, especially valuable for the *Gaspée* crisis.

Owing to certain practical limitations, my visit to Ann Arbor was shorter than I could have desired. The primary goal in reading the manuscripts, especially the Gage and Knox Papers, was to compare the originals with certain already printed references to Dartmouth. Thus, I am satisfied that Carter's edition of *General Gage's Correspondence* and the Historical Manuscripts Commission's calendar of William Knox's letters (*Various Collections,* VI, 1909) are essentially accurate. My footnote references in each case, consequently, are to the printed rather than the manuscript sources.

The South Carolina Archives Department, Columbia, South Carolina, possesses several collections which contain manuscripts relating to Lord Dartmouth's life and times. Transcriptions of original material in the Public Record Office provide a convenient source of information about Dartmouth's communications with Lieutenant-Governor Bull. The Journal of the colonial Council records Bull's consultations with his executive assistants, for example in the tea crisis. The "letter book" of the Charles Town Committee of Correspondence preserves copies of the letters received from the agent, Charles Garth in London. This last item is particularly enlightening with respect to the development of the coercive policy of 1774.

Part II: Printed works relating to British and American history in the Eighteenth-Century:

Many of the books and periodicals cited in the footnotes appear in Stanley Pargellis and D. J. Medley, editors, *Bibliography of British History: The Eighteenth Century, 1714-1789* (Oxford, 1951). Listed below are those works published after this useful bibliography appeared:

BOOKS

ALDEN, J. R., *The American Revolution, 1775-1783* (*New American Nation Series,* New York, 1954).

ARMYTAGE, Frances, *The Free Port System in the British West Indies: A Study in Commercial Policy, 1766-1822* (*Imperial Studies Series,* London, 1953).

BROOKE, John, *The Chatham Administration, 1766-1768* (London, 1956).

BURKE, Edmund, *Correspondence*: Vol. I (1744-1768), Copeland, ed. (Cambridge, 1958);

BURKE, Edmund, *Correspondence*: Vol. II (1768-1774), Sutherland, ed. (1960);

BURKE, Edmund, *Correspondence*: Vol. III (1774-1778), Guttridge, ed. (1961).

CHRISTIE, Ian, *The End of North's Ministry, 1780-1782* (London, 1958).

GIPSON, Lawrence Henry, *The Coming of the Revolution, 1763-1775* (*New American Nation Series,* New York, 1954).

GREENE, Jack P., *The Quest for Power: The Lower Houses of Assembly in the Southern Royal Colonies, 1689-1776* (Chapel Hill, 1963).

HARLOW, Vincent T., *The Founding of the Second British Empire*: Vol. I, "Discovery and Revolution" (London, 1952). Vol. II, "New Continents and Changing Values," published posthumously, 1964.

LABAREE, Benjamin Woods, *The Boston Tea Party* (New York, 1964).

LOVEJOY, David, *Rhode Island Politics and the American Revolution* (*Brown University Studies,* XXIII, Providence, 1958).

MACKESY, Piers, *The War for America, 1775-1783* (Cambridge, Mass., 1964).

MORGAN, Edmund S., ed., *Prologue to Revolution: Sources and Documents on the Stamp Act Crisis, 1764-1766* (Chapel Hill, 1959).

MORGAN, Edmund S. & Helen M., *The Stamp Act Crisis: Prologue to Revolution* (Chapel Hill, 1953).

PARES, Richard, *King George III and the Politicians* (Ford Lectures, Oxford, 1953).

RITCHESON, Charles R., *British Politics and the American Revolution* (Norman, Okla., 1954).

SHERRARD, O. A., *Lord Chatham and America* (London, 1958).

SOSIN, Jack M., *Whitehall and the Wilderness: The Middle West in British Colonial Policy, 1760-1775.* (Lincoln, Nebr., 1961).

TRUDEL, Marcel, *The Seigneurial Regime* (Canadian Historical Association Booklet #6, Ottawa, 1956).

UBBELOHDE, Carl, *The Vice-Admiralty Courts and the American Revolution* (Chapel Hill, 1960).

VALENTINE, Alan, *Lord George Germain* (Oxford, 1962).

WATSON, J. Steven, *The Reign of George III, 1760-1815* (*Oxford History of England,* Vol. XII, Oxford, 1959).

ARTICLES

GOEBEL, Dorothy Burne, "The 'New England Trade' and the French West Indies, 1763-1774: A Study in Trade Policy," *William and Mary Quarterly,* Third Series, XX (July 1963), 331-372.

GREENE, Jack P., "Bridge to Revolution: The Wilkes Fund Controversy in South Carolina, 1769-1775," *Journal of Southern History,* XXIX (February, 1963), 19-52.

LESLIE, William R., "The Gaspee Affair: A Study in Constitutional Significance," *Mississippi Valley Historical Review* XXXIX (September 1952), 233-256.

MAIER, Pauline, "John Wilkes and American Disillusionment with Britain," *William and Mary Quarterly,* Third Series, XX (July, 1963), 373-395.

PARES, Richard, "George III and the Politicians," *Transactions* of the Royal Historical Society, Fifth Series, Vol. I (London, 1951), 127-51.

SOSIN, Jack M., "The Massachusetts Acts of 1774: Coercive or Preventive," *Huntington Library Quarterly,* XXVI (May, 1963), 235-52.

VAN ALSTYNE, R. W., "Parliamentary Supremacy versus Independence: Notes and Documents," *Huntington Library Quarterly,* XXVI (May, 1963), 201-34.

INDEX

Aaron, witness in the affair of the *Gaspée,* 79

Adams, John, 157, 166

Adams, Samuel: opposed right of Parliament to legislate for the colonies, 93; comment on unifying effect of Tea Act, 97; account of Boston Tea Party by, 103; in Continental Congress, 146; no effort by Gage to apprehend, 166

Administration of Justice Act: providing for transportation for trial, 112-13

American Department: need for, 62-63; as a source of jobs, 63; connection of Bedfordites with, 63; housing of, 63-64; staff of, 64 and n.; relation with other colonial departments, 65-66; transfer of regiments by, 65-66; jealousy of, 67; turning point in Dartmouth's administration of, 106; Dartmouth's policy in last year in, 144-45; build-up in for proclamation of rebellion, 154; internal difficulties in, 164

Anne (1665-1714), 1

Apsley, Baron; *see* Bathurst

Bagot, Lady, 7

Barclay, David, intermediary between Franklin and Dartmouth, 133-34, 137-38; f a v o r e d acceptance of Olive Branch, 155

Barrington, Viscount: opposition to repeal of Stamp Act from, 31; request by for a Quartering Act, 105; repeal of tax laws proposed by, 138-39; shortage of British troops in America indicated by, 169

Barré, Colonel, 107, 127-28

Bathurst (Henry, Baron Apsley), Earl: support of Dartmouth's policy by, 114 and n.; interest of in province of Quebec, 120; work of in North's cabinet, 139; in North's cabinet, 190-91

Beattie, Dr., recipient of Lord Dartmouth's philanthropy, 10-11

Bedford, John Russell, 4th Duke, 15, 24: support of Stamp Act by, 30

Bedfordites, Whig faction: uncertain supporters in North ministry, 55-

56; connection of with American Department, 63; factor in Dartmouth's appointment, 69; criticism of Dartmouth's policy by, 108; conciliated by Lord North, 140; aggressive policy of, 144; strengthened by Weymouth appointment, 181

Bernard, Francis, Governor of Massachusetts, 26; on Massachusetts Government Bill, 111, 112

Board of Trade: powers and limitation of, 27, 193; reports from to Rockingham, 28; variety of issues before, 35, 39; shared responsibility of, 35-36, 40; reduced power of under Dartmouth, 36; interest of in trade problems, 37; instructions from for jury system for Quebec, 39; opposition of Pitt to, 42; absorbed by Secretary of State office, 58; work of under Dartmouth, 59-61; statistical study of colonies by, 59-60; expenses of, 60; action of on Ohio Company petition, 71

Boston Port Bill, 104, 105, 107, 108, 109, 110, 113, 115

Boston Tea Party, 96: arrival of the *Dartmouth* with cargo of tea, 98; destruction of tea, 98; unifying effect of, 99; movement for payment for, 102-03

Brickdale, Matthew: report from on Boston, 103 and n.

Briand, Monseigneur, head of the Catholic church in Canada: principal duties of, 127

Buckingham, Duchess of, 11 and n.

Buckinghamshire, Earl of: question on North Resolutions by, 144

Bull, William, Lieutenant-Governor of South Carolina: order by for storage of tea, 101-02; delay in dispatches from, 103-04

Burgoyne, General John: Adams letters intercepted by, 157; in command of Canadians, 171-72; defeat of, 189

Burke, Edmund, 27: policy of alliance between mercantile and political leaders of, 40; at Rockingham's home, 46; condemnation of Lord

Lewisham, George, Viscount, eldest son of Lord Dartmouth: education of, 11-12

Lewisham, L a d y (*née* Elizabeth Kaye), mother of L o r d Dartmouth: second marriage to Lord North and Grey, 2; death of, 3

Lewisham, Lord, father of Lord Dartmouth: early death of, 1

Livius, Peter, 59

Lyttelton, Lord, 15, 20; opposition to cider tax, 17-18; friendship of with Lord Dartmouth, 17-18; attack by on *Droit le Roi,* 18

Manchester, Duke of, 151

Mansfield, Earl of: firmer ministerial policy predicted by, 107-08; consultation with, 185

Mant, Major: application for western lands refused by Dartmouth, 39

Martin, Governor of North Carolina: flight of, 175

Masères, Francis, Attorney General of Quebec: promotion of plan for government of Quebec by, 120; approval of Bishop for Quebec, 127

Massachusetts, Government of, Act: changes in charter under, 105, 110-12; coercive features of, 108; end of compromise marked by, 114; repeal of proposed by Franklin, 136

Mercantilism: theoretical adherence to by Spain and Britain, 37; lax enforcement of, 37, 74; Grenville's orders for enforcement, 37, 74; complaints to Dartmouth on, 37-38; effect of Free Port Bill on, 38; colonial benefits under, 64-65, 196; effect of Seven Years' War on, 74-75; use of patrol ships resisted, 75; proposal for in Franklin's "Hints," 135

Moira, Earl of: land grant given to, 39

Molasses Act of 1733, 36

Montagu, Frederick, 57

Montagu, Admiral, 75, 76

Murray, Governor; instructions to for jury system in Quebec Province, 39

Massachusetts: and Stamp Act, 26; summons by for intercolonial con-gress, 26; change in British policy toward, 82; on payment by of governor's salary, 83-84, 88; delay requested from by Dartmouth, 83-84; concession offered and withdrawn, 85; replies by to governor's speech, 86, 87; Hutchinson, letters from, 90; petition from for removal of Hutchinson and Oliver, 90-91; elective Council of, 111-12; sympathy for, 116. *See also,* Boston Tea Party, Boston Port Bill, Massachusetts Government Act

Newcastle, Duke of: 17, 25, 27, 28, 31, 62: and Dartmouth's grand tour, 4-5; favored Dartmouth's appointment to Board of Trade, 5; leader of Old Whig group, 15, 16, 20; influence of on Dartmouth, 18, 19, 21-22, 196-97; on Stamp Act, 29; reforms of colonial administration proposed by, 40; plan by for new Rockingham ministry, 45

Newfoundland Fisheries: closing of to New England, 141

New England grievances: summary of sent to Dartmouth, 84

New York: considered loyal colony, 149, 167; resolution against violence passed by, 150; petitions prepared in, 150; limit of power of Parliament requested by, 151; treatment of petitions resented by, 151-52. *See* Tryon, Governor of New York

Newton, John, recipient of Lord Dartmouth's philanthropy, 10

North and Grey, Lord. *See* Guilford, Earl of

North, Brownlow, half brother of Lord Dartmouth, 3, 50

North, Frederick, "Lord North," step-brother and close associate of Lord Dartmouth: education and grand tour together, 2-4; favored cider tax bill, 16; political differences with Dartmouth, 22-23, 46, 50; Chancellor of the Exchequer, 46; p e r s o n a l friendship with Dartmouth, 46, 50, 51; cabinet offer from refused by Dartmouth, 49; paymaster in Chatham ministry, 50; and the John Wilkes affair, 51-

on, 27; h o p e s of Rockingham Whigs, 43; defense of East India Company by, 44-45; Bedford group joined Chatham's administration, 46; Rockingham group on the Boston Tea Party, 107; opposition to Quebec Act, 118

Whitefield, George, 9n., 13

Wilkes, John: opposition to cider tax, 15, 16; expulsion from House of Commons, 17-18; reopening of issue, 48-49, 51-52; motion by for impeachment of Lord North, 51;

support for by London mob, 51; quarrel with Tooke, 79

William III (1650-1702), 1

Wooldridge, Thomas: comment by on the affair of the *Gaspée,* 80

Woodsome Manor, Yorkshire property of Lord Dartmouth, 7, 45-46

Wright, James, Governor of Georgia: secured Board of Trade endorsement of purchase of Cherokee Lands, 59

Yorke, Charles: opposed repeal of Stamp Act, 31

DATE DUE

NOV 2 8 1974		
NOV 1 1 1975		
NOV 2 5 1975		
GAYLORD		PRINTED IN U.S.A.